iPad® and iPad Pro®

11th Edition

by Edward C. Baig
USA Today Personal Tech columnist

Bob LeVitus
Houston Chronicle "Dr. Mac" columnist

Bryan Chaffin
The Mac Observer Editor-in-Chief

for
dummies®
A Wiley Brand

iPad® and iPad Pro® For Dummies®, 11th Edition

Published by: **John Wiley & Sons, Inc.,** 111 River Street, Hoboken, NJ 07030-5774, www.wiley.com

Copyright © 2020 by John Wiley & Sons, Inc., Hoboken, New Jersey

Published simultaneously in Canada

No part of this publication may be reproduced, stored in a retrieval system or transmitted in any form or by any means, electronic, mechanical, photocopying, recording, scanning or otherwise, except as permitted under Sections 107 or 108 of the 1976 United States Copyright Act, without the prior written permission of the Publisher. Requests to the Publisher for permission should be addressed to the Permissions Department, John Wiley & Sons, Inc., 111 River Street, Hoboken, NJ 07030, (201) 748-6011, fax (201) 748-6008, or online at http://www.wiley.com/go/permissions.

Trademarks: Wiley, For Dummies, the Dummies Man logo, Dummies.com, Making Everything Easier, and related trade dress are trademarks or registered trademarks of John Wiley & Sons, Inc. and may not be used without written permission. iPad and iPad Pro are registered trademarks of Apple, Inc. All other trademarks are the property of their respective owners. John Wiley & Sons, Inc. is not associated with any product or vendor mentioned in this book. *iPad® and iPad Pro® For Dummies®,* 11th Edition is an independent publication and has not been authorized, sponsored, or otherwise approved by Apple, Inc.

For general information on our other products and services, please contact our Customer Care Department within the U.S. at 877-762-2974, outside the U.S. at 317-572-3993, or fax 317-572-4002. For technical support, please visit https://hub.wiley.com/community/support/dummies.

Wiley publishes in a variety of print and electronic formats and by print-on-demand. Some material included with standard print versions of this book may not be included in e-books or in print-on-demand. If this book refers to media such as a CD or DVD that is not included in the version you purchased, you may download this material at http://booksupport.wiley.com. For more information about Wiley products, visit www.wiley.com.

Library of Congress Control Number: 2020934546

ISBN 978-1-119-60797-7 (pbk); ISBN 978-1-119-74900-4 (ebk); ISBN 978-1-119-74901-1 (ebk)

Manufactured in the United States of America

SKY10031794_120321

Contents at a Glance

Table of Contents

Introduction

E very iPad is a magical device and the current iPad Pro lineup might be the most magical yet. But Apple has also released new versions of iPad, iPad mini, and iPad Air, and we think they're solid updates. New versions of Apple Pencil and Apple's Smart Keyboard line of external keyboards for iPad are also available. There's never been a better time to own an iPad, and there's never been a better time for many people to make iPad their main computing device. There, we said it, and it's true!

We hope you bought this book to find out how to get the most magic out of your iPad, regardless of its model. Our goal is to deliver the information you need in a light and breezy fashion. We expect you to have fun using your iPad and we hope you have fun spending time with us.

About This Book

We need to get one thing out of the way from the get-go. We think you're pretty darn smart for buying a *Dummies* book. To us, that says you have the confidence and intelligence to know what you don't know. The *Dummies* franchise is built on the core notion that everyone feels insecure about certain topics when tackling them for the first time, especially when those topics have to do with technology.

As with most Apple products, iPads are beautifully designed and intuitive to use. And though our editors may not want us to reveal this dirty little secret (especially on the first page, for goodness' sake), the truth is you'll get pretty far just by exploring the iPad's many functions and features on your own, without the help of this (or any other) book.

Okay, now that we've spilled the beans, we'll tell you why you shouldn't run back to the bookstore and request a refund. This book is chock-full of useful tips, advice, and other nuggets that should make your iPad experience all the more pleasurable. We'll even go so far as to say you won't find some of these nuggets anywhere else. So keep this book nearby and consult it often.

Foolish Assumptions

Although we know what happens when one makes assumptions, we've made a few anyway. First, we assume that you, gentle reader, know nothing about using an iPad or iPadOS, that you want to understand your iPad and its operating system without digesting an incomprehensible technical manual, and that you made the right choice by selecting this particular book.

We do our best to explain each new concept in full and loving detail. Perhaps that's foolish, but . . . oh, well.

One last thing: We also assume you can read. If you can't, please ignore this paragraph.

Icons Used in This Book

Little round pictures (or *icons*) appear in the left margin throughout this book. Consider these icons as miniature road signs, telling you something extra about the topic at hand or hammering a point home. Here's what the icons used in this book look like and mean.

These juicy morsels, shortcuts, and recommendations might make the task at hand faster or easier.

This icon emphasizes the stuff we think you ought to retain. You may even jot down a note to yourself on the iPad.

Put on your propeller beanie hat and insert your pocket protector; this text includes the truly geeky stuff. You can safely ignore this material, but if it weren't interesting or informative, we wouldn't have bothered to write it.

You wouldn't intentionally run a stop sign, would you? In the same fashion, ignoring warnings may be hazardous to your iPad and (by extension) your wallet. There, you now know how these warning icons work, for you have just received your very first warning!

We put a New icon next to anything that's new or improved in iPadOS.

Beyond the Book

We wrote a bunch of things that just didn't fit in the print version of this book. Rather than leave them on the cutting room floor, we've posted the most useful bits online in a cheat sheet for your enjoyment and edification.

To find them, go to www.dummies.com, and then type *iPad and iPad Pro For Dummies cheat sheet*. And here's what you'll find: info on using the iPad's buttons and icons, tips for mastering multitouch, and where to find additional help if your iPad is acting contrary.

Where to Go from Here

Why, go straight to Chapter 1, of course (without passing Go).

In all seriousness, we wrote this book for you, so please let us know what you think. If we screwed up, confused you, left out something, or — heaven forbid — made you angry, drop us a note. And if we hit you with one pun too many, it helps to know that as well. Because writers are people too (believe it or not), we also encourage positive feedback if you think it's warranted. So kindly send email to Ed at Baigdummies@gmail.com and to Bob at iPadLeVitus@boblevitus.com. You can contact Bryan at bryan2@macobserver.com. We do our best to respond to reasonably polite email in a timely fashion. Most of all, we want to thank you for buying our book. Please enjoy it along with your new iPad.

Note: At the time we wrote this book, all the information it contained was accurate for all Wi-Fi and Wi-Fi + Cellular iPads that support iPadOS. The book is also based on version 13 of the iPadOS operating system and version 12.9 of iTunes (for macOS Mojave and earlier) and Music 1.0 (for macOS Catalina and later). Apple is likely to introduce new iPad models and new versions of iOS and iTunes between book editions, so if the hardware or user interface on your new iPad or the version of iTunes on your computer looks a little different, be sure to check out what Apple has to say at www.apple.com/ipad. You'll no doubt find updates on the company's latest releases.

1

Getting to Know Your iPad

Get basic training for getting along with your iPad.

Enjoy a gentle introduction to your iPad.

Take a peek at your iPad hardware and software and explore the way it works.

Discover the joys of synchronization over USB or Wi-Fi and find out how to get your data — contacts, appointments, movies, songs, podcasts, books, and so on — from a computer (or iCloud) onto your iPad, quickly and painlessly.

Chapter **1**

Unveiling the iPad

ongratulations! You've selected one of the most incredible handheld devices we've ever seen. The iPad is a killer audio and video player, a great e-book reader, a powerful Internet communications device, a superb handheld gaming device, a still and video camera, and a platform for more than 4 million apps at the time this was written — and probably more by the time you read this.

REMEMBER

Following are all the iPad models covered in this book — because they all run iPadOS!

>> **iPad:** iPad Air 2 (2014), iPad 9.7-inch (2017), iPad 10.2-inch (2019)

>> **iPad mini:** iPad mini 4 (2015), iPad mini (2019)

>> **iPad Pro:** iPad Pro 12.9-inch (2015), iPad Pro 9.7-inch (2016), iPad Pro 2nd generation 12.9-inch (2017), iPad Pro 10.5-inch (2017), iPad Pro 12.9-inch 3rd generation (2018), and iPad Pro 11-inch (2019)

Note that because the five original full-sized iPads and the first three iPad mini models do not support iPadOS, they're not covered in this book. If you're the owner of one of those models, you can still find a lot of handy information here, but some things might look or work differently. You might want to rummage around for a previous edition of this book.

Moving right along, in this chapter, we offer a gentle introduction to all the pieces that make up your iPad, plus overviews of its revolutionary hardware and software features.

Exploring the iPad's Big Picture

The iPad has many best-of-class features, but perhaps its most notable feature is that it doesn't come with a physical keyboard or stylus. You can get them as options (Apple's first-generation $99 Apple Pencil, the second-generation $129 Apple Pencil, and the Smart Keyboard, which starts at $159), but they aren't required to use your iPad. Instead, every iPad requires a pointing device you're intimately familiar with: your finger.

Every iPad ever built has a beautiful Retina screen, easily the most beautiful screen we've ever seen on a tablet.

TIP

The screen rotates — that is, unless the screen orientation is locked. We tell you more about this feature shortly.

And we love the iPad's plethora of built-in sensors. It has an accelerometer that detects when you rotate the device from portrait to landscape mode — and instantly adjusts what's on the display.

A light sensor adjusts the display's brightness in response to the current ambient lighting conditions. Then there's a three-axis gyro that works with the accelerometer and built-in compass. And most models — since the iPad Air 2, iPad mini 4, 9.7-inch iPad, and all iPad Pro models — also include Apple's Touch ID sensor or Face ID. These features let you unlock your iPad with your fingerprint (Touch ID) or just by looking at it (Face ID)! We talk about both in detail later.

Last, but definitely not least, all iPads since the third generation include Siri, a voice-controlled personal assistant happy to do almost anything you ask (as long as your iPad is running iOS 6 or later).

In the following sections, we're not just marveling about the wonderful screen and sensors. Now it's time to take a brief look at the rest of the iPad's features, broken down by product category.

The iPad as a media player

We agree with the late Steve Jobs on this one: The iPad is magical — and without a doubt the best iPod (that is, media player) Apple has ever produced. You can enjoy all your existing media — music, audiobooks, audio and video podcasts, iTunes U courses, music videos, television shows, and movies, all on the gorgeous Retina display.

REMEMBER

If you can get a media file — be it video, audio, or whatever — on your iPad, you can watch or listen to it on your iPad. And, of course, you can always buy or rent content on your iPad in the iTunes Store. You can also watch streaming content from Netflix, Hulu, Apple's own Apple TV+ streaming service, and a host of others through apps.

The iPad as an Internet communications device

But wait — there's more! Not only is the iPad a stellar media player, it's also a full-featured Internet communications device with — we're about to drop some industry jargon on you — an email client that's compatible with most POP and IMAP mail services, plus it has support for Microsoft Exchange ActiveSync. (For more on this topic, see Chapter 5.) Also onboard is Safari, a world-class web browser that makes web surfing fun and easy on the eyes. Chapter 4 explains how to surf the web using Safari.

Another cool Internet feature is Maps, a killer mapping app that's improved in iPadOS. By using GPS or triangulation (Wi-Fi–only models), the iPad can determine your location, let you view maps and satellite imagery, and obtain driving directions and traffic information regardless of where you happen to be. You can also find businesses (such as gas stations, pizza restaurants, hospitals, and Apple Stores) with just a few taps.

TIP

Maps is useful over Wi-Fi but more useful and more accurate on cellular iPads.

We dare say that the Internet experience on an iPad is far superior to the Internet experience on any other handheld device.

The iPad as an e-book reader

Download the free Books app if you don't already have it, or any of the excellent (and free) third-party e-book readers such as the Kindle app from Amazon, and you'll discover a new way of finding and reading books. The Apple Book Store and News app (covered in Chapter 10) are chock-full of good reading at prices that are lower than what you'd pay for a printed copy. Better still, when you read an e-book, you're helping the environment and saving trees. Furthermore, some (if not many) titles include audio, video, or graphical content not available in the printed editions. Plus, a great number of good books are free. And best of all, you can carry your entire library in one hand. If you've never read a book on your iPad, give it a try. We think you'll like (or love) it.

The iPad as a multimedia powerhouse

The Retina display on all iPads since the third generation makes the experience even more extraordinary. You can use AirPlay to send your video out to Apple TV, too, and your iPad turns into a superb device for watching video on a TV, with support for output resolutions up to 4K.

And iPads include a pair of cameras and the FaceTime video-chatting app, taking the iPad's multimedia acumen to new heights. Chapter 8 gets you started with FaceTime.

The iPad as a platform for third-party apps

At the time of this writing, there were more than 4 million apps in the App Store, with hundreds of billions of downloads to date in categories such as games, business, education, entertainment, healthcare and fitness, music, photography, productivity, travel, and sports. The cool thing is that most of them, even ones designed for the iPhone, also run flawlessly on the iPad. And more than a million are designed *specifically* for the iPad's larger screen.

Chapter 10 helps you fill your iPad with all the cool apps your heart desires. We share our favorite free and for-pay apps in Chapters 18 and 19, respectively.

The iPad as a multitasking content production device

Apple has made the iPad more and more of a device for creating content as opposed to only consuming it. Writing, taking and editing pictures, recording and editing music or videos, and even putting together full-scale presentations — all of these tasks are even easier with iPadOS, especially on the iPad Pro. Split-screen views, support for the Files app, and the fastest processors in mobile computers have made the iPad a beast of a machine. We talk more about multitasking in Chapter 13.

What do you need to use an iPad?

To *use* your iPad, only a few simple things are required. Here's a list of everything you need:

>> An iPad

>> An Apple ID (assuming that you want to acquire content such as apps, TV shows and movies, music, books, and podcasts, which you almost certainly do)

>> Internet access — broadband wireless Internet access is recommended

Several years ago, we said you needed a computer with iTunes to sync your iPad. That's no longer true; these days you can activate, set up, update, back up, and restore an iPad wirelessly without ever introducing it to a computer.

If you do decide to introduce your iPad to your computer (and we think you should), you need one of the following for syncing (which we discuss at length in Chapter 3):

>> A Mac with a USB 2.0, 3.0, or C port, macOS version 10.8.5 or later, and iTunes 12.7 or later (for macOS Mojave and earlier) or Finder (macOS Catalina)

>> A PC with a USB 2.0 or 3.0 port, Windows 7 or later, and iTunes 12.7 or later

iTunes is a free download, available at www.itunes.com/download.

Touring the iPad Exterior

The iPad is a harmonious combination of hardware and software. In the following sections, we take a brief look at the hardware — what's on the outside.

On the top

On the top of your iPad, you find the sleep/wake button, headphone jack, and microphone, as shown in Figure 1-1. iPad Pro models have no headphone jack but do have two of their four speakers on top:

>> **Sleep/wake button:** This button is used to put your iPad's screen to sleep or to wake it up. It's also how you turn your iPad on or off. To put it to sleep or wake it up, just press the button. To turn it on or off, press and hold down the button for a few seconds.

Your iPad's battery will run down faster when your iPad is awake, so we suggest that you make a habit of putting it to sleep when you're not using it.

To wake it up, merely press the sleep/wake button again, or press the Home button on the front of the device (as described in a moment), or on iPad Pro, tap the screen.

If you use an Apple Smart Cover or Smart Case (or any third-party case that uses the Smart Cover mechanism), you can just open the cover to wake your iPad and close the cover to put it to sleep.

In Chapter 15, you can find out how to make your iPad go to sleep automatically after a period of inactivity.

» **Headphone jack:** This jack lets you plug in a headset. You can use pretty much any headphone or headset that plugs into a 3.5-mm stereo headphone jack. Apple no longer makes headphones with a headphone jack, but it does sell EarPods ($29), which connect via a Lightning connector, and AirPods (starting at $159), which connect via Bluetooth.

Throughout this book, we use the words *headphones, earphones,* and *headset* interchangeably. Strictly speaking, a headset includes a microphone so that you can talk (or record) as well as listen; headphones and earphones are for listening only. Either type works with your iPad, as do most wireless Bluetooth headsets such as Apple's AirPods and newer headsets with Lightning connectors.

» **Microphone:** The tiny dot — or two dots on some iPad Pro models — in the middle of the top is a pretty good microphone. (*Hint:* You'll sound better if you use a headset — any headset.)

» **Speakers (iPad Pro only):** iPad Pro has four speaker vents, two on the top and two on the bottom.

FIGURE 1-1:
iPad Pro models have speaker ports on the top, as well as the sleep/wake button. Some models have a headphone jack, too.

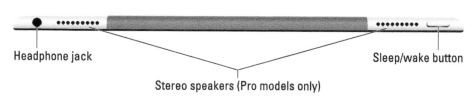

Headphone jack

Stereo speakers (Pro models only)

Sleep/wake button

On the bottom

On the bottom of your iPad are the speakers (two of the four speakers on iPad Pro models) and Lightning connector or USB-C connector, as shown in Figure 1-2:

>> **Speakers:** The speakers plays audio — music or video soundtracks — if you don't have a headset plugged in.

>> **Lightning or USB-C connector:** This connector has three purposes:

- *Recharge your iPad's battery:* Simply connect one end of the included cable to the iPad's Lightning or USB-C port and the other end to a USB or USB-C port, where appropriate.

- *Synchronize your iPad:* Connect one end of the same cable to the Lightning or USB-C connector and the other end to a USB or USB-C port on your Mac or PC.

- *Connect your iPad to a camera or television:* Make sure to use an adapter that works with the Lightning connector or the USB-C connector, depending on your iPad.

REMEMBER

If you connect your iPad to a USB port and get a *Not Charging* message, the USB port doesn't have enough power. Generally speaking, USB ports built into recent Macs and PCs, on powered hubs, or on the USB charging brick that came with your iPad will charge your iPad properly. Any USB data port connected to your Mac or PC will allow you to sync your iPad, whether or not it's charging.

FIGURE 1-2:
All full-size iPad models have speaker ports and a connection port on the bottom.

Speaker   Lightning or USB-C connector   Speaker

On the right side of your iPad are the volume up and volume down buttons, as shown in Figure 1-3. Press the upper button to increase the volume; press the lower button to decreases the volume.

TIP

The Camera app uses either volume button as an alternative shutter release button to the on-screen shutter release button. Press any of them to shoot a picture or start and stop video recording.

SIM card tray   Volume up and down buttons

On older iPads with cellular capabilities, you'll find the SIM card tray. On newer iPads and iPad Pro with cellular capabilities, the SIM card tray is on the right side. Wi-Fi-only models do not have a SIM card tray.

TIP

Apple used to include a SIM card eject tool with iPads and iPhones. If you don't have one lying around, you can straighten a paper clip and use it as a faux SIM card eject tool.

On the front and back

On the front and back of your iPad, you find the following (labeled in Figure 1-4):

- >> **Touchscreen:** You find out how to use the iPad's gorgeous high-resolution color touchscreen in Chapter 2. All we have to say here is: Try not to drool all over it.

- >> **Home button, Touch ID sensor, or Face ID:** No matter what you're doing, you can press the Home button at any time to display the Home screen, as shown in Figure 1-4. The Home button also doubles as a Touch ID sensor on most iPads, so you can use your fingerprint (or a passcode) to unlock your phone and authenticate purchases. Recent iPad Pro models do not have a Home button and rely on Face ID, not Touch ID. For iPads with Face ID, swipe up from the bottom of the screen to go back to the Home screen.

- >> **Front (FaceTime) camera:** The front camera is serviceable and delivers decent-enough video for video chats and such, but it's not particularly good for taking still photos. That is, unless your iPad is a Pro model, which offers 7-megapixel front camera photos (versus 1.2 megapixels on all other models).

- >> **App icons:** Each of the icons shown on the screen (see Figure 1-4) launches an included iPad app. You read more about these apps later in this chapter and throughout the rest of the book.

- >> **Rear camera:** The camera on the back, just below the sleep/wake button, is better than the one in front. Pro models have a 12-megapixel rear camera with an f/1.8 aperture; other iPads have an 8-megapixel rear camera with f/2.4 apertures. All iPads can record HD video at 1080p; Pro models can record video at up to 4K.

Front camera   App icon

FIGURE 1-4:
The front
of the iPad
10.2-inch:
a study in
elegant
simplicity.   Touchscreen   Home button

Status bar

The status bar, which is at the top of the screen, displays tiny icons that provide a variety of information about the current state of your iPad:

>> **Airplane mode:** Airplane mode should be enabled when you fly. It turns off all wireless features of your iPad — the cellular, 5G, 4G, LTE, 3G, GPRS, and EDGE networks; Wi-Fi; and Bluetooth — so you can enjoy music, video, games, photos, or any app that doesn't require an Internet connection while you're in the air.

Tap the Settings app and then tap the airplane mode switch on (so green is displayed). The icon shown in the margin appears on the left side of your status bar when airplane mode is enabled. You can also pull Control Center down from the top-right corner and tap the airplane mode icon to turn airplane mode on (the icon turns orange).

Disable airplane mode when the plane is at the gate before takeoff or after landing so you can send or receive email and iMessages.

REMEMBER

There's no need to enable airplane mode on flights that offer onboard Wi-Fi unless you have a cellular-equipped iPad. On such flights, it's perfectly safe to use your iPad's Wi-Fi while you're in the air (but not until the captain says so).

To use Wi-Fi in flight with a cellular iPad, first enable airplane mode and then reenable Wi-Fi.

» **Wi-Fi:** If you see the Wi-Fi icon, your iPad is connected to the Internet over a Wi-Fi network. The more semicircular lines that are lit (up to three), the stronger the Wi-Fi signal. If your iPad has only one or two semicircles of Wi-Fi strength, try moving around a bit. If you don't see the Wi-Fi icon on the status bar, Internet access with Wi-Fi is not currently available.

» **Personal hotspot:** You see this icon when you're sharing your Internet connection with computers or other devices over Wi-Fi. Personal hotspot is available for every iPad except the iPad 2 but may not be available in all areas or from all carriers. Additional fees may apply. Contact your wireless carrier for more information.

» **Syncing:** This icon appears on the status bar when your iPad is syncing with iTunes on your Mac or PC.

» **Activity:** This icon tells you that some network or other activity is occurring, such as over-the-air synchronization, the sending or receiving of email, or the loading of a web page. Some third-party apps use this icon to indicate network or other activity.

» **VPN:** This icon shows that you're currently connected to a virtual private network (VPN).

» **Lock:** This icon tells you when your iPad is locked. See Chapter 2 for information on locking and unlocking your iPad.

» **Screen orientation lock:** This icon appears when the screen orientation lock is engaged.

» **Location Services:** This icon appears when an app (such as Maps; see Chapter 6 for more about the Maps app) is using Location Services (GPS) to establish the location of your iPad.

» **Do not disturb:** This icon appears whenever do not disturb is enabled, silencing incoming FaceTime calls and alerts. See Chapter 15 for details on do not disturb.

» **Play:** This icon informs you that a song is currently playing. You find out more about playing songs in Chapter 7.

» **Bluetooth:** This icon indicates the current state of your iPad's Bluetooth connection. If you see this icon on the status bar, Bluetooth is on and a device (such as a wireless headset or keyboard) is connected. If the icon is gray, Bluetooth is turned on but no device is connected. If the icon is white, Bluetooth is on and one (or more) devices are connected. If you don't see a Bluetooth icon, Bluetooth is turned off. Chapter 15 goes into more detail about Bluetooth.

» **Bluetooth battery:** This icon displays the battery level of supported Bluetooth devices (while paired). Only certain devices — mostly headsets and speakers — support this feature. If you see this icon in your status bar, it's telling you the approximate battery level of whichever supported device is currently paired with your iPad.

» **Battery:** This icon shows the level of your battery's charge and also indicates when your device is connected to a power source. It's completely filled when your device isn't connected to a power source and your battery is fully charged. It then empties as your battery becomes depleted. You see an on-screen message when the charge drops to 20 percent or below, and another when it reaches 10 percent.

COMPARING WI-FI AND CELLULAR NETWORKS

As of this writing, wireless carriers offer several data networks relevant to the iPad. Only the third-generation and later iPads can take advantage of the speediest 4G or LTE networks. AT&T has a form of LTE the company misleadingly calls 5G. 3G is slower than 4G and LTE, and EDGE and GPRS are slower still. Your iPad starts by trying to connect to the fastest network it supports. If it makes a connection, you see the appropriate cellular icon on the status bar.

Most Wi-Fi networks, however, are faster than even the fastest 4G cellular network. So, because all iPads can connect to a Wi-Fi network if one is available, they do so, even when a cellular network is also available.

Last but not least, if you don't see 5G, 4G, LTE, 3G, GPRS, E (for EDGE), or the Wi-Fi icon, you don't currently have Internet access.

Discovering the Delectable Home Screen and Dock Icons

The iPad Home screen and dock display as many as 45 icons, with each icon representing a different built-in app or function. Because the rest of the book covers each and every one of these babies in full and loving detail, we provide brief descriptions here.

To get to your Home screen, tap the Home button or swipe up from the bottom of your display. If your iPad is asleep when you tap, the unlock screen appears. After your iPad is unlocked, you see whichever page was on the screen when it went to sleep. If that happens to have been the Home screen, you're golden. If it wasn't, merely tap the Home button or swipe up from the bottom of the screen again to summon your iPad's Home screen.

In the following sections, we tell you briefly about the icons preloaded on your iPad's first Home screen page, as well as the icons you find on the dock that are always accessible from each Home screen.

Home is where the screen is

If you haven't rearranged your icons, you see the following apps on the first Home screen, starting at the top left:

>> **FaceTime:** Use this app to participate in FaceTime video chats, as you discover in Chapter 8.

>> **Calendar:** No matter what calendar program you prefer on your Mac or PC (as long as it's iCal, Calendar, Microsoft Entourage, or Microsoft Outlook or online calendars such as Google or iCloud), you can synchronize events and alerts between your computer and your iPad. Create an event on one device, and the event is automatically synchronized with the other device the next time the two devices are connected. Neat stuff. You learn more about Calendar in Chapter 11.

>> **Clock:** The Clock app includes alarm clocks, timers, and more. You hear more about this nifty app in Chapter 12.

>> **Home:** The Home app is where you access and control your HomeKit smart home devices. Almost like a sci-fi movie, you can control lights, appliances, and surveillance cameras from an app or with your voice using Siri. You'll read much more about this great app, but you have to wait until Chapter 12.

>> **Photos:** This app is the iPad's terrific photo manager, which just keeps getting better. It lets you view and edit pictures in your library as well as from a camera or SD card (using the optional camera connection kit). You can zoom in or out, create slideshows, email photos to friends, crop, do a bit of image editing, and much more. And it's where you'll find the For You section, with photos intelligently grouped by Apple machine learning into relevant time and place groupings. To get started, see Chapter 9.

>> **Camera:** You use this app to shoot pictures or videos with your iPad's front- or rear-facing camera. You find out more in Chapters 8 (videos) and 9 (camera).

>> **Reminders:** With Reminders, you can, well, remind yourself to do something. If you ask Siri to remind you, it's added as a reminder in this app, too. You can even do location- and time-based reminders, which will be synced to your other Apple devices. Learn more about Reminders in Chapter 12.

>> **Notes:** This program enables you to type notes while you're out and about. You can send notes to yourself or to anyone else through the Sharing pane, or you can just save them on your iPad until you need them. For help using Notes, flip to Chapter 13.

>> **Voice Memos:** The Voice Memos app is a great way for you to talk to yourself. Have a thought for the next best-selling novel? Did inspiration just strike for your presentation at next week's meeting? Record anything you want in this app quickly and easily. For more about the Voice Memos app, turn to Chapter 12.

>> **Contacts:** This handy little app contains information about the people you know. Like the Calendar app, it synchronizes with the Contacts app on your Mac or PC (as long as you keep your contacts in Address Book, Contacts, Microsoft Entourage, Microsoft Outlook, or Google). If you create or edit a contact on one device, the contact is automatically synchronized with the other device the next time your devices are connected. Chapter 11 explains how to use the Calendar and Contacts apps.

>> **Maps:** View street maps, satellite imagery, transit information, and more for locations around the globe. Or ask for directions, traffic conditions, or even the location of a nearby pizza joint. We show you more about Maps in Chapter 6.

>> **Find My:** If your iPad (or iPhone, AirPods, or Mac) goes missing, use this app to determine its last known location. We look more closely at Find My in Chapter 15.

- **>> iTunes Store:** Tap this puppy to purchase music, movies, TV shows, audio-books, and more. You find more info about iTunes (and the Music app) in Chapter 7.

- **>> App Store:** This icon enables you to connect to and search the App Store for iPad apps you can purchase or download for free. Chapter 10 is your guide to buying and using apps from the App Store.

- **>> Books:** You use Books to read books, which you can buy in the Book Store. We love the Books app and discuss it more deeply in Chapter 7.

- **>> Podcasts:** Use the Podcasts app to listen to your favorite podcasts, which you download and subscribe to in the Podcast app itself. Learn more about the Podcasts app in Chapter 8.

- **>> TV:** This handy app is the repository for your movies, TV shows, and music videos. You add videos via iTunes on your Mac or PC or by purchasing them directly in the TV app. Check out Chapter 8 to find out more.

- **>> News:** This app is where you can find news from magazines, newspapers, and websites, and subscribe to Apple News+ for access to paid content from many mainstream sources. You read more about News in Chapter 7.

- **>> Stocks:** Long a staple on the iPhone, the Stocks app is now on the iPad too. Track AAPL and any other stock you want to follow using the app's clean and informative interface. You can also get news articles about the companies you're following.

- **>> Measure:** Use this app and the camera in your iPad to measure distances in the real world. Seriously, try it! Turn to Chapter 12 for more on the Measure app.

- **>> Settings:** Tap this icon to change settings for your iPad and its apps. With so many settings in the Settings app, you'll be happy to hear that Chapter 15 is dedicated exclusively to Settings.

Sittin' on the dock of the iPad

At the bottom of the iPad screen are the final five icons, sitting on the left side of a special shelflike area called the *dock*.

Suggested apps appear on the right side of the dock. These are apps you've used recently or apps that are open on your iPhone or Mac. In Figure 1-4, for example, the three suggested apps (from left to right) are App Store, Settings, and iTunes Store.

The icons on your dock are special because they are available on every Home screen.

By default, the five icons on the left side of the dividing line on the dock are as follows:

» **Messages:** The Messages app is a unified messaging platform for all Apple devices. You can exchange free, unlimited text or multimedia messages with any other device running iOS 5 or later or Mac OS X Mountain Lion or later. Find out more about Messages in Chapter 6.

» **Safari:** Safari is your web browser. If you're an iPhone or Mac user, you know that already. If you're a Windows user who hasn't discovered the wonderful Safari for Windows, think Internet Explorer or Edge on steroids. Chapter 4 shows you how to start using Safari on your iPad.

» **Music:** This icon unleashes all the power of an iPod right on your iPad so you can listen to music or podcasts. You discover how the Music app works in Chapter 7.

» **Mail:** This app lets you send and receive email with most POP3 and IMAP email systems and, if you work for a company that grants permission, Microsoft Exchange. Chapter 5 helps you start emailing from your iPad everyone you know.

» **Files:** This app (if enabled in Settings ⇨ iCloud ⇨ iCloud Drive) contains all documents you've saved to your iCloud Drive. Apple apps as well as many third-party apps know how to use it.

Feel free to add icons to or remove icons from the left side of the dock until it feels right to you. You can even remove the default apps Apple included. To add or remove dock icons, press and hold down on any icon and tap Rearrange Apps on the menu that appears. Your app icons will begin wiggling. Tap and drag a wiggling app icon to move it to or from the dock. When you're satisfied, press the Home button to exit wiggly mode and save your arrangement.

You can add many app icons to the dock. The first 12 will line up in the dock as you add them. If you add a 13th app to the dock, the number of recent and suggested apps on the right side of the dock will be limited to 2. And if you want still more apps on the dock, go to Settings ⇨ General ⇨ Multitasking & Dock and turn off Show Suggested and Recent Apps by tapping the toggle and turning it from green to white. You can now add up to 15 apps to the dock.

Two last points:

TIP

>> Notifications keep getting better with the updated iPadOS. We wanted to mention them even though they don't have an icon of their own. You hear much more about notifications in Chapter 12. To see them now (we know you can't wait), swipe from the top of your screen to the middle to make them appear. Then swipe from the bottom to put them away again.

This gesture works anytime — even when your iPad is locked. If it's locked, you'll see your most recent notifications when you swipe down. Then swipe up to see your older notifications.

>> We'd be remiss not to mention the even more useful Control Center, with controls for Wi-Fi, Bluetooth, audio playback, and more, all available from any screen in any app. You discover much more about Control Center in Chapter 14, but if you can't stand the suspense, put your finger in the top-right corner of your iPad screen and swipe down to check out Control Center (and then tap the Home button or swipe up from the bottom to put it away).

Chapter **2**

iPad Basic Training

By now you know that the iPad you hold in your hands is very different from other computers.

You also know that the iPad is rewriting the rule book for mainstream computing. How so? For starters, iPads don't come with a mouse or any other kind of pointing device. They lack traditional computing ports or connectors, such as USB. And they have no physical or built-in keyboard, though Apple will sell you a Smart Keyboard accessory for recent iPad models.

iPads even differ from other so-called tablet PCs, some of which feature a pen or stylus and let you write in digital ink. As we point out (pun intended) in Chapter 1, the iPad relies on an input device that you always have with you: your finger. Okay, some iPads can use Apple Pencil and other styluses, but what makes an iPad so powerful is that a stylus is optional.

Tablet computers of one form or another have been around since the last century. They just never captured the fancy of Main Street. Apple's very own Newton, an ill-fated 1990s personal digital assistant, barely made a dent in the market.

Technology — not to mention Apple itself — has come a long way since Newton. And tablets — led by the iPad brigade, of course — promise to become ever more prevalent, useful, and important.

If you own an iPhone, you already have a gigantic start in figuring out how to master the iPad multitouch method of navigating the interface with your fingers. If you've been using iOS 13, you have an even bigger head start. You have our permission to skim the rest of this chapter, but we urge you to stick around anyway because some aspects of iPadOS work in subtly different ways than on the iPhone. If you're a total novice, don't fret. Nothing about multitouch is painful.

Getting Started on Getting Started

You can set up your iPad with or without a Mac or PC. In Chapter 3, we show you how to set it up with a computer. But first, we show you how to set up your iPad without a computer.

TIP

Some users find it easier to do some iPad management tasks — such as iPadOS software updates or backing up — using iTunes on a Mac or PC. And having a local backup for your data can be a lifesaver.

Now, here are the two things you need to use your iPad:

>> **An Apple ID account:** You'll want an account to download content from iTunes and the App Store, and to take advantage of iCloud, including iCloud backups. Read Chapter 7 for details on how to set up an account. Like most things Apple, the process isn't difficult.

>> **Internet access:** Your iPad can connect to the Internet through Wi-Fi or cellular (if you bought an iPad with cellular capabilities). With Wi-Fi you can connect your iPad to cyberspace in your home, office, school, favorite coffeehouse, bookstore, or numerous other spots. If your iPad has cellular capabilities, you can connect anywhere.

In addition, if you want to back up your iPad to your Mac or PC, you will need one of the following:

>> A Mac running macOS Catalina 10.15 or later; use Finder to sync

>> A Mac running macOS El Capitan 10.11.6 through macOS Mojave 10.14.6 or later; use iTunes 12.8 or later to sync

>> A Windows PC running Windows 7 or later; use iTunes 12.10 or later to sync

You can go to www.itunes.com/download to fetch a copy of iTunes. Or launch your current version of iTunes and then choose iTunes ⇨ Check for Updates.

A Closer Look at Cellular Data on Your iPad

Wireless technology is constantly evolving, but support for cellular capabilities on mobile devices is everyday stuff now. You need to pay for a cellular plan with a carrier to use your iPad's cellular capabilities. Read on to learn more about your cellular options.

TECHNICAL
STUFF

In the United States, you can choose among AT&T, Sprint, Verizon Wireless, and T-Mobile. (Sprint and T-Mobile may have merged by the time you read this.) Most carriers offer some version of 4G wireless, with AT&T falsely claiming a 5G service that is just a rebranded 4G. Real 5G is still in the deployment stage, and Apple has not yet announced an iPad with 5G support.

Figuring out how much data you need beforehand isn't always easy, but it's simple enough to adjust along the way. If you're streaming a lot of music, T-Mobile for one provides a nice benefit: the capability to stream free on most major services, including Spotify and Apple Music.

The following are some of the offerings from the major US carriers when we published this book. But prices and the amount of data you get change so fast, you'll want to check current offerings and promotions. Also, in some instances, you must pay activation or other fees:

>> AT&T: Starting at $50 a month for 10GB

>> Sprint: Starting at $35 a month for 10GB

>> T-Mobile: Starting at $10 a month for 2GB

>> Verizon: Starting at $20 a month for 2GB

A friendly warning pops up on your iPad when you get close to your limit. At that point, you can pay more to add to your data bucket or start from scratch next month. And, as noted, prices are subject to change.

TIP

Whichever carrier you go with, we recommend finding a (secure) Wi-Fi network when streaming movies, lest you exhaust your data allotment in a hurry.

iPads with cellular service may include an Apple SIM card that theoretically allows you to bounce from one carrier to another. The process isn't always simple, however, because such SIM cards are sometimes locked down, either by Apple or by the carrier from which you buy the tablet. Moreover, the type of SIM card inside your iPad varies. Some models have nano-SIM cards. Others, including most early models dating all the way back to the original iPad, have a micro-SIM card. More recent models have both an embedded Apple SIM card and a tray for a nano-SIM card.

If you can't get your iPad to work with a chosen wireless carrier, check with that carrier for details.

Turning On and Setting Up the iPad

Unless your iPad is brand-spanking new and fresh out of the box, chances are that you've already performed the following steps. If you choose to use your iPad computer-free, these steps make up the entire setup process.

Apple has taken the time to partially charge your iPad, so you can set it up right away in one of two ways. We strongly encourage you to use the first method, automatic setup, because it's so easy. However, it does require you to have another iOS 11 or later device already set up and running with the same Apple ID.

If you don't have another device using iOS 11 or later, never fear! We also show you how to set up your iPad manually. In fact, you can skip straight down to the section called "Manual setup" to get started.

Automatic setup

Automatic setup enables you to transfer your settings and Apple ID-related data from one iPhone or iPad running iOS 11 or later, including iPadOS, to your iPad. As just mentioned, the device you're transferring from must be running the same Apple ID that you want to use on your new iPad. Depending on the choices you make during the setup process, some of these steps may be different for you.

1. **Begin the setup process:**

    a. *Press and hold down the sleep/wake button on the upper-right edge.* You see the Apple logo, followed by the word *hello* and similar greetings in a bunch of other languages.

    b. *When you see a* Press Home to Open *message (in English or another language), do so.* iPad Pro models with Face ID will say *Swipe Up to Open.* The language screen appears.

    c. *Tap to choose your language, followed by your country or region preferences.* The Quick Start screen appears, along with a blue Set Up Manually button. Resist the urge to tap that one!

2. **Pair the two devices:**

    a. *Bring your other iOS or iPadOS device close to your iPad.* And by close, we mean a couple of inches away. Make sure this other device is unlocked, and look for the Set Up New iPad pop-up notification. The automatic setup magic has begun!

TECHNICAL STUFF

The pairing process uses the camera on your existing device to view shifting dots on your new device described in the next step. This security procedure makes it difficult for someone to hijack the pairing process and steal your Apple ID and other data.

b. *On the second device, tap the gray Continue button.* Your second device displays the instruction *Hold Your New iPad Up to the Camera,* while the iPad gets a cool screen with a rotating 3D blob of dots. (The dots are a code, similar to a QR code, generated by your iPad.)

c. *Hold your other device over the iPad you're setting up until the camera is positioned over the blob of dots, as shown in Figure 2-1.* After the camera captures the blob of dots, your other device will say *Finish on New iPad,* while your new iPad asks you to *Enter Passcode of Your Other Device.*

d. *On your new iPad, enter the passcode from your other device.* This passcode is now the one for your iPad, too. (You can change it later, as detailed in Chapter 15.) As soon as you enter the passcode successfully, your iPad automatically displays the Touch ID screen (for iPads with Touch ID) or the Face ID screen (for iPad Pro models with Face ID).

FIGURE 2-1:
Maneuvering an iPad to pair with an existing iOS or iPadOS device for automatic setup.

3. **Set up Touch ID or Face ID:**

   To set up Touch ID on iPad models that support Touch ID:

   a. *Tap Continue.*

   b. *Tap the Home button each time you're asked.* With each touch, sensors comprehensively map your fingerprint.

   c. *When asked, tap Continue to adjust your grip, and continue the process until the Complete screen appears.*

   To set up Face ID on iPad Pro models that support Face ID:

   a. *Tap Continue.* The front camera activates.

   b. *When asked, turn your head in different directions until your entire face is scanned.*

   c. *After completing one scan, complete a second scan when asked.*

4. **On the Complete screen, tap Continue.**

The screen displays *Setting Up Your Apple ID* while your other device and your iPad exchange information, including Contacts, Calendar, and Keychain passwords. Your other device also copies over all your Wi-Fi settings, even passwords, so your iPad automatically joins your networks. This process could take a few minutes. When it's finished, the Apps & Data screen appears.

5. **Choose how to set up your iPad by tapping one of the options and following the on-screen prompts.**

Your four choices are Restore from iCloud Backup, Restore from iTunes Backup, Move Data from Android, and Don't Transfer Apps & Data. When the process is complete, the Terms and Conditions screen appears.

6. **Tap Agree to accept the terms and conditions, and then tap Agree again on the pop-up dialog that appears.**

When you tap Agree the second time, the Transfer Settings from your Other iPad screen appears. If you were using an iPhone, it would be the Transfer Settings from Your iPhone screen. They both do the same things, including allowing Siri to use your personal information when handling your requests; allowing apps and Maps to use Location Services, and sharing your analytics and diagnostics with Apple.

7. **Tap Continue.**

The Apple Pay screen appears.

8. **Confirm or set up Apple Pay.**

If Apple Pay is set up on your other iOS or iPadOS device, confirm each credit card you've set up. Otherwise, you can now add credit cards one at a time or set up Apple Pay later by tapping the Set Up Later in Settings button. (Learn more about Apple Pay in Chapter 15.)

9. **Tap Continue.**

If you already have an Apple Card set up on your other iOS or iPadOS device, the Get Daily Cash Every Time screen appears.

10. **If you have an Apple Card, tap Set as Preferred Card and follow the on-screen instructions.**

You can make your Apple Card the default credit card for Apple Pay transactions. You can also set up Apple Pay cash on your iPad.

11. **Decide whether or not to share your analytic data with developers.**

In Step 6, you chose whether or not to share analytics data with Apple. Now you're asked if you want to share analytics with developers. If you agree to share with developers, you're not just trusting Apple; you're trusting all those developers, too. When we set up our devices, we often skip this permission.

12. **Tap Continue to cycle through a series of screens highlighting new features of iPadOS specific to your iPad model.**

At the end, the Get Started screen appears.

13. **Tap Get Started.**

You are taken to the Home screen! That's it! You're now ready to use your iPad.

If you ever need to restore your iPad to factory condition, follow the preceding steps to set it up again.

Manual setup

If you've already gone through the automatic setup process, skip this section. If you want to know how to manually set up your iPad, however, you're in the right place. In the interest of space, we won't repeat details for instructions that are identical to what we explained in the "Automatic setup" section. Also, depending on the choices you make during the setup process, some of these steps may be different:

1. **Begin the setup process:**

   a. Press and hold down the sleep/wake button on the upper right edge. You see the Apple logo, followed by the word *hello* and similar greetings in a bunch of other languages.

   b. When you see a Press Home to Open *message (in English or another languages), do so.* The language screen appears.

   c. Tap to choose your language, followed by your country or region preferences. The Quick Start screen appears, along with a blue Set Up Manually button.

2. **Tap the Set Up Manually button.**

3. **Tap to choose an available Wi-Fi network, provide a password (if necessary), and then tap the blue Join button.**

Certain iPad models may allow you to choose a cellular network, if available, and set up or change your Wi-Fi network later. (See Chapter 15 for setting up Wi-Fi in Settings.) After you tap Join, your iPad automatically advances to the Data & Privacy screen.

4. **Tap Continue to acknowledge the Data & Privacy icon and its meaning.**

Apple takes your privacy seriously, calling privacy a human right! The icon you see at the top of this screen appears whenever your iPad asks to use your personal information.

You advance to the Set Up Touch ID or Set Up Face ID screen, depending on your iPad model.

5. **Set up Touch ID or Face ID:**

   To set up Touch ID on iPad models that support Touch ID:

   a. Tap Continue.

   b. Tap the Home button each time you're asked. With each touch, sensors comprehensively map your fingerprint.

   c. When asked, tap Continue to adjust your grip, and continue the process until the Complete screen appears.

   To set up Face ID on iPad Pro models that support Face ID:

   a. Tap Continue. The front camera activates.

   b. When asked, turn your head in different directions until your entire face is scanned.

   c. After completing one scan, complete a second scan when asked.

6. **Tap Continue to Create a passcode.**

   Type a 6-digit passcode to unlock your iPad. When the Re-enter Your Passcode screen appears, type your passcode again. The Apps & Data screen appears.

7. **Choose how to set up your iPad by tapping one of the options and following the on-screen prompts.**

   Your four choices are Restore from iCloud Backup, Restore from Mac or PC, Move Data from Android, and Don't Transfer Apps & Data. When the process is complete, the Apple ID screen appears.

8. **If you don't have an Apple ID or you've forgotten it:**

   a. Tap the Forgot Password or Apple ID? button.

   b. Set up a new account or bypass this step until later by choosing Settings ⇨ Apple ID.

   The Terms and Conditions screen appears.

9. **If you have an Apple ID:**

   a. Enter your Apple ID credentials.

   b. If you have activated two-factor authentication (sometimes called 2FA), approve this login on one of your other Apple devices, and then enter the passcode displayed on that device.

   c. If you use a different Apple ID for iCloud than you do for iTunes, you can enter both by tapping the Use Different Apple IDs for iCloud & iTunes? button, and entering your credentials for both.

When your Apple ID has been set up, the Terms and Conditions screen appears.

10. **Tap Agree to accept the terms and conditions, and then tap Agree again on the pop-up dialog that appears.**

When you tap Agree the second time, the Express Settings screen appears.

11. **Tap Continue to automatically set up Location Services and iPad Analytics through the Express Settings screen.**

With one tap of your finger, Apple makes it possible to set up Location Services and iPad Analytics at once. We recommend you do so, though you can choose to customize these settings by tapping Customize Settings.

Location Services are key to making the most out of your iPad by letting iOS and your apps know where you are. Data analytics are key to Apple learning more about how you use your iOS devices, including problems and other information. We think the company's privacy policies are best in class, and Apple has committed to anonymizing the data it collects so that it can't be tied to a specific user.

When Express Settings is finished, the Keep Your iPad Up to Date screen appears.

12. **Tap Continue to automatically install iPadOS updates on your iPad.**

Apple very much wants you to allow your iPad to update automatically. We think this is a good idea, but if you think differently, choose the Install Updates Manually option to keep control over when your iPad is updated.

When you tap Continue, the Apple Pay screen appears.

13. **Tap Continue, and then confirm or set up Apple Pay.**

If you have Apple Pay already set up with your Apple ID, you'll be asked to confirm each credit card you've set up. Otherwise, you can now add credit cards one at a time or set up Apple Pay later by tapping the Set Up Later in Settings button. (Learn more about Apple Pay in Chapter 15.)

14. **Tap Continue.**

The Siri screen appears.

15. **Tap Continue again to acknowledge how to use Siri.**

Siri is activated by default. Although you can turn her off in Settings, we strongly recommend that you keep this feature on and use it. Siri is a good voice assistant, and Apple is improving her steadily.

16. **Decide whether or not to share your analytic data with developers.**

In Step 11, you chose whether or not to share analytics data with Apple. Now you're asked if you want to share analytics with developers. If you agree to share with developers, you're not just trusting Apple; you're trusting all those developers, too. When we set up our devices, we often skip this permission.

17. **Tap Continue.**

Your iPad cycles through a series of screens highlighting new features of iPadOS specific to your iPad model.

18. **Tap Get Started.**

You are taken to the Home screen! That's it! You're now ready to use your iPad.

REMEMBER

If you ever need to restore your iPad to factory condition, follow the preceding steps to set it up again.

SECURITY USING YOUR FINGER OR YOUR FACE

Every iPad covered in this book is equipped with either Touch ID, a fingerprint scanner cleverly embedded in the Home button, or Face ID.

With Touch ID and a gentle press of any designated finger, you bypass your passcode. (Setting up passcode safeguards is a good idea, and is something we touch on in the chapter on settings, Chapter 15.)

What's more, you can use your own digit (not the numerical kind) to authenticate iTunes and App Store purchases, and to access your iCloud Keychain passwords or even third-party password keepers. (Go to Settings ⇨ Touch ID & Passcode and make sure that the iTunes & App Store switch is turned on.) You can also use Touch ID to authorize Apple Pay purchases on the web (but not in bricks-and-mortar retail stores).

Face ID is much like Touch ID in terms of how you use it, but instead of touching your finger to a fingerprint sensor you look into your camera. The camera has a special Face ID sensor that uses infrared and other camera data to carefully and securely measure your face. As of this writing, only recent iPad Pro models come with Face ID. We've been using it on iPhone and iPad Pro for years, and we love it.

Locking the iPad

We can think of several sound reasons for locking your iPad:

>> You don't want to turn it on inadvertently.

>> You want to keep prying eyes at bay.

>> You have a persistently inquisitive child.

>> You want to spare the battery some juice.

Apple makes locking the iPad a cinch.

REMEMBER

You don't need to do anything to lock the iPad; it happens automatically as long as you don't touch the screen for a minute or two. As you find out in Chapter 15, which is all about settings, you can also set the amount of time your iPad must be idle before it automatically locks.

Can't wait? To lock the iPad immediately, press the sleep/wake button.

TIP

If you have an iPad with a Smart Cover (or a third-party equivalent), opening and closing the cover locks and unlocks your iPad, but the Smart Cover has the advantage of awakening your iPad without making you tap the Home button (though you may still have to enter a passcode).

Unlocking the iPad is easy, too. Here's how:

1. **Press the sleep/wake button, or press the Home button on the front of the screen.**

2. **Do one of the following:**

   ● *If you have Touch ID, use one of your registered fingers to press the Home button to unlock the iPad and go to your Home screen.*

   ● *If you have Face ID, just look at the camera.*

   ● *If you don't have Touch ID or Face ID, or your iPad was just restarted, press Home with another finger and enter your passcode.*

   See Chapter 15 to find out how to password-protect your iPad.

Mastering the Multitouch Interface

The iPad, like the iPhone, dispenses with a physical mouse and keyboard in favor of a virtual keyboard — a step that seemed revolutionary several years ago but is just-how-it-is today.

In the following sections, you discover how to move around the multitouch interface with ease. Later, we home in on how to make the most of the keyboard.

Training your digits

Rice Krispies have *Snap! Crackle! Pop!* Apple's response for the iPad is *Tap! Flick! Pinch!* Oh yeah, and *Drag!*

Fortunately, tapping, flicking, pinching, and dragging are not challenging gestures, so you can master many of the iPad's features in no time:

>> **Tap:** Tapping is the single most important element of multitouch interfaces. Tap to open, tap to play, tap to select, tap to shoot (in games). Sometimes, you *double-tap* (tapping twice in rapid succession), which has the effect of zooming in (or out) of web pages, maps, and emails. Or you *tap-and-hold* to move something on the screen.

>> **Flick:** A flick of the finger on the screen lets you quickly scroll through lists of songs, emails, and picture thumbnails. Tap the screen to stop scrolling, or merely wait for the scrolling list to stop.

>> **Pinch/spread:** Place two fingers on the screen and spread them apart to zoom in on images, web pages, text, videos, and more. Or pinch your fingers together to make things smaller. These gestures will quickly become second nature!

>> **Drag:** Here's where you slowly press your finger against the touchscreen without lifting it. You might drag to move around a web page or map that's too large for the iPad's display area.

>> **Drag downward from the top of the screen:** This special gesture displays notifications. Press your finger at the very top of the screen and drag downward.

>> **Drag downward from the top right of the screen:** This time, you're calling up Control Center, a handy repository for music controls, airplane mode (see Chapter 15), Wi-Fi, Bluetooth, do not disturb, mute, volume, orientation lock, timer (Clock app), camera, AirPlay, and brightness controls. Check out Figure 2-2 for one view of Control Center.

- >> **Drag downward on any screen without starting at the very top of the screen:** This action summons Search, a discussion for later in this chapter.

- >> **Drag from left to right on the first Home screen:** You're summoning the Today screen, where you see the appointments and reminders you have coming up, get app suggestions and News stories, and access Search. The today view is available on the lock screen and the Home screens.

- >> **Drag from right to left on the lock screen:** This shortcut action summons the iPad's camera app.

- >> **Swipe from right edge of the screen:** You can pull in a temporary overlay of another open app, a *slide-over* feature we get to later in this chapter. This action requires that you go to Settings⇨Homescreen & Dock⇨Multitasking and enable the Allow Multiple Apps switch.

FIGURE 2-2:
We think you'll call on Control Center a lot.

- >> **Four-finger swipes and pinches:** To quickly multitask or switch among or view running apps (see the later section, "Multitasking"), use four fingers to swipe upward. Swipe left or right (only one finger required) to switch between recently used apps. Pinch using four fingers to jump to your Home screen. Swipe up (one finger will do the trick) on an app's thumbnail to quit it.

Later in the chapter, you read about a couple of new ways to employ your digits, at least on certain models: slide over and split view.

Navigating beyond the Home screen

The Home screen, which we discuss in Chapter 1, is not the only screen of icons on your tablet. After you start adding apps from the iTunes App Store (see Chapter 10), you may see a row of two or more tiny dots just above the main apps parked at the bottom of the screen. Those dots denote additional Home screens each containing up to 30 additional icons, not counting the additional icons on your iPad's dock.

You can have up to 15 Home screens. You can also have more or fewer icons on your dock, but we can't think of a decent reason why you'd want to ditch any of them. In any case, more on these in a moment.

Here's what you need to know about navigating among the screens:

>> To navigate between screens, flick your finger from right to left or left to right across the middle of the screen, or tap directly on the dots. The number of dots you see represents the current number of screens on your iPad. The all-white dot denotes the screen you're currently viewing. Flicking — or swiping — from right to left from the first Home screen brings up the aforementioned Today screen.

>> Make sure you swipe and not just tap, or you'll probably open one of the apps on the current screen instead of switching screens.

>> Press the Home button to jump back to the Home screen. You can also swipe up from the bottom of the screen. Doing so the first time takes you back to the last-viewed Home screen. A second time takes you to the first Home screen.

TIP

>> You can now put as many as 15 apps and as little as none on the dock. The dock also shows the three most recently opened apps on the right side of the divider line, making for a quick return to an app. You can access the dock from an open app by swiping up from the bottom of your screen.

Select, cut, copy, and paste

You can select and copy content from one place on the iPad and then paste it elsewhere, just like you can with a Mac or PC. You might copy text or a URL from the web and paste it into an email or a note. Or you might copy a bunch of pictures or video into an email.

Here's how you to exploit the copy-and-paste feature:

1. **Select a word by tapping and holding it or double-tapping it.**

2. **Drag the *grab points* (handles) to select a larger block of text or to contract the text you've already selected, as shown in Figure 2-3.**

   Dragging grab points may take a little practice.

| Cut | Copy | Paste | Replace... | B I U | Look Up | Share. | Indent Right |

This is a test of the emergency broadcast system and only a test.

FIGURE 2-3:
Drag the grab handles to select text.

3. **Tap Copy.**

   If you were deleting text from a document you created, instead of copying and pasting, you would tap Cut instead.

4. **Open the Mail program (see Chapter 5) and start composing a message.**

5. **When you decide where to insert the text you just copied, tap the cursor.**

   Up pops the Select, Select All, Paste, Quote Level, Insert Photo or Video, and Add Document commands, as shown in Figure 2-4. (We get to the last three options in Chapter 5.)

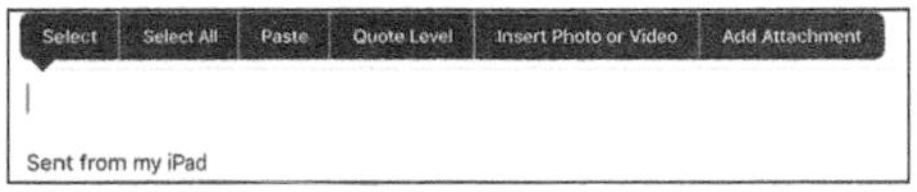

   | Select | Select All | Paste | Quote Level | Insert Photo or Video | Add Attachment |

   Sent from my iPad

   FIGURE 2-4:
   Tap Paste and text will appear.

6. **Tap Paste to paste the text into the message.**

TIP

If you made a mistake when you were cutting, pasting, or typing, shake the iPad. Doing so undoes the last edit (provided that you tap the Undo Paste or Undo option when it appears and keep the shake feature enabled in Settings ➪ Accessibility ➪ Touch ➪ Shake to Undo).

You might also see these options:

- *Auto-Correct:* If you happen to select a word with a typo, the iPad might underline that word. If you tap the underlined work, the iPad might show you the word it thinks you meant to spell. Tap that suggested word to accept it.

- *Predict:* A predictive word feature reveals up to three word or phrase options in buttons just above the keyboard. If one of these words or phrases is what you had in mind, tap the appropriate button.

- *Replace:* The iPad may show you possible replacement words. For example, replacement words for *test* might be *fest, rest,* or *text.* Tap the word to substitute it for the word you originally typed.

- *Indent Right or Left:* Pretty self-explanatory. With this option, you can indent highlighted text to the right or left.

- *Look Up:* Tap your selected word for a definition, courtesy of the *New Oxford American Dictionary,* the *Oxford Dictionary of English,* an Apple dictionary, or a foreign language dictionary if you've downloaded any dictionaries onto your iPad. But Look Up goes well beyond definitions and includes searches that extend to the App Store, Apple Music, Twitter, the web, Wikipedia, and more.

Multitasking

Through *multitasking*, you can run numerous apps in the background simultaneously and easily switch from one app to another. The following examples illustrate what multitasking enables you to do on your iPad:

>> A third-party app, such as Slacker Personal Radio, can continue to play music while you surf the web, peek at pictures, or check email. Without multitasking, Slacker would shut down the moment you opened another app.

>> A navigation app can update your position while you're listening to, say, Pandora Internet radio. From time to time, the navigation app will pipe in with turn-by-turn directions, lowering the volume of the music so you can hear the instructions.

>> If you're uploading images to a photo website and the process is taking longer than you want, you can switch to another app, confident that the images will continue to upload behind the scenes.

>> You can leave voice notes in the Evernote app while checking out a web page.

Multitasking couldn't be easier — and it only gets better in iPadOS. Your iPad can anticipate your needs. For example, if it detects, over time, that you tend to turn to your social networking apps around the same time every morning, it will make sure the feeds are ready for you.

Here's another example. Double-press the Home button or swipe up from the bottom of your screen to display the app switcher. You see preview pages with icons just above them for any open apps. Scroll to the left to see more apps. Tap the preview screen for the app you want to switch to; the app remembers where you left off. If you hold the tablet sideways in landscape mode, as shown in Figure 2-5, the previews for your apps appear sideways, too.

To remove an app from the multitasking rotation, swipe up on the app's preview. Poof — it's gone.

Now let's look at some other tricks that make multitasking even more powerful.

Splitting the screen

You can exploit all that gorgeous screen real estate on your iPad to make multitasking even more productive.

FIGURE 2-5:
Scroll to the left to see the apps you've recently used or are still running.

For starters, there's a feature called *slide over.* Launch the first app you want to use and then swipe up from the bottom of the screen to bring out the dock. Drag an app off the dock, and iOS 11 will make a tray on the right side of the screen where you can drop that app. Now it's running side by side with your first app! This split view mode is shown in Figure 2-6. Drag the gray bar between the two apps to resize them.

Safari   Resizer Mail

FIGURE 2-6:
iPadOS split view in action with Safari on the left and Mail on the right.

In Safari, you have two ways to open in split view when using the iPad in landscape mode. The first way is to long-press a link on a web page, which opens several options, including a preview of the link. Drag that preview to the side to open it in split view.

The second way requires you to have Tabs turned on. Go to Settings ➪ Safari and toggle Show Tab Bar so that it turns green. In the Safari app, you can then drag a tab to the right edge of the screen and release, and a new split view is created.

We bet you can think of all sorts of reasons to run two apps at the same time. Maybe you're composing a message to a friend in the Mail app while scrolling through Safari in the smaller panel to find a place to have lunch. Or perhaps you're sketching in one app while using a photo in another as a reference point.

Drag down the gray handle at the top of the side app and the iPad switches to pop-over mode. Instead of running side by side, your first app now runs underneath the second one.

When you're finished with that secondary app, just slide it away by dragging the gray handle in the middle to the right side of the screen. The slide-over feature works with Apple's own apps and some third-party apps. Apps that don't support it can still have a second app running on top of them, as described in the preceding tip.

Picture-in-picture

There's a good possibility that your television at home has a picture-in-picture feature that enables you to watch one channel in the main portion of the TV screen while checking out a second channel in a small window on the screen. You don't really want to miss any of the action in the big game now, do you?

Since iOS 9, your iPad has had the same feature. The picture-in-picture feature on the iPad works when you're on a FaceTime video call, watching a video stored on your iPad, or streaming a video from one of the many streaming video services. These topics are reserved for Chapter 8.

Picture-in-picture couldn't be simpler. While watching a video, press (not tap) the Home button, or simply swipe up from the bottom of the screen. The video picture shrinks into a small window hanging out in the lower-right corner of the display.

You can pause the video or shut it down by tapping the controls that appear in this diminutive video window. (Tap the window if you don't see the controls.) If you want the video to take over the entire iPad screen, tap the leftmost picture control inside the video window, shown in Figure 2-7.

Meanwhile, if the video window is blocking a portion of the screen that you want to see, you can drag it to another space.

Organizing icons into folders

Finding the single app that you want to use among apps spread out over 15 screens may seem like a daunting task. But Apple felt your pain and added a handy organizational tool:

FIGURE 2-7:
Like some TVs, the iPad has a picture-in-picture feature.

folders. The Folders feature lets you create folder icons, each containing apps that pertain to the name that Apple assigned or you gave to that folder.

To create a folder, follow these steps:

1. **Press your finger against an icon until all the icons on the screen wiggle.**

2. **Decide which apps you want to move to a folder and then drag the icon for the first app on top of the second app.**

   The two apps now share living quarters inside a newly created folder. Apple names the folder according to the category of apps inside the folder.

3. **(Optional) Change the folder name by tapping the X on the bar where the folder name appears and typing a new name.**

To launch an app inside a folder, tap that folder's icon and then tap the icon for the app that you want to open.

You have plenty of room for all your apps on the iPad. Indeed, you can put as many as 16 apps inside a folder, stash up to 30 apps or folders per page (not counting up to 15 apps on the dock), and have as many as 15 pages.

When you drag all the apps from a folder, the folder automatically disappears.

Printing

iPadOS's AirPrint feature allows you to print wirelessly from the iPad to an AirPrint-capable printer, available from all major printer manufacturers.

AirPrint works with Mail, Photos, Safari, and Books (PDF files). You can also print from apps in Apple's iWork software suite, as well as third-party apps with built-in printing.

REMEMBER

An AirPrint printer doesn't need any special software, but it does have to be connected to the same Wi-Fi network as the iPad.

To print, follow these steps:

1. **Tap the share icon, and then tap the Print command.**

   The icon is shown in the margin.

2. **In the Printer Options bubble that appears, tap Select Printer to select a printer, which the iPad locates in short order.**

3. **Depending on the printer, specify the number of copies you want to print, the number of double-sided copies, and a range of pages to print.**

   Graphics that appear may even show you how much ink is left in the printer.

4. **When you're happy with your settings, tap Print.**

If you display the preview pages while a print job is underway, the Print Center icon appears with all your other recently used apps. A badge indicates how many documents are in the print queue, along with the currently printing document.

Proactive search

Using the Safari browser (see Chapter 4), you can search the web via Google, Yahoo!, Bing, or DuckDuckGo. If you've added a foreign language keyboard, other options may present themselves. For example, with a Chinese keyboard enabled, you can summon the Baidu search engine.

You can search also for people and programs across your iPad and within specific apps, using a combination of Search and Siri. We show you how to search within apps in the various chapters dedicated to Mail, Contacts, Calendar, and Music.

Searching across the iPad is based on the powerful Search feature familiar to Mac owners. Search can search for news and trending topics, local restaurants, movie times, and content in Apple's own iTunes Store, App Store, and Book Store.

Moreover, with Siri teaming up with the Search feature, you'll also see circled icons representing the contacts you engage with the most, the people you are next scheduled to meet, as well as eateries, shops, and other places of possible interest nearby.

Searches are also proactive, meaning that the device gets to know you over time and makes suggestions accordingly. It attempts to read your mind. The tablet might surface the News app, for example, if it learns that you turn to it every morning (while enjoying your coffee). Or if you're in a particular area, you may see the news that's trending in your location.

Here's how the Search feature works:

1. **Swipe down from the center of any screen to access Search.**

   A bar slides into view at the top of the screen.

2. **Tap the bar and use the virtual keyboard to enter your search query.**

   The iPad spits out results the moment you type a single character; the list narrows as you type additional characters.

   The results are pretty darn thorough. Say that you entered *Ring* as your search term. Contacts whose last names have *Ring* in them show up, along with friends who might have done a trapeze act in the now defunct Ringling Bros. circus. All the songs on your iPad by Ringo Starr show up too, as do such song titles as "Ring-A-Ling," from the Black-Eyed Peas if that happens to be in your library. The same goes for apps, videos, audiobooks, events, and notes with the word *Ring*. You'll see web and App Store references as well.

3. **Tap any listing to jump to the contact, ditty, or app you seek.**

TIP

At the bottom of the Search results list, you can tap to move your search query to the web (using your designated search engine). You can search the Maps app too.

You can enable Suggestions by choosing Settings ⇨ Siri & Search to summon results from the web, iTunes, the App Store, movie showtimes, nearby locations, and more. A separate switch lets you enable Suggestions in Look Up when taking advantage of the Look Up feature.

The Incredible, Intelligent, and Virtual iPad Keyboard

As you know by now, instead of a physical keyboard, several virtual English-language or (depending upon what you chose during setup) foreign-language keyboard layouts slide up from the bottom of the iPad screen, including variations on the alphabetical keyboard, the numeric and punctuation keyboard, the more punctuation and symbols keyboard, and the emoji keyboard.

Indeed, the beauty of a software keyboard is that you see only the keys that are pertinent to the task at hand. The keyboards in Safari, for example, differ from the keyboards in Mail. In Mail, you'll see a Return key (and the @ symbol when typing in an address field). The similarly placed key in Safari is labeled Go, as shown in Figure 2-8.

FIGURE 2-8:
The keys on the Mail (top) and Safari (bottom) keyboards.

TIP

See the little gray letters and numbers at the top of most keys in Figure 2-8? If you swipe down on one of these keys instead of tapping it, you'll get that second character instead of the main one. Try it!

Before you consider how to *use* the keyboard, we want to share a bit of the philosophy behind its so-called *intelligence*. Knowing what makes this keyboard smart can help you make it even smarter when you use it. The keyboard

>> Has a built-in English dictionary that includes words from today's popular culture. Apple uses machine learning to quickly identify new trending words, too. Dictionaries in other languages are automatically activated when you use a given international keyboard, as described in the sidebar "A keyboard for all borders," later in this chapter.

>> Adds your contacts to its dictionary automatically.

>> Uses complex analysis algorithms to predict the word you're trying to type.

>> Suggests corrections as you type. It then offers you the suggested word just below the misspelled word. When you decline a suggestion and the word you typed is *not* in the iPad dictionary, the iPad adds that word to its dictionary and offers it as a suggestion if you mistype a similar word in the future.

TIP

Actively decline incorrect suggestions by tapping the characters you typed as opposed to the suggested words that appear. This helps train your intelligent keyboard.

>> Reduces the number of mistakes you make as you type by intelligently and dynamically resizing the touch zones for certain keys. The iPad increases the zones for keys it predicts might come next and decreases the zones for keys that are unlikely or impossible to come next. Cool!

Anticipating what comes next

The keyboard takes an educated stab at the next word you mean to type and presents what it surmises to be the best possible word choices front and center. Say you're in the Messages app and the last message you received was an invitation to lunch or dinner. Above the row of keys on the iPad keyboard, you'd see buttons with three word suggestions: *Dinner, Lunch,* and *Not sure* (as shown in Figure 2-9). If one of those was the appropriate response, you could tap the button to insert its text into your reply.

A KEYBOARD FOR ALL BORDERS

Apple expanded the iPad's reach globally with international keyboard layouts for dozens of languages. To access a keyboard that isn't customized for Americanized English, tap Settings ➪ General ➪ Keyboard ➪ Keyboards ➪ Add New Keyboard. Then flick through the list to select any keyboard you want to use. Up pops the list shown in the figure, with custom keyboards for German, Italian, Japanese, and so on. Apple even supplies four versions of French (including keyboards geared to Belgium, Canadian, and Swiss customers) and several keyboards for Chinese. Heck, you can even find Australian, Canadian, Indian, Singapore, and UK versions of English.

Have a multilingual household? You can select as many of these international keyboards as you might need by tapping the language in the list.

When you're in an app that summons a keyboard, tap the international keyboard key (globe icon) in the lower left until the keyboard you want to call on shows up. (If you see an emoji key with a smiley face, tap it to switch to the globe icon.) Tap again to choose the next keyboard in the corresponding list of international keyboards that you turned on in Settings. If you keep tapping, you come back to your original keyboard. Or press against the globe icon until you see the list of all the keyboards you've added. You'll also see the Predictive switch above the list of keyboards that you've added to your iPad.

To remove a keyboard that you've already added to your list, tap the Edit button in the upper-right corner of the Keyboard settings screen displaying your enabled keyboards and then tap the red circle with the white horizontal line that appears next to the language to which you want to say *adios*.

(continued)

(continued)

Meanwhile, your iPad keypad is even more fluent with iPadOS. You can now type in two languages at once, without switching keyboards. You can type with any pair of the following languages: English, French, German, Italian, Portuguese, and Spanish. This multilingual typing feature is also supported for English and Chinese.

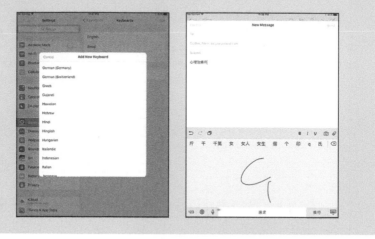

If you wanted to respond with something different than the three options presented by Apple, you'd just type your response with the regular QWERTY keys. As you type additional letters and words, the three suggested word choices above the keyboard change in real time. For instance, if you start by typing *That's a* in your message, the new trio of word choice buttons that show up might be *great,* *good,* and *very.*

To exploit the predictive text feature, make sure the Predictive setting is turned on (as it is by default). Go to Settings ➪ General ➪ Keyboards, and slide the Predictive switch to on.

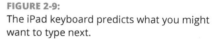

FIGURE 2-9:
The iPad keyboard predicts what you might want to type next.

Discovering the special-use keys

The iPad keyboard contains several keys that don't actually type a character. Here's the scoop on each of these keys:

» **Shift:** If you're using the alphabetical keyboard, the shift key switches between uppercase and lowercase letters. You can tap the key to change the case, or hold down shift and slide to the letter you want to be capitalized.

» **Typewriter:** Enable the Split Keyboard option (tap Settings ⇨ General ⇨ Keyboards), and you can split the keyboard in a thumb-typist-friendly manner, as shown in Figure 2-10. When you're ready to split your keyboard, press and hold down the typewriter icon key, and tap Split on the menu. From that menu you can also dock the keyboard to the bottom of the screen. When you want to bring the keyboard back together, press and hold down the typewriter icon key again and choose either Merge or Dock and Merge from the menu. Another option in the typewriter key is Floating. Tap Floating to shrink your keyboard to a smaller version that you can then drag. Tap and drag the gray bar at the bottom of the floating keyboard to drag it where you want it; if you drag to the bottom of the screen, you redock the keyboard and expand it to its full size.

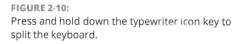

FIGURE 2-10:
Press and hold down the typewriter icon key to split the keyboard.

» **#+= or 123:** If you're using a keyboard that shows only numbers and symbols, the traditional shift key is replaced with a key labeled #+= or 123. Pressing that key toggles between keyboards that just have symbols and numbers.

» **Emoji:** Tap this key and you can punctuate your words by adding smiley faces and other emojis.

» **International keyboard:** You see this key only if you've turned on an international (or third-party) keyboard, as explained in the nearby sidebar "A keyboard for all borders."

» **Delete:** Tapping this key (otherwise known as the backspace key) erases the character immediately to the left of the cursor.

» **Return:** This key moves the cursor to the beginning of the next line. You might find this key labeled Go or Search, depending on the app you're using.

>> **Dictation:** Tap the microphone icon and start talking. The iPad listens to what you have to say. Tap the key again, and the iPad attempts to convert your words into text. You can use this dictation feature in many of the instances in which you can summon the keyboard, including the built-in Notes and Mail apps, as well as many third-party apps. See Chapter 14 for more on dictation.

WARNING

When you use dictation, the things you say are recorded and sent to Apple, which converts your words into text. Just make sure to proofread what you've said because the process isn't foolproof. Apple also collects other information, including your first name and nickname, the names and nicknames of folks in your contacts list, song names in Music, and more. Apple says it anonymizes this information, which helps the Dictation feature perform its duties. If any of this freaks you out, however, tap Settings ⇨ General ⇨ Keyboard and slide the Enable Dictation switch to off. You can also restrict the use of dictation in Settings, as explained in Chapter 15.

On the top row of the keyboards that pop up in certain apps — Mail and Notes, for instance — tap the Aa button at the top left of the keyboard to find **B**, *I*, U, and s formatting keys. These permit you to bold, italicize, underline, or strikethrough selected text, respectively. Other formatting options, depending on the app you're using, might include paragraph alignment, ordered and unordered lists, font colors, and more.

To the left of the three alternative word suggestions on various keyboards, you'll see icons for undoing or redoing your last steps, plus a third icon that pastes the last selected word or passage that you copied. Such options are visible in both images that make up Figure 2-8, but they may differ depending on the app you're using.

What you see also varies by what you do. For example, after you select text in the Mail app, a scissors icon appears on the top row of the virtual keyboard; when you tap the icon, it cuts the selected text.

Choosing an alternative keyboard

Good as the keyboards that Apple supplies to your iPad are, you can choose an alternative keyboard from a third-party app developer, including SwiftKey, Swype, and Fleksy keyboards. You can fetch new keyboards in the App Store. Some are free; others require a modest sum.

After you've downloaded a keyboard, visit Settings ⇨ General ⇨ Keyboard ⇨ Keyboards ⇨ Add New Keyboard and select the keyboard of choice. Then press and hold down on the international keyboard key (globe icon) on the iPad's own keyboard, and select your new keyboard from the list that appears. Alternatively, keep tapping the globe icon until the keyboard you want takes over.

Finger-typing on the virtual keyboards

The virtual keyboards in Apple's multitouch interface just might be considered a stroke of genius. Or they just might drive you nuts. If you're patient and trusting, in a week or so, you'll get the hang of finger-typing — which is vital to moving forward, because you rely on a virtual keyboard to tap a text field, enter notes, type the names of new contacts, and so on.

Apple has built intelligence into its virtual keyboard, so it can correct typing mistakes on the fly or provide helpful word choices by predicting what you're about to type next. The keyboard isn't exactly Nostradamus, but it does an excellent job of coming up with the words you have in mind. Apple is also increasingly relying on deep neural network technology to improve accuracy even more.

As you start typing on the virtual keyboard, we think you'll find the following additional tips helpful:

TIP

>> **See what letter you're typing.** As you press your finger against a letter or number on the screen, the individual key you press darkens until you lift your finger, as shown in Figure 2-11. That way, you know that you struck the correct letter or number.

>> **Slide to the correct letter if you tap the wrong one.** No need to worry if you touched the wrong key. You can slide your finger to the correct key because the letter isn't recorded until you release your finger.

>> **Tap and hold down to access special accent marks, alternative punctuation, or URL endings.** Sending a message to an overseas pal? Keep your finger

FIGURE 2-11:
The ABCs of virtual typing.

pressed against a letter, and a row of keys showing variations on the character for foreign alphabets pops up, as shown in Figure 2-12. This row lets you add the appropriate accent mark. Just slide your finger until you're pressing the key with the relevant accent mark and then lift your finger.

FIGURE 2-12:
Accenting your letters.

Meanwhile, if you press and hold down the .? key in Safari, it offers you the choice of .us, .org, .edu, .com, or .net with additional options if you also use international keyboards.

» **Tap the space bar to accept a suggested word, or tap the suggested word to decline the suggestion.** Alas, mistakes are common at first. Say that you meant to type a sentence in the Notes app that reads, "I am fixing an important . . ." But because of the way your fingers struck the virtual keys, you actually entered "I am fixing an *importsnt* . . ." Fortunately, Apple knows that the *a* you meant to press is next to the *s* that showed up on the keyboard, just as *t* and *y* and *e* and *r* are side by side. So the software determines that *important* was indeed the word you had in mind and, as Figure 2-13 reveals, places it front and center among the three predictive text buttons. Note that the suspect word is highlighted. To accept the suggested word, merely tap the space bar. And if for some reason you actually did mean to type *importsnt* or maybe *imports to,* tap those choices instead among the predictive buttons that appear.

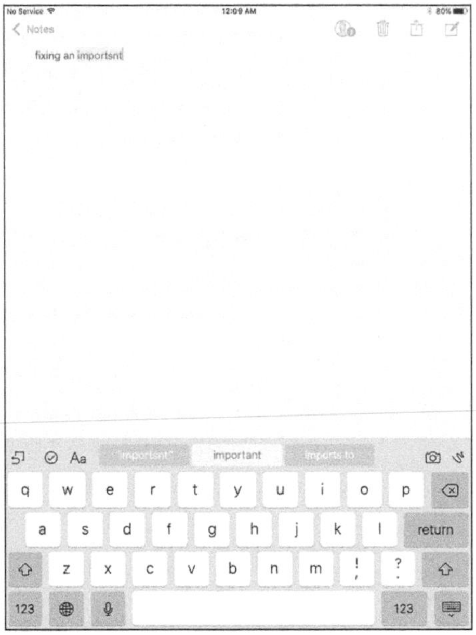

FIGURE 2-13:
Fixing an *important* mistake.

If you don't appreciate these features, you can turn off Auto-Correction and Predictive in Settings. See Chapter 15 for details.

Because Apple knows what you're up to, the virtual keyboard is fine-tuned for the task at hand, especially when you need to enter numbers, punctuation, or symbols. The following tips help you find common special characters or special keys that we know you'll want to use:

>> **Putting the @ in an email address:** If you're composing an email message (see Chapter 5), a dedicated @ key pops up on the main Mail keyboard when you're in the To: field choosing whom to send a message to. That key disappears from the first view when you tap the body of the message to compose your words. You can still get to the @ by tapping the 123 key.

>> **Switching from letters to numbers:** When you're typing notes or sending email and want to type a number, symbol, or punctuation mark, tap the 123 key to bring up an alternative virtual keyboard. Tap the ABC key to return to the first keyboard. This toggle isn't hard to get used to, but some may find it irritating. Meanwhile, after tapping the 123 key, the shift key shifts into a #+= key. Tap #+= to summon additional character and symbol keys.

>> **Adding apostrophes and other punctuation shortcuts:** If you press and hold down the exclamation mark/comma key, a pop-up offers the apostrophe. If you press and hold down the question mark/period key, you'll see the option to type quotation marks.

If you buy any current iPad Pro model or the 10.2-inch iPad, you'll likely want to consider purchasing one of the optional Smart Keyboard covers. Ranging from $159 to $199, these accessories are pricey, but you just might be tempted to go with a physical keyboard. You may be tempted also by the Apple Pencil (first generation costs $99 and second generation is $129). For more on iPad accessories, let us direct you to Chapter 17.

We already mentioned that iPads don't *need* a stylus, but sometimes you might want to use one anyway. If the Apple Pencil is too pricey for you, check out some of the many third-party options. Wacom sells various Bamboo Stylus models, starting around $15. It's a potentially useful tool for those with too broad, oily, or greasy fingers, or those who sketch, draw, or jot notes. You can find lower-priced styluses as well.

Editing mistakes

We think typing with abandon, without getting hung up over mistyped characters, is a good idea. The self-correcting keyboard can fix many errors (and occasionally introduce errors of its own). That said, plenty of typos are likely to turn up, especially in the beginning, and you have to correct them manually.

TIP

A neat trick for doing so is to hold your finger on the line of text you want to edit. A cursor will appear, and you can then slide your finger to the spot where you need to make the correction. Then use the delete key (also called the backspace key) to delete the error and press whatever keys you need to type the correct text.

And with that, you are hereby notified that you've survived basic training. The real fun is about to begin.

Chapter **3**

Synchronicity: Getting Stuff to and from Your iPad

We have good news and . . . more good news. The good news is you can easily set up your iPad so your contacts, appointments, reminders, events, mail settings, bookmarks, books, music, movies, TV shows, podcasts, and photos are synchronized between your computer and your iPad (or other iDevices). And the more good news is that after you set up your iPad, your contacts, appointments, events, and everything else we just mentioned can be kept up to date automatically on all of those devices.

This communication between your iPad and computer is called *syncing* (short for *synchronizing*). Don't worry: It's easy, and we walk you through the entire process in this chapter.

Another form of syncing is moving files to and from your iPad and other iDevices or to and from a Mac or PC. You can do so via iTunes with macOS Mojave and earlier and Windows, or you can do it using Finder in macOS Catalina and later. You can also wirelessly transfer files via AirDrop!

In this chapter, you find out how to sync all the digital data your iPad can handle, right after a short interlude about Apple's iCloud service.

TIP

The information in this chapter is based on iTunes version 12.9, Finder in macOS Catalina 10.15.2, and iPadOS version 13.1, the latest and greatest when these words were written. If your screens don't look exactly like ours, you probably need to upgrade to iTunes 12.9 or higher (PCs and Macs using macOS Mojave or earlier) or macOS 10.15 or higher (Macs using macOS Catalina). To do so, choose iTunes ⇨ Check for Updates (PCs and Macs using macOS Mojave or earlier) or choose ⇨ System Preferences and click the Software Update icon (Macs using macOS Catalina or later). You may also need to update your iPad to iPadOS 13.1 or higher (on your iPad, tap Settings ⇨ General ⇨ Software Update). All of these updates are free and offer useful features not found in their predecessors.

A Brief iCloud Primer

Apple's iCloud is a complete data synchronization and wireless storage solution. In a nutshell, iCloud stores and manages your digital stuff — music, photos, contacts, events, and more — and makes it available to all your computers and iDevices automatically.

iCloud pushes information such as email, calendars, contacts, reminders, and bookmarks to and from your computer and to and from your iPad and other iDevices, and then keeps those items updated on all devices without any effort on your part. iCloud also includes nonsynchronizing options, such as Photo Stream and iCloud photo sharing (see Chapter 9) and email (see Chapter 5).

Your free iCloud account includes 5GB of storage, which is all many users will need. If you have several devices (including Macs and PCs) or like saving data in the cloud, you'll probably need more storage; 50GB, 200GB, and 2TB upgrades are available for $1, $3, and $10 a month, respectively.

A nice touch is that music, apps, periodicals, movies, and TV shows purchased from the iTunes Store, as well as your photo stream and iTunes Match content (see Chapter 7), don't count against your 5GB of free storage. Books (formerly iBooks) don't count against your 5GB either, but audiobooks do. You'll find that the things that do count — such as mail, documents, account information, settings, and other app data — don't use much space, so 5GB might last a long time.

Conversely, if you use iCloud Photos and take a lot of photos and videos with your iDevice cameras, you're going to fill up your free 5GB pretty fast.

REMEMBER

If you're not using iCloud Photos (lovingly described in Chapter 9), you might want to sync your iPad photos with a computer every so often and then delete the photos from the iPad. Otherwise, over time, those photos will take up a lot of space and eventually fill up your iPad.

If you plan to go PC-free, as described in Chapter 2, but still want to have your email, calendars, contacts, and bookmarks automatically synchronized between your computers and other iDevices (and believe us, you do), here's how to enable iCloud syncing on your iPad:

1. **On your Home screen, tap Settings.**

2. **At the top of the Settings list, tap your name.**

3. **Tap iCloud**

   A list of apps appears.

4. **Tap any individual on/off switch to enable or disable iCloud sync.**

   Your choices are Mail, Contacts, Calendars, Reminders, Notes, Safari (Bookmarks), and several other apps with on/off switches.

In the same list are three items that don't have switches: Photos, Keychain, and iCloud Backup. Tap any of these tabs to reveal more controls and options:

>> **Photos:** Enable or disable three iCloud services — iCloud Photos, My Photo Stream, and Shared Albums — with the by-now familiar on/off switches. See Chapter 9 for details.

>> **Keychain:** Enable Apple's Keychain password service. Keychain keeps passwords and credit card information you save up to date on all devices you approve. The info is encrypted and can't be read by Apple (or, we hope, by anyone else).

>> **iCloud Backup:** Enable or disable this service, which backs up your iPad's photo library, accounts, documents, and settings whenever your iPad is plugged in to power, locked, and connected to Wi-Fi. Tap the Back Up Now button to initiate a backup, well, now.

TIP

Tap Manage Storage (near the top of the screen) to manage iCloud storage or upgrade your storage plan. Tap Share with Family (near the top of the Storage screen) to add or remove family members and shared payment methods from your Family Sharing plan (which you read more about in Chapter 15).

You find out much more about iCloud in the rest of this chapter and several other chapters, so let's move on to syncing your iPad.

Getting in Sync

You can sync your calendars, reminders, bookmarks, and other data and documents among your iDevices and computers via iCloud, iTunes (macOS Mojave or earlier and Windows), Finder (macOS Catalina or later), or a combination of the three.

WARNING

While we're talking about syncing, it's important to remember that although you can back up your iPad to iCloud, you'll need to sync it with a Mac or PC to have a local backup, too. We strongly believe that a single backup is never enough. The best practice is to maintain at least two different backups: one in iCloud and another stored locally on your Mac or PC.

Sync prep 101

Synchronizing your iPad with your computer is similar to syncing an iPhone with your computer. That is to say, it's easy! But even if you've never used an iPhone, iTunes (Windows or macOS Mojave and earlier), or the Finder app (macOS Catalina), the process isn't difficult. Follow these steps:

1. **Start by connecting your iPad to your computer with the Lightning-to-USB or USB-C cable that came with your iPad or iPad Pro.**

    When you connect your iPad to your computer, iTunes (or Finder in macOS Catalina) should launch automatically. For Windows or macOS Mojave and earlier, if iTunes doesn't launch automatically, try launching it manually. In macOS Catalina, Finder is always launched.

2. **If you see an alert on your Mac or PC asking whether you want iTunes to open automatically when you connect this iPad, click Yes or No, depending on your preference.**

    You can change this setting later, so don't give it too much thought.

3. **If this is the first time you've introduced your iPad to iTunes or Finder:**

    a. *When an alert on your Mac or PC asks "Do you want to allow this computer to access information on this iPad?" click Continue.*

    b. *On your iPad screen, when you see an alert asking, "Trust this computer?" tap Trust. Enter your passcode if requested, put down the iPad, and go back to iTunes or Finder on your computer.*

4. **Click the iPad icon, shown in the margin and near the top left of the iTunes window or in the left sidebar of a Finder window.**

TIP

If you don't see the iPad icon and you're positive it's connected to a USB port *on your computer* (not the keyboard, monitor, or hub), try restarting your computer.

5. **For Windows PCs and Macs running macOS Mojave or earlier, if you use more than one iDevice with this computer, select your iPad in the drop-down list of all your devices that appears when you click the iPad icon.**

   The Welcome to Your New iPad screen appears.

6. **Click Set Up as New iPad or select a backup from the Restore from This Backup drop-down menu, and then click Continue.**

REMEMBER

   See Chapter 16 for the scoop on restoring from iCloud or iTunes backups. For this example, we tapped Set Up as New iPad.

   The Sync with iTunes screen appears.

7. **Click the Get Started button.**

   The iPad screen appears, as shown in Figure 3-1.

8. **In the list on the left, click Summary, as shown in Figure 3-1.**

   If you don't see a Summary tab, make sure your iPad is still connected. If you don't see your iPad's name near the top-left corner of the iTunes window, as shown in Figure 3-1, go back to Step 1 and try again.

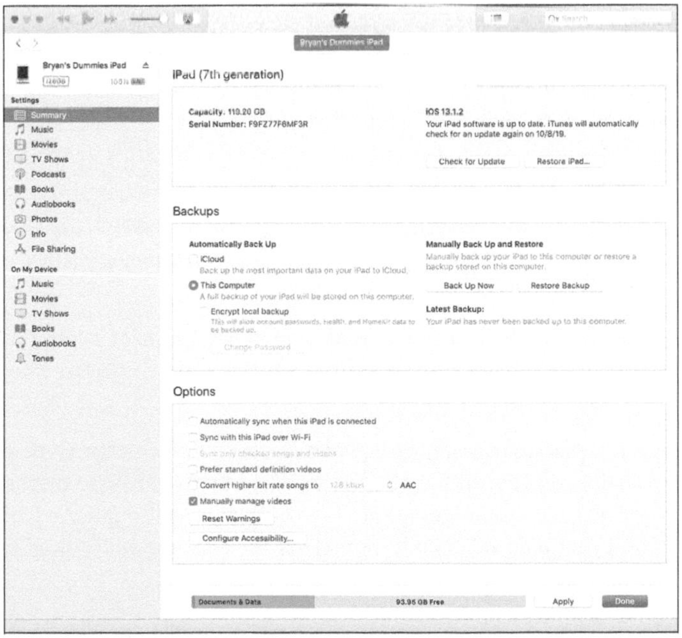

FIGURE 3-1:
The Summary pane is relatively painless.

9. **(Optional) If you want to rename your iPad, click its name and type a new one.**

In Figure 3-1, we renamed ours *Bryan's Dummies iPad.*

On the Summary pane, you can set any options you want from the Options area:

>> **Automatically Back Up:** Select iCloud or This Computer as your preferred location for automatic backups. If you're backing up to This Computer, select the check box for Encrypt Local Backup to automatically include your saved passwords, Health, and HomeKit data in your automatic backups, which we recommend.

>> **Automatically sync when this iPad is connected:** Select this option if you want your iPad to sync every time you connect it to your Mac or PC. If you don't select this option, your iPad will be synced only when you back up or when you manually sync.

>> **Sync with This iPad Over Wi-Fi:** If you want to sync automatically over your Wi-Fi connection, select the check box.

WARNING

If you choose to sync wirelessly, your iPad and computer must be on the same Wi-Fi network and your iPad must be plugged into a power source for syncing to occur.

>> **Sync Only Checked Songs:** If you want to sync only items that have check marks to the left of their names in your iTunes library, select this check box. If you choose to use Apple's iTunes Match cloud-based storage (described in Chapter 7), this option will appear dimmed and be unavailable.

>> **Prefer Standard Definition:** If you want high-definition videos you import to be automatically converted into smaller standard-definition video files when you transfer them to your iPad, select this check box.

Standard-definition video files are significantly smaller than high-definition video files. You'll notice the difference when you watch the video on your iPad, but you can have more video files on your iPad because they take up less space.

WARNING

The conversion from HD to standard definition takes a *long* time, so be prepared for very long sync times when you sync new HD video and have this option selected.

If you plan to use Apple's digital AV adapter (choose the Lightning or USB-C version, as appropriate) or Apple TV (starting at $149) to display movies on an HDTV, consider going with high definition. Although the files will be bigger and your iPad will hold fewer videos, the HD versions look spectacular on a big-screen TV.

>> **Convert Higher Bit Rate Songs to 128/192/256 Kbps AAC:** If you want songs with bit rates higher than 128, 192, or 256 Kbps converted into smaller AAC files when you transfer them to your iPad, select this check box and choose the lower bit rate from the drop-down menu.

A *higher* bit rate means the song will have better sound quality but use more storage space. Songs you buy in the iTunes Store or on Amazon, for example, have bit rates of around 256 Kbps. So a four-minute song with a 256-Kbps bit rate is around 8MB; convert it to 128-Kbps AAC, and it's roughly half that size (that is, around 4MB) while sounding almost as good.

Everyone's hearing is different: Some people can't tell the difference between higher and lower bit rate music, while others think listening to lower bit rate files is little better than fingernails down a chalkboard! Song file size has become less important as iPad storage has increased and more people listen to music through streaming services. (See Chapter 7 for more on Apple Music.) If you're picky about your music quality, don't convert it. If you aren't picky and are concerned about storage on your iPad, convert it.

>> **Manually Manage Videos:** To turn off automatic syncing in the Video panes, select this check box.

One more thing: If you decide to select the Prevent iPods, iPhones, and iPads from Syncing Automatically check box on the Devices tab in iTunes Preferences (that's iTunes ⇨ Preferences on a Mac and Edit ⇨ Preferences on a PC), you can still synchronize manually by clicking the Sync or Apply button in the lower-right corner of the window.

TECHNICAL STUFF

Why the Sync *or* Apply button? Glad you asked. If you've changed *any* sync settings since the last time you synchronized, the Sync button instead says Apply. When you click that button — regardless of its name — your iPad will start to sync.

Backing Up Your iPad

Whether you know it or not, your iPad backs up your settings, your app data, photos and videos you shoot, and other information whenever you connect to a computer and use iTunes to sync with, update, or restore your iPad.

Backups are saved automatically and stored in iCloud by default, or you can choose to back up to your computer by clicking the appropriate button in the iTunes Summary pane, as described in the preceding section.

If anything goes wonky, or you get a new iPad, you can restore most (if not all) of your settings and files that aren't synced with iCloud or iTunes on your computer. Or, if you've backed up an iPhone, an iPod touch, or another iPad, you can restore the new iPad from the older device's backup.

Regardless of whether you back up locally or to iCloud, you should encrypt your backups. Unless you enable encryption, important data such as website and Wi-Fi passwords won't be backed up. Because backups to iCloud are encrypted by default with the Apple ID password associated with the account, you don't have to do anything else if you choose iCloud backups. But if you back up to your computer, encryption is turned off by default. So enable the Encrypt Local Backup check box (refer to Figure 3-1).

We strongly recommend that you encrypt your backups. Simply select the check box and type a password (and don't forget it), and you'll never have to think about it again.

TIP

One last thing: Many users maintain both types of backup — iCloud and computer — and that is what we strongly recommend. To do so, merely enable This Computer instead of iCloud (or iCloud instead of This Computer) and click the Back Up Now button. When the backup is finished, switch it back (or not). Either way, you now have a backup on your hard drive and a second backup in iCloud. Although your iCloud backups use up some of your iCloud space, redundancy in backups is a good thing.

Disconnecting the iPad

If your iPad is connected and syncing, you'll see the sync icon next to the device (as shown in Figure 3-2). At the same time, a message appears at the top of the iTunes window to inform you that your iPad is syncing, as shown at the top of Figure 3-2.

When your iPad is connected and not syncing, you'll see the eject icon (shown in the margin) to the right of its name rather than the sync icon.

When the sync is finished, the sync icon in Figure 3-2 stops spinning and morphs back into an eject icon, and the message at the top of the window disappears.

WARNING

If you disconnect your iPad before the sync finishes, all or part of the sync may fail. Although early termination of a sync isn't usually a problem, it's safer to cancel the sync and let it finish gracefully than to yank the cable out while a sync is in progress. So just don't do that, okay?

Sync icon   Click to cancel sync

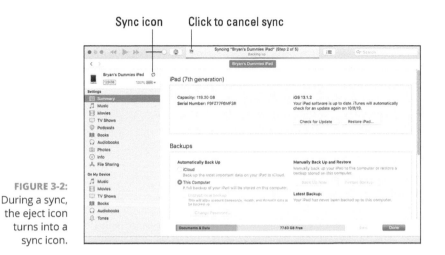

FIGURE 3-2:
During a sync,
the eject icon
turns into a
sync icon.

To cancel a sync properly and disconnect your iPad *safely* from your Mac or PC, first hover your cursor over the animated sync icon in the left column in iTunes (see Figure 3-2) or Finder until it becomes an x-in-a-circle. Then click the x-in-a-circle and the sync will stop.

Synchronizing Your Data

Your next order of business is to tell iTunes what data you want to synchronize between your iPad and your computer.

To get started, first select your iPad by clicking the iPad icon (or the devices drop-down menu, if you have more than one iDevice) near the top left of the iTunes window. Then click the Info tab, which is the last tab in the Settings list on the left.

If you're using iCloud to sync contacts, calendars, bookmarks, or notes — which we recommend — you won't be able to enable these items in iTunes. Turn off iCloud syncing on your iPad (choose Settings ⇨ iCloud) for items you want to sync with your Mac or PC.

The Info pane has three sections: Sync Contacts, Sync Calendars, and Advanced, which we look at one by one. One last thing: To use your iPad with a Google or Yahoo! account, you must sign in with the appropriate account on your iPad, as described in Chapter 5. After you've added the account to your iPad, you can enable contact or calendar syncing with it in the Settings app under Mail, Contacts, and Calendars.

Contacts

In Figure 3-3, note that the section is named Sync Contacts because this image was captured on a Mac. Contacts (formerly known as Address Book) is the Mac application that syncs with your iPad's Contacts app.

If you use a PC, you see a drop-down list that gives you the choices of Outlook, Google Contacts, Windows Address Book, or Yahoo! Address Book. Don't worry — the process works the same on either platform.

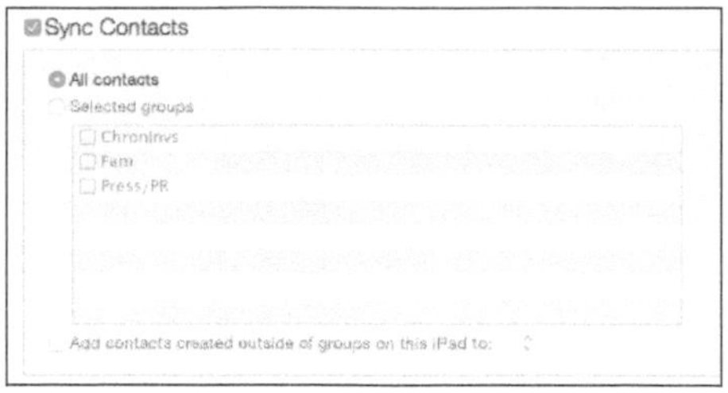

FIGURE 3-3:
Want to synchronize your contacts? This is where you set up things.

The iPad syncs with the following address book programs:

>> **Mac:** Contacts and other address books that sync with Contacts, such as Microsoft Outlook

>> **PC:** Windows Contacts (Vista, Windows 7 or later), Windows Address Book (XP), Microsoft Outlook, and Microsoft Outlook Express

>> **Mac and PC:** Yahoo! Address Book and Google Contacts

You can sync contacts with multiple apps.

The Contacts section has the following options:

>> **All Contacts:** One method is to synchronize all your contacts, as shown in Figure 3-3. This will synchronize every contact in your Mac or PC address book with your iPad's Contacts app.

>> **Selected Groups:** You can synchronize any or all groups of contacts you've created in your computer's address book program. Just select the appropriate check boxes in the Selected Groups list, and only those groups will be synchronized.

>> **Add Contacts Created Outside of Groups on This iPad To (iTunes on macOS Mojave or earlier or Windows) or Add New Contacts from This iPad To (macOS Catalina):** Enable this option and you can choose a group from the pop-up menu. New contacts created on this iPad will belong to the group you select.

If you sync with your employer's Microsoft Exchange calendar and contacts, all personal contacts and calendars already on your iPad might be wiped out.

Calendars

The Sync Calendars section of the Info pane determines how synchronization is handled for your appointments, events, and reminders. You can synchronize all your calendars, as shown in Figure 3-4. Or you can synchronize any or all individual calendars you've created in your computer's calendar program. Just select the appropriate check boxes.

FIGURE 3-4:
Set up sync for your calendar events here.

The iPad syncs with the following calendar programs:

>> **Mac:** Calendar

>> **PC:** Microsoft Exchange and Outlook 2003, 2007, 2010, and later

>> **Mac and PC:** Google Calendar and Yahoo! Calendar

Advanced syncing

Every so often, the contacts, calendars, mail accounts, or bookmarks on your iPad get so screwed up that the easiest way to fix things is to erase that information from your iPad and replace it with information from your computer.

If that's the case, go to the Advanced section of the Info pane and click to select the Contacts or Calendars check boxes (or both). Then, the next time you sync, that information on your iPad will be replaced with the contacts or calendars from your computer.

Because the Advanced section is at the bottom of the Info pane and you have to scroll down to see it, you can easily forget that the Advanced section is there.

Synchronizing Your Media

If you chose to let iTunes manage synchronizing your data automatically, welcome. This section looks at how you get your media — your music, podcasts, videos, and photos — from your computer to your iPad.

REMEMBER

Podcasts and videos from your computer are synced only one way: from your computer to your iPad. If you delete a podcast or a video that got onto your iPad via syncing, the podcast or video will not be deleted from your computer when you sync.

That said, if you buy or download any of the following items from the iTunes Store, Book Store, or App Store *on your iPad*, the item *will* be copied back to your computer automatically when you sync:

>> Songs

>> Podcasts

>> Videos

>> E-books and audiobooks from the Book Store.

>> Playlists you created on your iPad

And if you save pictures from email messages, the iPad camera, web pages, or screen shots, these too can be synced.

You use the Music, Movies, TV Shows, and Photos panes to specify the media you want to copy from your computer to your iPad. The following sections explain the options you find in each pane.

To view any of these panes, make sure your iPad is still selected and then click the appropriate tab in the list of Settings on the left.

The following sections focus only on syncing. If you need help acquiring apps, music, movies, podcasts, or anything else for your iPad, just flip to the most applicable chapter for help.

TIP

The last step in each section is "Click the Sync or Apply button in the lower-right corner of the window." You have to do this only when selecting that item for the first time and if you make any changes to the item after that.

Music, music videos, and voice memos

To transfer music to your iPad, select the Sync Music check box in the Music pane. You can then select the option for Entire Music Library or Selected Playlists, Artists, Albums, and Genres. If you choose the latter, select the check boxes next to particular playlists, artists, albums, and genres you want to transfer. You also can choose to include music videos or voice memos or both by selecting the appropriate check boxes near the top of the pane (see Figure 3-5).

FIGURE 3-5: Use the Music pane to copy music, music videos, and voice memos from your computer to your iPad.

HOW MUCH SPACE DID I USE?

If you're interested in knowing how much free space is available on your iPad, look near the bottom of the iTunes window while your iPad is connected. You'll see a chart that shows the contents of your iPad, color-coded for your convenience. As you can see in the figure, this iPad has 77.67GB of free space. Hover your cursor over any color to see a bubble with info on that category, as shown for Documents & Data in the figure.

You can find similar information about space used and space remaining on your iPad by tapping Settings ⇨ General ⇨ iPad Storage. You can also see how much storage each of your apps is using.

WARNING

If you choose Entire Music Library and have more songs in your iTunes library than storage space on your iPad, the sync will fail and the capacity bar at the bottom of the screen will display your overage.

WARNING

Music, podcasts, and video are notorious for using massive amounts of storage space on your iPad. If you try to sync too much media content, you see lots of error messages. Forewarned is forearmed. One solution is to create one or more iPad-specific playlists and sync only those. You might also listen to podcasts with the Podcasts app, which can stream episodes (in addition to letting you download them). Streamed episodes don't take up storage on your iPad!

Finally, if you select the Automatically Fill Free Space with Songs check box, iTunes fills any free space on your iPad with music. We strongly recommend against choosing this option because, you can easily run out of space for pictures and videos you shoot or documents you save (to name just a few of the possible consequences of filling your iPad with songs outside your control).

Movies

To transfer movies to your iPad, select the Movies pane in the sidebar on the left (macOS Mojave or earlier or Windows) or select your iPad in the Finder sidebar (macOS Catalina or later), and then click Movies. Next, select the Sync Movies check box and then, from the pop-up menu, choose an option for movies you want to include automatically. In Figure 3-6, we are choosing to automatically include all movies using iTunes. If you choose an option other than All, you can optionally select individual movies and playlists by selecting the boxes in appropriate sections.

FIGURE 3-6: Your choices in the Movies pane determine which movies are copied to your iPad.

TV shows

The procedure for syncing TV shows is almost the same as the one for syncing movies. First, select the Sync TV Shows check box to enable TV show syncing. Then select the Automatically Include check box. Next, choose how many episodes to include from the pop-up menu and whether you want all shows or only selected shows from the second pop-up menu. If you want to also include individual episodes or episodes on playlists, select the appropriate check boxes in the Shows, Episodes, and Include Episodes from Playlists sections of the TV Shows pane.

Podcasts

To transfer podcasts to your iPad, select the Sync Podcasts check box in the Podcasts pane. Then you can automatically include however many podcasts you want by making selections from the two pop-up menus, the same way you did for TV Shows.

Books and Audiobooks

By now we're sure you know the drill: You can sync all your e-books and audiobooks as well as just sync selected titles by choosing the appropriate buttons and check boxes in the Books and Audiobooks panes. We talk more about the Books app in Chapter 7.

Photos

To sync photos between computers and iDevices, you must enable iCloud Photos (formerly known as iCloud Photo Library).

You can also *copy* photos to your iPad from the Photos app (Mac only) or any folder on your computer that contains images (Mac or PC).

To enable iCloud Photos, choose one of the following:

» **On your iPad:** Choose Settings ➪ *yourname* ➪ iCloud ➪ Photos, and then turn on iCloud Photos.

» **On your Mac:** Choose System Preferences ➪ Apple ID, and then select the check box for iCloud Photos.

» **On your PC:** Download and launch iCloud for Windows. Click Options (next to Photos), select iCloud Photos, click Done, and then click Apply. Now enable iCloud Photos on all your Apple devices.

You can also choose to use My Photo Stream and iCloud photo sharing, and customize the location of your upload and download folders.

When you turn on iCloud Photos on your PC, My Photo Stream is turned off automatically. If you want to send new photos to devices that don't use iCloud Photos, turn My Photo Stream back on.

Now, connect your iPad to your computer and return to iTunes (Windows PC or macOS Mojave or earlier) or Finder (macOS Catalina and later). Select the Photos tab, and then select the Sync Photos check box and the Automatically Include check box. Next, choose an application or folder from the pop-up menu.

If you choose an application that supports photo albums (such as Photoshop Elements, Aperture, or Photos), projects (Aperture), events (Photos), facial recognition and places (Aperture or Photos), or any combination thereof, you can automatically include recent projects, events, or faces by making a selection from the same pop-up menu.

Note that although Photoshop Elements includes features called Places and Faces, those features are not supported by your iPad.

TIP

You can also type a word or phrase in the search field (an oval with a magnifying glass) to search for a specific event or events.

If you choose a folder full of images, you can create subfolders inside it that will appear as albums on your iPad.

If you've taken any photos with your iPad or saved images from a web page, an email, an MMS message, or an iMessage since the last time you synced, the appropriate program launches (or the appropriate folder is selected) when you connect your iPad, and you have the option of uploading the pictures on your iPad to your computer.

Manual Syncing

This chapter has focused on automatic syncing thus far. Automatic syncing is great; it selects items to sync based on criteria you've specified, such as genre, artist, playlist, and album. But it's not efficient for transferring a few items — songs, movies, podcasts, or other files — to your iPad.

The solution? Manual syncing. With automatic syncing, iTunes updates your iPad automatically to match your criteria. With manual syncing, you merely drag individual items to your iPad.

TIP

Automatic and manual sync aren't mutually exclusive. If you've set up automatic syncing, you can still sync individual items manually.

You can manually sync music, movies, TV shows, podcasts, and iTunes U lessons but not photos and info such as contacts, calendars, and bookmarks.

TIP

Want to see which songs, movies, TV shows, and other media are already on your device? iTunes users can use the On My Device section in the sidebar (if the sidebar isn't displayed, choose View➪Show Sidebar). macOS Catalina users should select their iPad in the sidebar, and then click the Files tab.

To configure your iPad for manual syncing:

1. **Connect your iPad to your computer via USB-to-Lightning, USB-C, or Wi-Fi.**

   If iTunes doesn't open automatically, open it manually.

2. **iTunes users should click the iPad icon to the right of the media kind drop-down menu. Finder users should click their iPad in the sidebar.**

   If you have more than one iDevice, the iPad icon becomes a drop-down menu listing all your connected iDevices. Click the icon to display the menu with your devices, and then select the device you want.

   In Finder, you see all connected iOS and iPadOS devices in the sidebar of all windows.

3. **(Optional) Click the Summary tab. In the Options section, select Manually Manage Music and Videos.**

   This step disables automatic syncing for music and videos.

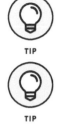

TIP

   If you're happy with automatic syncing and just want to get some audio or video from your computer to your iPad, feel free to skip this step.

You can wirelessly transfer a file, photo, movie, and anything you can share from your iPad to another Apple device by using AirDrop — and vice versa! Both devices must be on the same Wi-Fi network, nearby, unlocked, and the destination device much be set to allow AirDrop file transfers (go to Settings➪General➪AirDrop). To transfer a file using AirDrop, tap the share icon for a file and then the AirDrop icon that appears on the Sharing pane. Nearby, unlocked devices on the same Wi-Fi network will appear. Choose which device to send the file to, and wait until the AirDrop pane says Sent. This method is great for getting a small number of files to and from your iPad quickly.

That's pretty much all you need to know to sync files automatically or manually. And if you haven't figured out how to watch movies or listen to audio on your iPad yet, it's only because you haven't read Part 3 on multimedia, where watching and listening to your iPad are made crystal clear.

2

The Internet iPad

IN THIS PART . . .

Explore Safari, the best web browser to ever to grace a handheld device. Take advantage of links and bookmarks; and, how to view every open web page on any of your other Apple devices in Safari on your iPad.

Set up email accounts and send and receive real honest-to-goodness email messages and attachments.

Discover the amazing world of iMessage and the Messages app; the joy and usefulness of animoji and memoji; how you can send and receive money through the Messages app with Apple Pay Cash, and more.

Chapter **4**

Going on a Mobile Safari

Y ou feel like you're holding the web right in the palm of your hand.

Sure, that's something Apple might say, but a lot of truth is behind it. The spectacular Retina display combined with Apple's snappy AX family of chips makes browsing on Apple's tablets an absolute delight. With the 64-bit A12X Fusion chip and embedded M10 coprocessor in the newest iPad Pro models, browsing on an iPad has never been better.

In this chapter, you discover the pleasures — and the few roadblocks — in navigating cyberspace on your iPad.

Surfin' Dude

The Apple Safari web browser is a major reason that the Internet on the iPad is every bit the Internet you've come to expect on a more traditional computer. Safari for the Mac and for Windows are two of the very best web browsers in the business. In our view, Safari on the iPhone has no rival as a smartphone browser. Safari on the iPad is even more appealing.

Exploring the browser

We start our cyberexpedition with a quick tour of the Safari browser. Take a gander at Figure 4-1. Not all browser controls found on a Mac or a PC are present, but Safari on the iPad still has a familiar look and feel. We describe these controls and others throughout this chapter.

Blasting off into cyberspace

Surfing the web begins with a web address, of course.

TIP

Here are a few tips for using the keyboard in Safari (see Chapter 2 for more help with using the virtual keyboard):

Previous page
Next page
Bookmarks/reading list/history
Website settings
Smart search field
Share pane
View open tabs
Reload web page
Add tab
Share

FIGURE 4-1:
The iPad's Safari browser.

>> Because so many web addresses end with the suffix .com (pronounced *dot com*), the virtual keyboard has a few shortcuts worth noting. Press and hold your finger against the .? key, and you'll see that .com option as well as other common web suffixes (.us, org, .edu, and .net). Some options appear only if you've selected an international keyboard (as discussed in Chapter 2).

>> The moment you tap a letter, you see a list of web addresses that match that letter. For example, if you tap the letter *E* (as we did in the example shown in Figure 4-2), you see web listings for eBay, ESPN, and others. Tapping *U*, *H*, or *M* instead may display listings for *USA TODAY*, *The Houston Chronicle*, or *The Mac Observer* (shameless plugs for the publications where Ed, Bob, and Bryan, respectively, write).

>> In iPadOS, each key on the virtual keyboard has two values. Tap, and you get the darker letter, number, or symbol. Swipe down on a key, and you get the letter, number, or symbol in gray, at the top of the key.

TIP Siri can lend a hand, um, voice, as you surf. If you call upon Siri and ask the voice genie inside the iPad to open the Safari app, Siri obliges. If you mention a specific website to Siri — "ESPN.com," say — Siri opens the site or at the very least your designated search engine (Google, Bing, or Yahoo!), as discussed later in this chapter. And that web page will open in a new tab, so you don't lose whatever pages are already open.

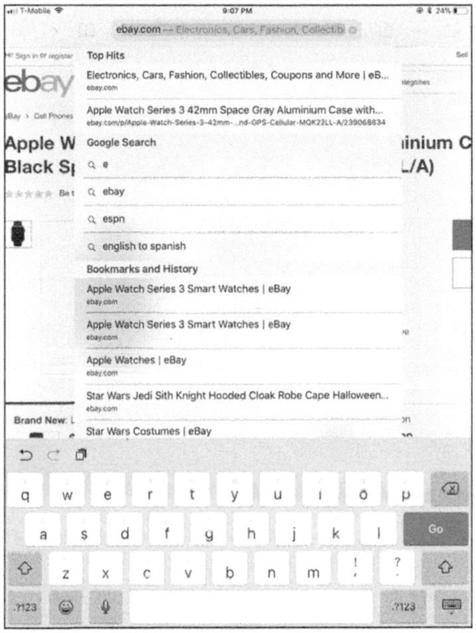

FIGURE 4-2:
Web pages that match your search letter.

When you tap certain letters, the iPad has three ways to determine websites to suggest:

>> **Bookmarks:** The iPad suggests websites you've bookmarked from Safari or other browsers on your computer (and synchronized, as we describe in Chapter 3). More on bookmarks later in this chapter.

>> **History:** The iPad suggests sites from the history list — those cyberdestinations where you recently hung your hat, including websites you've visited on your other Apple devices. Because history repeats itself, we also tackle that topic later in this chapter.

>> **Smart search field:** When you type an address in the search field, you see icons for sites you frequent most often, and you can tap any of those icons to jump immediately to those sites.

You might as well open your first web page now — and it's a full *HTML* page, to borrow from techie lingo:

1. **Tap the Safari icon docked at the bottom of the Home screen.**

   If you haven't moved the Safari icon, it's a member of the Fantastic Five on the dock (along with Messages, Mail, Music, and Files). Chapter 1 introduces the Home screen.

2. **Tap the smart search field (refer to Figure 4-1).**

3. **Begin typing the web address, or *URL*, on the virtual keyboard that slides up from the bottom of the screen.**

4. **Do one of the following:**

   - *To accept one of the bookmarked (or other) sites that show up in the list, merely tap the name.* Safari automatically fills in the URL in the address field and takes you where you want to go.

   - *Keep tapping the proper keyboard characters until you enter the complete web address for the site you have in mind, and then tap the Go key on the right side of the keyboard.*

REMEMBER

   You don't need to type **www** at the beginning of a URL. So if you want to visit www.theonion.com, for example, typing **theonion.com** is sufficient to transport you to the humor site.

TECHNICAL STUFF

Safari in iPadOS is a desktop browser first — even more so than it was when iPad ran Apple's iOS. When you pull up a website on your iPad, it no longer defaults to the mobile version, because Apple takes steps behind the scenes to make sure your iPad is requesting the full desktop version of every website.

TIP

You can still pull up the mobile version of a website, though we can't imagine why you'd want to. Simply tap the AA icon in the smart search field and tap Request Mobile Website in the pane that appears. This action affects only the current site.

Zoom, zoom, zoom

Zooming in can let you read and see what you want, without enlisting a magnifying glass. Better yet, it's easy to zoom in, and we show you how.

Try these neat tricks for starters:

>> **Unpinch the page to zoom.** Sliding your thumb and index finger together and then spreading them apart (or, as we like to say, *unpinching*) zooms in

and out of a page. By way of example, check out Figure 4-3, which shows two views from Apple's web page for the 2019 Mac Pro. In the first view, you see what the page looks like when you first open it. In the second view, we've zoomed in to get a closer look at the ventilation holes — and come on, we're all thinking they look like aliens.

>> **Press down on a page and drag it in any direction, or flick through a page from top to bottom.** You're panning and scrolling, baby.

>> **Rotate the iPad to its side.** This action reorients from portrait view to a widescreen landscape view. The keyboard is also wider, making it a little easier to enter a new URL. However, this little bit of rotation magic won't happen if you set and enabled the screen orientation lock feature, which we describe in Chapter 1.

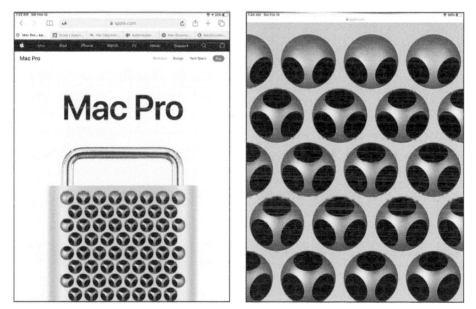

FIGURE 4-3:
Unpinch to
zoom in.

Reading clutter-free web pages with reader view

It's all too easy to get distracted reading web pages, what with ads, videos, and other clutter surrounding the stuff you want to take in. Reader view can remove most of those distractions, but you need to activate it first.

When you first pull up a new web page that has reader view available, the URL bar briefly displays *Reader View Available*. To activate reader view, tap the AA icon, which appears to the left of the URL, as shown in Figure 4-4. If Show Reader View is blue in the pane that appears, tap it to switch to reader view. If Show Reader View appears dimmed, reader view is not available on this site.

Tap for clutter-free reading

FIGURE 4-4:
Reducing
clutter when
reading.

Finding Your Way around Cyberspace

In this section, we discuss ways to navigate the Internet on your iPad by using links and tabs.

Looking at lovable links

Because Safari functions on the iPad in the same way browsers work on your Mac or PC, text links that transport you from one site to another typically are underlined, are shown in blue, red, or bold type, or appear as items in a list. Tap the link to go directly to the site or page.

Other types of links lead to different outcomes:

>> **Map address link:** Tapping an address might launch the Maps app.

>> **Email address link:** Tap an email address, and the iPad opens the Mail app (see Chapter 5) and populates the To field with that address. The virtual keyboard is also summoned so you can add other email addresses and compose a subject line and message. For this feature to work, your Mail app must be set up (see Chapter 5).

TIP

To see the URL for a link, press your finger on the link and hold it there until a preview of the linked web page pops up, along with a list of options (see Figure 4-5). You can use this method also to preview where a linked image will take you.

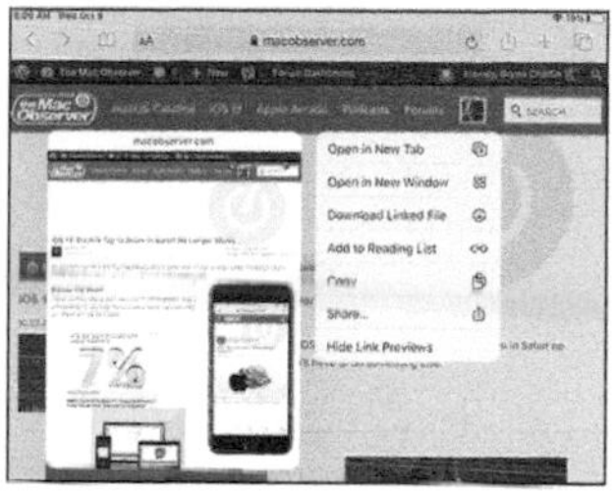

As for the link options shown in Figure 4-5, here's what three of them do:

FIGURE 4-5:
Tap and hold down on a link to see a preview and other options.

>> **Open in New Tab:** Opens the link in a new tab.

>> **Copy:** Copies the link's URL to your iPad's Clipboard so you can paste it elsewhere.

>> **Share:** Tap to open the same sharing options presented when you tap the share icon.

Not every web link cooperates with the iPad because it doesn't support some common web standards.

Tabbed browsing

When we surf the web on a Mac or PC, we rarely go to a single web page and call it a day. In fact, we often have multiple web pages open at the same time. Sometimes we choose to hop around the web without closing the pages we visit. Sometimes a link automatically opens a new page without closing the old one, whether we want it to or not.

Safari on the iPad, like the desktop version of Safari (and other browsers), lets you open multiple pages. After you have one page open, you have two ways to open additional web pages in Safari so they appear on the tab bar at the top of the screen (rather than replace the page you're currently viewing):

» **Tap the + icon near the top-right corner of the browser.** A tab named Favorites appears, as shown in Figure 4-6. Now type a URL, tap a bookmark or an icon for a favorite or frequently visited site, or initiate a search, and the result will appear on this tab.

» **Hold your finger on a link until a list of options appears (refer to Figure 4-5), and then tap Open in New Tab.**

New tab

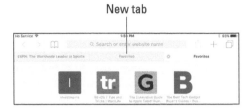

FIGURE 4-6:
A new tab, ready to display any page you choose.

To switch tabs, just tap the tab you want to view. To close a tab, tap the gray x-in-a-circle that appears on the left edge of the active tab.

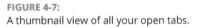 You can manage tabs in one other way. Tap the view open tabs icon in the top-right corner of the browser (labeled in Figure 4-1 and shown in the margin) to summon thumbnail views of your open web pages, as shown in Figure 4-7. You can tap the X on any thumbnail to close it. From here you can also go into private browsing mode (discussed later in this chapter) or check out iCloud tabs, the topic we're about to dive into.

Surfing your iCloud tabs

FIGURE 4-7:
A thumbnail view of all your open tabs.

Although the iPad is your likely traveling companion just about everywhere you go, we know you also browse the web from your smartphone or personal computer. If that smartphone happens to be an iPhone and the computer is a Mac (or a Windows PC running Safari), you can take advantage of iCloud tabs, a feature that lets you resume reading web pages you started looking at on those other devices. Tap the view open tabs icon (shown in the margin) to bring up tab view.

Doing the splits

When you rotate an iPad running iPadOS in landscape mode, you can display a split view in Safari, with two web pages each claiming half the screen. For instance, maybe you're trying to decide between two cars or exploring different places to go on vacation.

In typical Apple fashion, you can arrive at this split view in more than one way:

>> Drag a tab to the left or right edge of the screen and release.

>> Tap and drag any link in a web page to the left or right edge of the screen and release.

To exit split view, drag the gray handle in the middle of your display to the left or right edge of the screen and release. If you drag to the right, the window on the left side takes over the entire screen. If you drag to the left, the window on the right side takes over your screen.

Revisiting Web Pages

Surfing the web would be a drag if you had to enter a URL every time you wanted to navigate from one page to another. To find those favorite websites in the future, the iPad provides bookmarks, web clips, reading lists, and history lists.

Book(mark) 'em, Danno

You already know how useful bookmarks are and how you can synchronize bookmarks from the browsers on your computer. It's equally simple to bookmark a web page directly on the iPad. Follow these steps:

1. **Make sure the page you want to bookmark is open, and then tap the share icon (shown in the margin) at the top of the screen.**

    You have many options beyond bookmarking when you tap the share icon (refer to Figure 4-1, though not all the options are visible in the figure), as you discover later in this chapter.

2. **Tap Add Bookmark.**

   A new Add Bookmark window opens with a default name for the bookmark, its web address, maybe a logo, and its folder location.

3. **Give the bookmark a name and folder location:**

   - *Accept the default bookmark name and default bookmark folder:* Tap Save.

   - *Change the default bookmark name:* Tap the *x*-in-a-circle next to the name, enter the new title (using the virtual keyboard), and then tap Save.

   - *Change the location where the bookmark is saved:* Tap the suggested Location field, which likely shows Favorites, tap the folder where you want the bookmark to be kept so that a check mark appears, and then tap Save.

To open a bookmarked page after you set it up, tap the bookmarks icon, which is to the left of the smart search field. (Refer to Figure 4-1.)

REMEMBER

If you don't see bookmarks right away after tapping the bookmarks icon, make sure the leftmost of the three tabs at the top of the bookmarks menu is highlighted. The other tabs are for the reading list and your history.

If the bookmark you have in mind is buried inside a folder, tap the folder name first and then tap the bookmark you want.

Altering bookmarks

If a bookmarked site is no longer meaningful, you can change it or get rid of it:

TIP

- » **To remove a bookmark (or folder),** tap the bookmarks icon and then tap Edit. Tap the red circle next to the bookmark you want to toss off the list, and then tap Delete.

  To remove a single bookmark or folder, you can also swipe its name from right to left and then tap the red Delete button.

- » **To change a bookmark name or location,** tap Edit at the bottom-right corner of the Bookmarks window. Tap a given bookmark, and an Edit Bookmark window appears, with the name, URL, and location of the bookmark already filled in. Tap the fields you want to change. In the Name field, tap the gray *x*-in-a-circle and then use the keyboard to enter a new title. In the Location field, tap the location name and scroll up or down the list until you find a new home for your bookmark.

- » **To create a new folder for your bookmarks,** tap Edit and then tap New Folder. Enter the name of the new folder, and choose where to put it.

>> **To move a bookmark up or down in a list,** tap Edit and then drag the three bars to the right of the bookmark's name to the bookmark's new resting place.

If you take advantage of iCloud, the web pages you've bookmarked on your Mac and on your other iOS devices will be available on the iPad, and vice versa.

Saving to your reading list

When you visit a web page you'd like to read, but just not now, the reading list feature is sure to come in handy, including when you're offline. Here's how it works:

>> **Saving a page for later:** Tap the share icon and then tap Add to Reading List. Or, if you see a link to a page you'd like to read later, press on the link until a list of options appears (refer to Figure 4-5) and then tap Add to Reading List. The first time you add an article to your reading list, you may be asked if you would like to automatically save reading list articles for offline viewing. Tap Save Automatically or Don't Save Automatically, as you want.

>> **Reading a page on your reading list:** Tap the bookmarks icon and tap the page in the reading list, as shown in Figure 4-8.

>> **Keeping track of what you've read:** Tap Show Unread to display only those items you haven't read yet. Tap Show All to show all the items in the reading list.

>> **Removing items from the reading list:** Swipe the item from right to left, and then tap its red Delete button. If you swipe a little farther to the left, you can tap Mark Read instead.

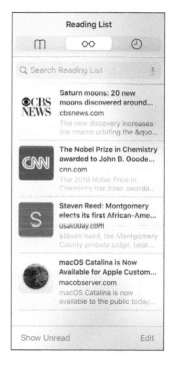

FIGURE 4-8:
Tap a page in the reading list to read it.

Finally, don't forget you can share your reading list (and bookmarks) among your computers and iDevices with iCloud, as described in Chapter 3.

Clipping a web page

You frequent lots of websites, some way more than others. For example, perhaps you consult the train schedule several times during the day. In their infinite wisdom, the folks at Apple let you bestow special privileges on frequently visited sites, not just by bookmarking pages but also by affording them unique Home screen icons. Creating one is dead simple. Follow these steps:

1. **Open the web page in question, and tap the share icon (shown in the margin).**

2. **Tap Add to Home Screen; you may have to scroll through the options to find it.**

   Apple creates an icon out of the area of the page that was displayed when you saved the clip, unless the page has its own custom icon.

3. **Type a new name for your web clip or leave the one Apple suggests.**

4. **Tap Add.**

   The icon appears on your Home screen.

TIP

As with any icon, you can remove a web clip by pressing and holding down on its icon until it starts to wiggle. Tap the X in the corner of the icon, and then tap Delete. You can also move the web clip to a more preferred location on one of your Home screens or on the dock.

Letting history repeat itself

Sometimes you want to revisit a site you failed to bookmark, but you can't remember the darn destination or what led you there in the first place. Good thing you can study the history books.

Safari records the pages you visit and keeps the logs on hand for several days. Here's how to access your history:

1. **Tap the bookmarks icon and then tap the history icon (clock) at the top of the pane that appears.**

2. **Tap the day you think you hung out at the site.**

   Sites are listed under such headings as This Morning, Thursday Evening, or Thursday Morning, or segregated by a specific date.

3. **When you find the listing, tap it.**

   You're about to make your triumphant return.

To clear your history so no one can trace your steps, tap Clear in the bottom-right corner of the history list. You can clear the last hour, clear only the day when you tapped Clear, clear today and yesterday, or clear all your history. Alternatively, starting on the Home screen, tap Settings ⇨ Safari ⇨ Clear History and Website Data. With both methods, per usual, you have a chance to back out without wiping the slate clean.

When you clear your history from settings, your history, cookies, and browsing data will be removed from all the devices signed into iCloud. If that was not your intention, tap Cancel.

Saving web pictures

You can capture most pictures you come across on a website — but be mindful of any potential copyright violations, depending on what you plan to do with the images. To copy an image from a website, follow these steps:

1. **Tap and hold down on the image.**

   A preview of the image you have selected appears, along with a pop-up menu offering the following options: Share, Add to Photos, and Copy.

2. **Tap Add to Photos, as shown in Figure 4-9.**

   Saved images end up in your Photos, where they can be synced back to a computer.

   Tap Copy instead, and you can paste the image into an email or as a link in a program such as Notes. Tap Share to display the regular Sharing pane.

Share...	⬆
Add to Photos	⬇
Copy	▨

FIGURE 4-9:
Hold your finger against a picture in Safari to save it to the iPad.

Sharing Your Web Experiences

When you find a great website you just must share, tap the share icon (shown in the margin) or tap Share after pressing down on a link, and you find these sharing options:

» **One Tap Suggestions:** The top row in the iPadOS Sharing pane is one of the best new features in iPadOS. It contains people and places Siri thinks you're most likely to want to share with, such as nearby AirDrop devices, as described next, as well as a combination of your most-used and recent Messages contacts. Sharing with your closest friends and family is now even easier!

- **AirDrop:** Share the page with other people who have compatible devices and AirDrop. You'll need to turn on AirDrop in Control Center (swipe down from the top-right corner of the screen). Then choose whether to make your iPad discoverable to everyone or only people in your contacts.

- **Messages:** Send a link to the web page in a text or an iMessage.

- **Mail:** The Mail program opens, with a new message containing a link for the page and the name of the site or page in the Subject line.

- **News:** Using this option isn't so much sharing as opening the web page you're viewing in Apple's News app. Tap the News icon to go to the Apple News version of that article.

- **Reminders:** Add to a new reminder a link to the web page you're viewing so you don't forget! If you tap Options, you can be reminded on a given day or location.

- **Notes:** Your iPad opens a pane that allows you to save the web page as an attachment in an existing or new note. Tap Save to finish the process and return to Safari.

- **Books:** Convert the web page you're viewing into a PDF that is then added to your Books library.

- **More:** Display other recent apps — including social networking apps such as Twitter, Facebook, Tencent Weibo, and others.

TIP

Your list may not look exactly like the list we described, which was based on a clean iPad set up just for this book. If you've been using your iPad for a while, you'll see your frequently used apps.

- **Copy:** Copy the page in question.

- **Add to Reading List:** See the "Saving to your reading list" section for details.

- **Add Bookmark:** Bookmark a web page.

- **Add to Favorites:** When you tap the + button to add a new tab, you see a page of icons representing the web pages you visit most often. Tap Add to Favorites to add the web page you're viewing to this most-favored-nation-status grouping.

- **Find on Page:** Type a word you want to find. Matching words are highlighted; use the up and down arrows that appear to cycle through each mention. Tap Done when you're finished.

- **Add to Home Screen:** We discuss this feature in the "Clipping a web page" section.

- **Print:** Print to an AirPrint printer. You can choose the number of copies you want. Tap Print to complete the job.

>> **Markup:** Convert the web page to a PDF you can then draw on! Use the brush palette that appears at the bottom of the screen to choose a color, a type of pen, and other markup controls. Tap Done to either save or delete the PDF.

Launching a Mobile Search Mission

Most of us spend a lot of time using search engines. And the ones we summon most often are Google, Yahoo!, and Microsoft's Bing, at least in the United States. If you're in China, chances are you search using Baidu. All these search options are available on the iPad, along with DuckDuckGo, a search engine that doesn't track your web footsteps.

Apple combines the address bar and search fields into a single, convenient, unified strip called the *smart search field,* following the path taken on most popular web browsers for PCs and Macs. Although you can certainly use the virtual keyboard to type *google.com, yahoo.com, bing.com,* or other search engines into this field, Apple doesn't require that tedious effort. Instead, just type your search query directly in the box.

To conduct a web search on the iPad, tap the smart search field. You immediately see icons for your favorite web destinations. But when you start typing in the smart search field, a Google (or other) search mission commences, with live guesses shown at the top.

You see other search suggestions as you start tapping additional letters. In Figure 4-10, for example, typing the letters **ap** yields such suggestions as Applebees, Apple Store, and Apple Watch. Tap any search result that looks promising, or tap Go on the keyboard to immediately land on the top hit. Or keep tapping out letters until you generate the search result you want.

You can also find a search word or phrase on the web page you have on-screen. If there's a match, you'll see an On This Page entry at the bottom of the smart search results. If you tap that result, the smart search pane vanishes, and the Find on Page pane comes up from the bottom of your screen.

To switch the search field from the current search engine to another search engine on your iPad, check out the "Smart Safari Settings" section, later in this chapter.

As mentioned earlier in this chapter, Siri can open Safari — all you have to do is ask. Of course, much of what Siri can do is web-centric. So now is as good a time as any to recommend Chapter 14, where you get an excellent sense of all Siri can do.

Through the search engine suggestions and Safari suggestions features, you can get potentially useful information even if you don't explicitly search for it. If you search the name of a movie, for example, Safari will also provide showtimes at nearby theaters without being asked. If you're not comfortable with this feature, you can turn it off in Settings.

FIGURE 4-10:
Running a search on the iPad.

Private Browsing

Don't want to leave any tracks while you surf? Turn on private browsing for a "what happens in Safari stays in Safari" tool. Those truly bent on staying private will also want to tap Clear History, as we mention earlier in this chapter.

To go incognito, tap the view open tabs icon (labeled in Figure 4-1), and then tap the Private button at the upper-right corner of the screen. After private browsing is on, any traces of your visit to nonono.com (or wherever) are nowhere to be found. Your history is wiped clean, open tabs don't appear in iCloud tabs, and your autofill information is not stored anywhere. To remind you that you're browsing privately, the Safari interface takes on a darker shade.

To come out of hiding, tap the view open tabs icon again and then tap Private again to turn it off.

The history of pages you've visited can be useful and a huge timesaver, so don't forget to disable this option when you're finished.

Be mindful of your settings on other machines. If you run Safari on both an iPad and a Mac, but choose to go private only on Apple's tablet, your Mac browsing history will still show up in your history list on the iPad. Safari browsers marked private on the iPad will still bring in sites from iPhones or Macs via iCloud. Mark things private across all devices to keep things really private.

Smart Safari Settings

Along with the riches galore found on the Internet are places in cyberspace where you're hassled. You might want to take action to protect your privacy and maintain your security.

To get started, tap the Settings icon on the Home screen and then tap Safari.

The following settings enable you to tell your iPad what you want to be private and how you want to set your security options:

>> **Search Engine:** Tap the search engine you desire — just as long as that search engine happens to be Google, Yahoo!, Bing, DuckDuckGo, or if you've enabled a Chinese keyboard, Baidu. Other settings found here let you determine whether the iPad can make search engine suggestions and Safari suggestions, features touched on earlier in this chapter.

>> **Quick Website Search:** Determine whether or not to use website shortcuts when you're searching within a website. For example, you can type **wiki FDR** to show Wikipedia entries for Franklin Roosevelt.

>> **Preload Top Hit:** We talk about the smart search field throughout this chapter. Here you get to choose whether the iPad can preload the top hit in the background.

>> **AutoFill:** Safari can automatically fill out web forms by using your personal contact information, usernames, and passwords, or information from your other contacts. Tap AutoFill and then tap the on/off switch to enable or disable AutoFill.

- Tap Use Contact Info if you're comfortable using the information found about your contacts.

- Tap My Info to select yourself in your contacts so that Safari knows which address, phone number, email address, and other information to use when it fills in a form.

- Tap Credit Cards to manage and enter the credit card numbers you're comfortable sharing. Tap Saved Credit Cards to view the cards you've saved on your tablet or to add others.

WARNING

Turning on AutoFill can compromise your security if someone gets hold of your iPad. It can also affect security across all your iCloud-enabled devices.

» **Frequently Visited Sites:** This setting controls whether Safari in iPadOS displays your most frequently visited websites when you first open a new tab. Tap the toggle to disable it, changing it from green to white.

» **Favorites:** Apple lets you quickly access favorite bookmarks when you enter an address, search, or create a tab. Tap the category of sites for which you'd like to see icons (News, Business, Technology, whatever). A check mark appears next to your selection. Or leave the default category setting as Favorites.

» **Show Favorites Bar:** If you enable this option, you'll see Safari's bookmarks bar between the smart search field and tab bar.

» **Block Pop-Ups:** *Pop-ups* are web pages that appear whether or not you want them to. Often, they're annoying advertisements. But on some sites, you welcome the appearance of pop-ups, so remember to turn off blocking under such circumstances.

» **Downloads:** Tap through to decide where the files you download to your iPad will reside, in iCloud drive or directly on your iPad. If you choose the iCloud Drive option, the files will be available on all of your Apple devices signed into iCloud drive.

» **Show Tab Bar:** You can display open tab buttons in a bar near the top of the Safari display, another matter of personal preference.

» **Show Icons in Tabs:** Turn this feature on to have website icons displayed in each of your open tabs.

» **Open New Tabs in Background:** If you enable this setting, new tabs that you open in Safari will load even if you're reading a different page in another tab.

» **Close Tabs:** Tap through to decide whether you want to close tabs manually — which we recommend — or have them closed automatically after one day, one week, or one month.

» **Prevent Cross-Site Tracking:** Apple is the tech leader in protecting your privacy, and no close second exists. The Prevent Cross-Site Tracking feature makes it difficult for Google, Facebook, and the myriad of advertising trackers on the Internet to track you as you go from site to site. This feature is enabled by default, and we recommend you keep it enabled.

- >> **Block All Cookies:** *Cookies* are tiny bits of information a website places on the iPad when you visit so that the site recognizes you when you return. You need not assume the worst; most cookies are benign.

  If this concept wigs you out, take action and block cookies from third parties and advertisers: Tap the Always Block option, and you will theoretically never again receive cookies on the iPad. Or choose to accept cookies only from the website you're currently visiting or only from the websites you visit. You can also tap Always to accept cookies from all sites. Tap Safari to return to the main Safari Settings page.

REMEMBER

  If you set the iPad so that it doesn't accept cookies, certain web pages won't load properly, and other sites such as Amazon won't recognize you or make any of your preferred settings or recommendations available.

- >> **Fraudulent Website Warning:** Safari can warn you when you land on a site whose producers have sinister intentions. The protection is better than nothing, but don't let down your guard because this feature isn't foolproof. The setting is on by default.

- >> **Check for Apple Pay:** If you come to a website that accepts Apple Pay (Apple's mobile payments service), the site can check whether you have Apple Pay enabled on your tablet. If you're not comfortable with this idea, make sure this switch is off.

- >> **Clear History and Website Data:** You met this option earlier. Tap it to erase everything in Safari's history, leaving nary a trace of the pages you've visited.

- >> **Page Zoom:** Apple offers several settings for controlling what happens on every website, starting with Page Zoom. Tap Page Zoom to change the default setting for every website. You have options ranging from 50% to 300%, which is useful if you find yourself constantly adjusting the zoom level for new web pages.

- >> **Request Desktop Website:** Earlier in this chapter, we talk about how Safari for iPadOS requests the desktop version of every website, rather than the mobile version. If you want to turn off this feature for some reason, tap Request Desktop Website and toggle the All Websites switch from green to white. Turning off this feature allows the server to decide whether you get the website's mobile version or desktop version.

- >> **Reader:** Tap the Reader category, and then tap the All Websites toggle to green if you want to view in reader mode every website you visit.

- >> **Camera, Microphone, or Location:** You set up all three features in the same way. Tap through Camera, Microphone, or Location to control how websites request access to these features on your iPad. By default, they're all set to Ask, which means a website must ask for your permission before accessing one of these features.

>> **Automatically Save Offline:** Tap the toggle for this setting to have your iPad automatically save to your iPad any web page you added to your reading list so you can read the page offline, without an Internet connection.

>> **Advanced:** The Advanced category has several settings most iPad users will never need to worry about. But because we love you, dear reader, we're going to explain just in case! Tap Advanced to access the following additional settings.

- Tap *Website Date* to view and manage the data cached by websites you've visited. They're listed in order by how much data they've saved, showing only the top ten by default. Tap Show All Sites to see the rest. If you tap and slide to the left on an individual website, you reveal a red Delete button. Tap Delete to remove that site's data. Tap and slide back to the left to hide the Delete button after you're finished with the site. Tap the Remove All Website Data to remove all cached data from every site at once.

- Tap to toggle *JavaScript* on or off. Be careful when turning off JavaScript, however, because it adds advanced functionality to websites.

- Tap the *Web Inspector* toggle to enable the capability to inspect different elements of a website. This feature is typically used by developers and isn't something the rest of us will ever need to think about. Similarly, the *Remote Automation* feature is a developer feature, and we do not recommend that you enable it.

- Tap the *Experimental Features* category to unveil a wealth of different things Apple is experimenting with in WebKit, the engine that powers Safari. We strongly recommend that you leave this entire section alone, unless you're a developer who needs to access these features to develop a website.

Chapter **5**

The Email Must Get Through

O n any computing device, emails come and go with a variety of emotions. Messages may be amusing or sad, frivolous or serious. Electronic missives on the iPad are almost always touching. Because, you know, you're touching the display to compose and read messages.

Okay, so we're having a little fun, but the truth is that Apple's Mail on the iPad is a modern app designed to send and receive plain-text emails, as well as rich HTML email messages formatted with font and type styles and embedded graphics.

Furthermore, your iPad can read several types of file attachments, including (but not limited to) PDFs, JPG images, Microsoft Word documents, PowerPoint slides, and Excel spreadsheets, as well as stuff produced through Apple's own productivity software, notably Pages, Keynote, and Numbers. Better still, all this sending and receiving of text, graphics, and documents happens in the background, so you can surf the web or play a game while your iPad quietly and efficiently handles your email behind the scenes. Apple even lets you grant VIP status to important senders so there's almost no chance you'll miss mail from the people who matter most.

In this chapter, you learn the ins and outs of the Mail app: sending and viewing emails, working with attachments, setting up and managing email accounts, and more.

Prep Work: Setting Up Your Accounts

First things first. To use Mail, you need an email address. You get a free email account (for example, *yourname*@iCloud.com) from Apple as part of iCloud. If you need to create a new iCloud account, go to Settings ➪ Passwords & Accounts ➪ Add Account ➪ iCloud. Then tap Create a new Apple ID and follow the onscreen directions.

If you have broadband Internet access (that is, a cable modem, FiOS, or DSL), you may have received one or more email addresses when you signed up. If you're one of the handful of readers who doesn't already have an email account, you can get one for free from Google Gmail (`https://gmail.com`), Microsoft Outlook (`https://outlook.live.com/`), or numerous other service providers.

You can add as many as you want to your mail or just stick with the one that comes with your iCloud account.

TIP

Many so-called free email providers add a bit of advertising to the end of your outgoing messages, or they sift through your email to add to their profile of you, which they then use to sell advertising. If you'd rather not be a billboard for your email provider, use Apple's excellent iCloud email, the address(es) that came with your broadband Internet access (*yourname*@comcast.net or *yourname*@att.net, for example), or pay a few dollars a month for a premium email account.

Finally, while the rest of the chapter focuses on the Mail app, you can also use Safari to access most email systems, if that's your preference. You can also install separate Gmail, Outlook, and other dedicated email apps from the App Store.

Setting up your account the easy way

Chapter 3 explains the option of automatically syncing the email accounts on your Mac or Windows PC with your iPad. If you chose the automatic syncing option when you set up your iPad, your email accounts should already be configured properly. And if you signed in with an iCloud account while setting up your iPad (read Chapter 2), you should already be good to go with your iCloud email account. If so, you may proceed directly to the later section "See Me, Read Me, File Me, Delete Me: Working with Messages."

TIP

If you haven't yet chosen to sync your accounts on your iPad but want to set up your account the easy way now, go to Chapter 3, read about syncing email accounts, and then sync your iPad with your Mac or PC. Then you, too, can proceed directly to the section "See Me, Read Me, File Me, Delete Me: Working with Messages," later in this chapter.

Remember that syncing email accounts doesn't have any effect on your email messages; it merely synchronizes the *settings* for email accounts so you don't have to set them up manually on your iPad.

Setting up your account the less-easy way

If you don't want to sync the email accounts on your Mac or PC, you can set up an email account on your iPad manually. It's not quite as easy as clicking a box and syncing your iPad, but it's not rocket science either. Here's how you get started:

>> **If you don't have an email account on your iPad:** The first time you launch Mail, you see the Welcome to Mail screen. Your choices are iCloud, Microsoft Exchange (business email), Google (Gmail), Yahoo!, AOL, Outlook.com, and Other.

Merely tap the account type you want to add to the iPad and follow the steps in the upcoming "Setting up an account with another provider" or "Setting up corporate email" section.

>> **If you have one or more email accounts on your iPad and want to add a new account manually:** Tap Settings on the Home screen and then tap Passwords & Accounts ⇨ Add Account.

You see an Add Account screen, shown in Figure 5-1, with the same account options that appear on the Welcome to Mail screen. Proceed to one of the next three sections, depending on the type of email account you selected.

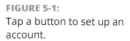

FIGURE 5-1:
Tap a button to set up an account.

Setting up an email account with iCloud, Gmail, Yahoo!, AOL, or Microsoft Outlook

If the account you want to create is with iCloud, Gmail (Google), Yahoo!, AOL, or Outlook, follow these steps:

1. **Tap the appropriate button on the Welcome to Mail screen (refer to Figure 5-1).**

2. **Tap Create Account, as shown in Figure 5-2.**

   Each service is different and wants different information from you. Most will ask for your name and other identifying information. Follow the on-screen instructions until the process is finished.

   That's all there is to setting up your account. You can now proceed to "See Me, Read Me, File Me, Delete Me: Working with Messages."

Setting up an account with another provider

If your email account is with a provider other than iCloud, Microsoft Outlook, Gmail (Google), Yahoo!, or AOL, you have a bit more work ahead of you. You need a bunch of information about your email account you may not know or have handy.

We suggest you scan the following instructions, note the items you don't know, and go find the answers before you continue. To find the answers, look at the documentation you received when you signed up for your email account or visit the account provider's website and search there.

Here's how you set up an account:

1. **Starting at the Home screen, tap Settings ⇨ Passwords & Accounts ⇨ Add Account ⇨ Other.**

2. **Tap Add Mail Account.**

3. **Fill in the name, address, password, and description in the appropriate fields, and then tap Next.**

   With any luck, that's all you'll have to do. The iPad will look up and retrieve your account settings. If that doesn't happen, continue with Step 4.

4. **Tap the button at the top of the screen that denotes the type of email server this account uses, IMAP or POP, as shown in Figure 5-3.**

5. **Fill in the Internet hostname for your incoming mail server, which looks something like mail.*providername*.com.**

6. **Fill in your username and password.**

7. **Enter the Internet hostname for your outgoing mail server, which looks something like smtp.*providername*.com.**

FIGURE 5-2: The Create Account button is below the login option offered for people who already have accounts.

8. **Enter your username and password in the appropriate fields.**

9. **Tap the Next button in the upper-right corner to create the account.**

   You're now ready to begin using your account. See the section "See Me, Read Me, File Me, Delete Me: Working with Messages."

TIP

Rarely, outgoing mail servers don't need your username and password. The fields for these items on your iPad note they're optional. Still, we suggest you fill them in anyway. Doing so saves you from having to add them later if your outgoing mail server does require an account name and a password, which almost all do these days.

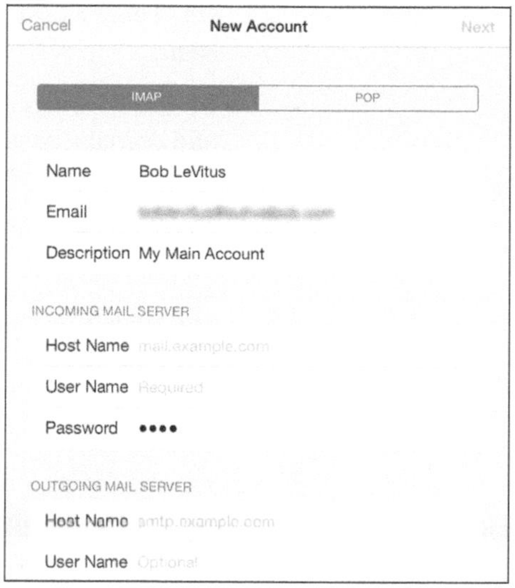

| Cancel | New Account | Next |

| IMAP | POP |

Name   Bob LeVitus

Email   ▒▒▒▒▒▒▒▒▒▒▒▒ com

Description My Main Account

INCOMING MAIL SERVER

Host Name mail.example.com

User Name Required

Password   ••••

OUTGOING MAIL SERVER

Host Name smtp.example.com

User Name Optional

FIGURE 5-3:
If you set up an IMAP or a POP email account, you may have a few more fields to fill in before you can rock.

Setting up corporate email

The iPad makes nice with the Microsoft Exchange servers that are a staple in large enterprises, as well as many smaller businesses.

What's more, if your company supports Microsoft Exchange ActiveSync, you can exploit push email so messages arrive pronto on the iPad, just as they do on your other computers. (To keep everything up to date, the iPad also supports push calendars and push contacts.) For push to work with Exchange Server, your company must support one of the last several iterations of Microsoft Exchange ActiveSync (most companies are). If you run into a problem, ask your company's IT or tech department.

Setting up Exchange email isn't particularly taxing, but you might have to consult your employer's techie-types for certain settings.

Start setting up your corporate email on your iPad by following these steps:

1. **Tap the Microsoft Exchange listing on the Welcome to Mail or Add Account screen.**

   Refer to Figure 5-1.

2. Fill in your name and the description you want for your account. Then tap Next.

3. On the next screen, enter your name, email address, password, server, and domain, assuming the Microsoft Autodiscover service didn't already find it. Then tap Next.

   You might need to contact your company's IT support to fill in any information you don't know.

4. Choose which information you want to synchronize through Exchange by tapping each item you want.

   You can choose Mail, Contacts, Calendars, Reminders, and Notes. When one of these switches is turned on, it turns green, as in Figure 5-4; otherwise, what you see appears dimmed.

Cancel	Exchange	Save
Mail		●
Contacts		●
Calendars		●
Reminders		●
Notes		●

FIGURE 5-4:
Keeping your mail, contacts, calendars, and reminders in sync.

5. Tap Save.

WARNING

The company you work for doesn't want just anybody having access to your email — heaven forbid your iPad is lost or stolen — so your bosses may insist you change the passcode lock in Settings on your iPad. (The passcode lock is different than your email account password.) Now if your iPad ends up in the wrong hands, your company can wipe the contents clean remotely.

If you're moonlighting at a second job, you can configure more than one Exchange ActiveSync account on your iPad; there used to be a limit of just one such account per device.

See Me, Read Me, File Me, Delete Me: Working with Messages

Now that your email accounts are all set up, it's time to figure out how to receive and read the stuff. Fortunately, you did most of the heavy lifting when you set up your email accounts. Getting and reading your mail is a piece of cake.

You can tell when you have unread mail by looking at the Mail icon at the bottom of your Home screen. The cumulative number of unread messages across all your email inboxes appears in a little red badge in the upper right of the icon.

TIP

The badge display is the default behavior. If you don't care for it, turn it off in Settings ➪ Notifications ➪ Mail.

In the following sections, you find out how to read messages and attached files and then send messages to the trash, or maybe a folder, when you've read them. Or, if you can't find a message, check out the section on searching your email messages. Reading email on an iPad versus a desktop or notebook computer is similar, except you have the advantage of the iPad's touchscreen.

Reading messages

To read your mail, tap the Mail icon on the Home screen. Remember that what appears on-screen depends on whether you're holding the iPad in landscape or portrait mode, as well as what was on the screen the last time you opened the Mail app:

>> **Landscape:** With the iPad in landscape mode, you see the Mailboxes section (see Figure 5-5), which, as its name suggests, is a repository for all the messages across all your accounts. The number to the right of Inbox (2 in Figure 5-5) matches the number on the Mail icon on your home page. Again, it's the cumulative tally of *unread* messages across all your accounts. If you have more than one email account set up, Inbox will instead say All Inboxes.

See all emails

Emails from your VIPs

Compose new email

Move message

Delete or archive message

FIGURE 5-5: When you're holding the iPad sideways, Mail looks something like this.

Below the Inbox or All Inboxes listing are the inboxes for your individual accounts. On our test device shown in Figure 5-5, we had just set up a new account, so it looks all clean and pretty. Depending on how you use email, yours might look considerably busier. Each individual inbox you have displays the number of unread messages for that one account.

In this view, you can also see the available subfolders for your accounts (Drafts, Sent, Junk, Trash, and so on). If you have multiple accounts, tap through to each account to see its subfolders.

Check out the VIP, mailbox, too. The VIP mailbox lists all messages from senders you deem most important. We tell you how to give someone VIP status in the later section, "More things you can do with messages."

REMEMBER

Depending on the last time the Mail app was open, you may see previews of the messages in your inbox. Previews display the name of the sender, the time the message arrived, the subject header, and the first two lines of the message. (In Settings ⇨ Mail ⇨ Preview, you can change the number of lines shown in the preview from one line to five, or even to no preview lines.)

>> **Portrait:** When you hold the iPad in portrait mode, as shown in Figure 5-6, the last incoming message fills the entire screen. You have to tap Inbox (in the upper-left corner of the screen) to summon a panel that displays other accounts or message previews. You can summon the panel also by swiping from the left edge of the screen to the right. The panel overlays the message that otherwise fills the screen.

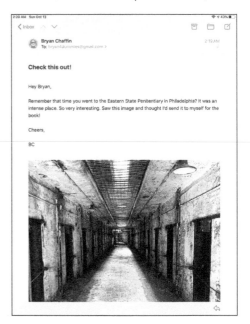

Messages are displayed in *threads*, or conversations, making them easy to follow, but you can still view accounts individually. To read your email:

1. **If the email mailbox you want to see isn't front and center, tap Mailboxes button in the upper-left corner of the screen to summon the appropriate one.**

FIGURE 5-6:
When you're holding the iPad in portrait mode, the message fills the screen.

Again, your button may say All Inboxes, Mailboxes, or some other folder name, or it may say the name of the email account currently open. Within an email account, you can see the number of unread messages in each mailbox.

2. **(Optional) To summon new messages, swipe down the left panel that lists your accounts or mailboxes and immediately release.**

   If you see a spinning gear, the iPad is searching for new mail.

3. **Swipe down one of the inboxes or accounts to refresh that specific mailbox. To summon the unified inbox, tap All Inboxes instead.**

   If a blue dot appears next to a message, the message hasn't been read.

4. **Tap a message to read it.**

5. **When you've finished reading, tap the Mailboxes button in the upper-left corner of the message.**

   The button might carry a different name, depending on which account you have open. For example, it may say Exchange or Inbox.

6. **Read additional messages.**

   When a message is on-screen, you see at the top the buttons for managing incoming messages, most of which you're already familiar with:

   - *In portrait mode:* If the message list pane isn't visible, drag from the left edge of the screen to the right, and then scroll up or down until you see the message you want to read. Tap the message so that it takes over the entire screen.

   - *In landscape mode (and from within an account):* Tap a preview listing to the left of a message to read the next or previous message or any other visible message. Scroll up or down to find other messages you may want to read, and tap the appropriate message.

Threading messages

Apple lets you display related messages as *threads*. The beauty of this arrangement is you can easily trace an email conversation. When you organize messages by thread, the related messages appear as a single entry in the preview pane mailbox, with a right-pointing arrow in a circle to indicate that the message is indeed part of a larger ongoing exchange. When you tap that listing, all messages that make up the threaded conversation appear in the larger pane on the right, though you may have to scroll up or down to see them all. Figure 5-7 (left) shows Bryan and Bryan (it's a thing!) hanging together by a thread. If you tap an individual message from the thread in the pane on the right, you can swipe to quickly reply to the message, forward it, or mark it unread. These are the same options you see when you swipe a preview in the message list.

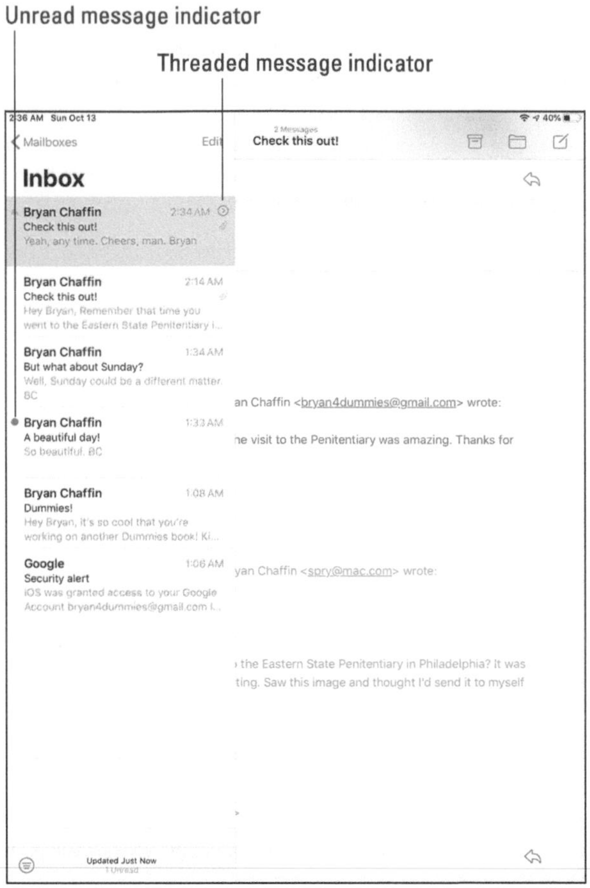

FIGURE 5-7:
Your emails
are hanging
together by a
thread.

When you look at a message that's part of a thread, the number at the top of the screen tells you how many individual messages make up the entire conversation.

To turn on threading, go to the Home screen and tap Settings ⇨ Mail, and then tap on Organize by Thread so the toggle turns green. You can also choose whether to display the most recent message in a thread on top, and whether to complete the thread so all messages in the conversation are shown, even if you subsequently moved some messages to other mailboxes.

Managing messages

Managing messages typically involves either moving the messages to a folder or deleting them. To herd your messages into folders, you have the following options:

>> **To create a folder to organize messages you want to keep:** Open the Mail app and tap Edit in the Mailboxes column. If you're in portrait mode you may have to first tap the blue Mailboxes button in the upper-left corner of your screen to reveal the Mailboxes column. In the column of mailboxes on the left side of the screen, tap Edit. Then tap New Mailbox at the bottom. Type a name for the mailbox and choose a location for it.

>> **To file a message in another folder:** Tap the move message icon (refer to Figure 5-5). When the list of mailboxes appears, tap the folder where you want to file the message. Watching the message fly and land in the designated new folder is cool.

>> **To read a message you've filed:** Tap the folder where the message now resides and then tap the header or preview for the message in question.

>> **To delete, move, or mark multiple messages:** Tap Edit. In both portrait and landscape views, Edit appears at the top of your inbox or another mailbox when its mail folder is selected. Tap Edit, and it becomes a Cancel button, and Mark All, Move, and Trash buttons appear at the bottom of the list. Tap each message you want to select so that a check mark appears; Mark All becomes Mark, Move All becomes Move, and Trash All becomes Trash:

- *Tap Trash* to delete all selected messages.

- *Tap Move* to move all selected messages to another folder in the same or another Mail account, and then tap the new folder or mailbox (or both) in which you want those messages to hang out.

- *Tap Mark* to mark all selected messages read (or unread) or flagged (or unflagged), or to move messages to the Junk folder.

>> **To delete a single message:** Tap the delete message (trash can) icon in that open message. If you tap the delete message icon by mistake, you have a chance to cancel, provided the Ask Before Deleting switch is turned on in Settings ➪ Mail.

>> **To delete a single message without opening it:** Swipe one finger to the left across the message in the mailbox list, and then tap the red Trash button that appears to the right of the message. You'll also see a Flag option and a More button. Tapping More gives you, well, more options: reply, forward, mark it as unread, move it to junk or elsewhere, or have the iPad send a notification when someone replies to the message or thread.

TIP

In certain Mail accounts, Gmail being one, the Trash option may be replaced by an Archive option, depending on your preference. That means you're not getting rid of a message but stashing it or, to be precise, saving the message in your All Mail folder. If the Archive option does present itself, you can turn the feature on or off in Settings ➪ Mail.

Searching emails

With Search, you can quickly and easily search through a bunch of messages to find the one you want to read — such as that can't-miss stock tip from your broker. In the search box at the top of a mailbox preview pane, type *Dummies* or whichever search term seems relevant. You'll notice a couple of things right off the bat. You can confine your query to just the current mailbox or widen the search to include all your mailboxes, as Figure 5-8 shows. What's more, Apple has helpfully organized the search results, so senders who have *dummies* as part of their name are separated from the subject headings of email messages that include the search term.

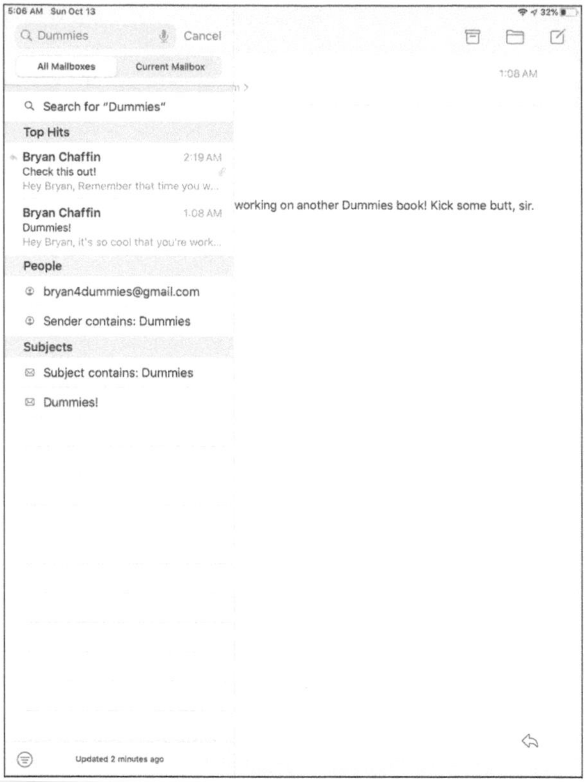

FIGURE 5-8:
Searching your email is easy.

Next, for a more granular search, tap Search for "Dummies," which is below the search field and is preceded by a magnifying glass (refer to Figure 5-8). You have the option of searching for *dummies* in the body or subject of email messages. (For more on Search, see Chapter 2.)

Search within Mail is quite powerful. For example, you can search by time frame by typing something along the lines of *March meetings.* You can also search to find just flagged messages from your VIPs *(flag unread VIP).*

TIP

Siri can also find emails on your behalf. For example, ask her to find all the emails from a particular person in a particular month, or have Siri run a search similar to the Dummies example we just used.

If you're using Exchange, iCloud, or certain IMAP-type email accounts, you may even be able to search messages stored on the server.

Don't grow too attached to attachments

Your iPad can receive email messages with attachments in a wide variety of popular file formats. Which file formats does the iPad support? Glad you asked:

>> **Images:** .jpg, .tiff, .gif, .png

>> **Microsoft Word:** .doc, .docx

>> **Microsoft PowerPoint:** .ppt, .pptx

>> **Microsoft Excel:** .xls, .xlsx

>> **Web pages:** .htm, .html

>> **Apple Keynote:** .key

>> **Apple Numbers:** .numbers

>> **Apple Pages:** .pages

>> **Preview and Adobe Acrobat:** .pdf

>> **Rich Text:** .rtf

>> **Text:** .txt

>> **Contact Information:** .vcf

WARNING

If the attachment is a file format the iPad doesn't support (for example, an Adobe Photoshop .psd file), you see the name of the file in your email, but you can't open it on your iPad, at least not without an assist from a third-party app you may have installed.

Here's how to read a supported attachment:

1. **Open the email that contains the attachment, which you can identify by a little paper clip icon.**

    Another option is to conduct a search for *Messages with Attachments*.

2. **Tap the attachment.**

    The attachment typically appears at the bottom of the message, so you might need to scroll down to see it.

    In some cases, the attachment downloads to your iPad and opens automatically. In other instances, you may have to tap the button representing the attachment to download it.

3. **Read or (in the case of a picture) eyeball the attachment.**

    Tap the attachment (in the case of a document), and you can likely read it immediately. Tap Done to return to the message text.

TIP

Alternatively, tap and hold down on the attachment in the email, and then tap the app from the presented options. Among the possible choices: Tap Quick Look for a quick peek at the attachment, or tap Markup and Reply to add your comments to a document before whisking it back to the sender. You can also add the attachment to iCloud Drive or Notes, or import it to Apple's Pages word processor should that app resides on your tablet. Third-party apps you added to your iPad may also become available as a destination for said attachment.

More things you can do with messages

Wait! You can do even more with your incoming email messages:

>> **To see all recipients of a message:** Assuming you can't see all the names of the people receiving the message, tap the triangle to the right of the recipient. That name expands to show everyone to whom the email was sent or cc'd as a recipient.

>> **To add an email recipient or sender to your contacts:** Tap the name or email address at the top of the message and then tap Create New Contact or Add to Existing Contact.

>> **To make a sender a VIP:** Tap the name or email address at the top of the message and then tap Add to VIP. You may want to give VIP status to important people in your life, such as your significant other, family members, boss, or doctor. A star appears next to any incoming messages from a VIP. You can summon mail from all your VIPs by tapping the VIP folder in the list of Mailboxes. To demote a VIP to an NVIP (not very important person), tap the name or email at the top of the message and then tap Remove from VIP.

>> **To mark a message as read or unread:** Tap and slide the message to the right to reveal three buttons: More, Flag, and Delete. Tap the More button to mark the message as unread if you've already read it, or read if it's already been marked as unread.

Choose Mark as Unread for messages you may want to revisit at some point. The message is again included in the unread message count on the Mail icon on your Home screen, and its mailbox again has a blue dot next to it in the message list for that mailbox.

>> **To flag, reply to, or delete a message:** Tap and slide the message to the left to reveal three buttons for Reply, Flag, and Delete. Tap Reply for quick access to Reply, Reply All, and Forward. Tap Flag to flag the message so it will turn up in any search for flagged messages. Tap Delete to quickly delete the message.

>> **To access other controls for your open email message:** Tap the Reply button at the bottom of the screen to reveal another way to access the options we already mentioned, as well as Archive (for Gmail and other services that support this feature), Move to Junk, Move to Other Folders, Notify Me, and Print. The options you see may differ, depending on the features supported by your email service.

>> **To zoom in on and out of a message:** Use the pinch and unpinch gestures, at which we suspect you now excel. See Chapter 2 if you need help with your touchscreen moves.

>> **To follow a link in a message:** Tap the link. Links are typically displayed in blue but sometimes appear in other colors, or underlined, or both. If the link is a URL, Safari opens and displays the web page. If the link is a phone number, the iPad gives you the chance to add it to your contacts, copy it, call it using FaceTime Audio or your iPhone (through the Handoff feature), or send a message. If the link is an address, the Maps app opens and displays the location. If you tap a date, you can create an event on that date or display it in Calendar. And last but not least, if the link is an email address, a new preaddressed blank email message is created.

TIP

>> If the link opens Safari, Contacts, or Maps and you want to return to your email, tap Mail in the upper-left corner of the display. Or press the Home button on the front of your iPad and then tap the Mail icon. Or double-press the Home button or swipe up from the bottom and select the Mail icon on the dock.

Darling, You Send Me (Email)

Sending email on your iPad is a breeze. You'll encounter several subspecies of messages: pure text, text with a photo, a partially finished message (a *draft*) you want to save and complete later, or a reply to an incoming message. You can also forward an incoming message to someone else — and in some instances print messages. The following sections examine these message types one at a time.

Sending an all-text message

To compose a new email message, tap Mail on the Home screen. As before, what you see next depends on how you're holding your iPad. In landscape mode, your email accounts or email folders are listed in a panel along the left side of the screen, with the message filling the larger window on the right. In portrait mode, your view will depend on what you were viewing the last time you opened the Mail app. If you don't see the Mailboxes folder, tap the blue Mailboxes button in the upper-left corner.

Now, to create a message, follow these steps:

1. **Tap the compose new message icon (labeled in Figure 5-5).**

   The New Message screen appears, like the one shown in Figure 5-9.

2. **Type the names or email addresses of the recipients in the To field, or tap the + symbol to the right of the To field to choose one or more contacts from your iPad's contacts list.**

TIP

   If you start typing an email address, email addresses that match what you typed appear in a list below the To or Cc field. If the correct one is in the list, tap it to use it.

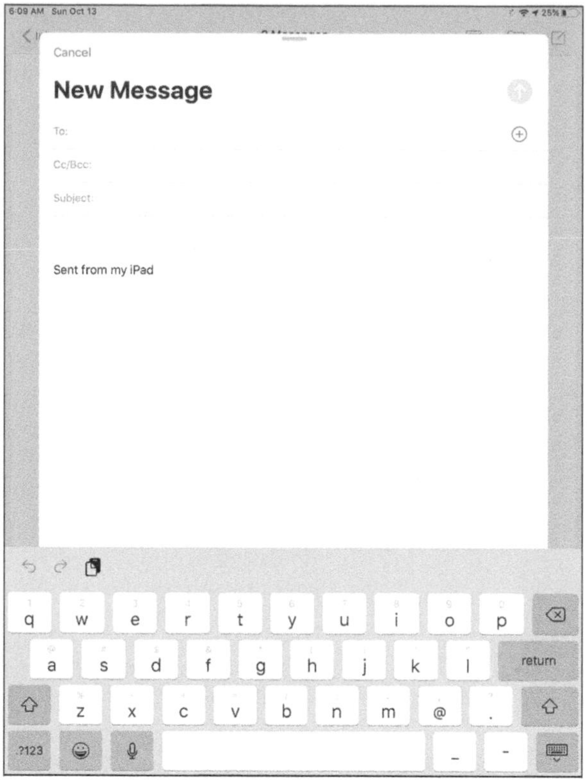

FIGURE 5-9:
The New Message screen is ready for you to start typing.

As part of the intelligent and proactive iPadOS, your iPad may suggest people you typically include when you start to address a message.

3. **(Optional) To break the Cc/Bcc, From field into separate Cc, Bcc, and From fields, tap the field.**

   The Cc/Bcc label stands for *carbon copy/blind carbon copy. Carbon copy* (a throwback term from another era) is kind of an FYI to a recipient. It's like saying, "We figure you'd appreciate knowing this, but you don't need to respond."

   When using Bcc, you can include a recipient on the message, but other recipients can't see that this recipient has been included. Bcc is great for those secret agent emails! Tap the respective Cc or Bcc field to type names. Or tap the + symbol that appears in those fields to add a contact.

4. **(Optional) If you tap From, you can choose any of your email accounts on the fly — assuming you have more than one account set up on the iPad.**

5. **In the subject field, type a subject.**

   The subject is optional, but it's considered poor form to send an email without one.

6. **In the message area, type your message.**

   The message area is immediately below the Subject field. You have ample space to get your message across.

7. **Tap the Send button in the upper-right corner of the screen.**

   Your message wings its way to its recipients almost immediately. If you aren't in range of a Wi-Fi network or a cellular network when you tap Send, the message is sent the next time you're in range of one of these networks.

Formatting text in an email

One of the goodies in Mail is the capability to format email text by underlining, bolding, or italicizing it. First you select the text by pressing your finger against the screen until you see the options to select some or all text. You can also double-tap a single word to select it, and then expand the selection by dragging the selection handles to include more words.

After making your selection, you'll have various other options: Cut, Copy, Paste, BIU, Replace, Look Up, Share, Quote Level, Insert Photo or Video, and if you tap the right arrow in the context menu, Add Document, Scan Document, and Insert Drawing. To format text, tap the BIU button. Then apply whichever style (bold, italics, underline) suits your fancy.

If you tap Quote Level (if you don't see it, tap the right-pointing arrow after selecting a word), you can quote a portion of a message you're responding to. *Note:* Increase Quote Level must be turned on in Mail Settings. You can also increase or decrease the indentation in your outgoing message.

If you tap Replace, you're provided with alternative word choices to the word you selected. Tap one of the alternative options to select it.

If you tap Look Up, you can summon a definition from the *New Oxford Dictionary* or another available dictionary, as well as see suggestions, if appropriate, from iTunes, the App Store, nearby locations, movie showtimes, and more.

Sending a photo or video with an email message

Sometimes a picture is worth a thousand words, and a video can be priceless. When that's the case, follow these steps to send an email message with a photo or video attached:

1. **Tap the Photos icon on the Home screen.**

2. **Find the photo or video you want to send.**

3. **Tap the share icon at the top of the screen (and shown in the margin).**

4. **Tap the Mail button.**

   An email message appears on-screen with the photo or video already attached. The image may appear to be embedded in the body of the message, but the recipient receives it as a regular email attachment.

   On the Cc/Bcc line of your outgoing message, you see the size of the attached photo. If you tap the size of the image shown, a new line appears, giving you the option to choose an alternative size among Small, Medium, Large, or Actual Size. Your choice affects both the visible dimensions and file size of the photo (with the actual size of the file measured in kilobytes or megabytes reported for each possible choice). You don't have the option of modifying your video size.

5. **Choose what size photo you want to send.**

6. **Address the message and type whatever text you like, as you did for an all-text message previously, and then tap the Send button.**

You have an alternative way of inserting pictures (or videos) in your outgoing mail messages. When you're in the composition window of a new email and your cursor is in the body of that new email, you see the insert photo or video icon just above the keyboard. Tap the icon to reveal a menu that allows you to go to your Photo library, where you can choose from your existing photos and videos, or to Take Photo or Video. Tap Take Photo or Video to open the camera interface, where you can take a new photo or video.

When you 're finished, tap Retake for a do-over or tap Use Photo (or Video) to attach the image you just took to your email.

Adding an attachment to an email message

In addition to attaching photos and videos to an email, you can attach documents. When you're in the composition window of a new email with the keyboard displayed and the cursor in the body field, tap the add document icon to reveal a menu that allows you to add or scan a document.

Tap the Add Document option to open a files-based interface for navigating the files on your device, on iCloud Drive, or on any third-party file-hosting service you may have added to your iPad. Simply navigate to and tap the document you want to attach, and it will be attached automatically to your email.

Tap the Scan Document option to turn your iPad into a mobile scanner! The iPad is just accessing your camera so you can take a picture of the document you want to send. But it offers some additional controls, such as adjusting which portion of the image is included in your attachment. Tap the camera button to take the image. You can then drag the corners of the selection area to adjust your image. When you're satisfied, tap the Keep Scan button at the bottom right of your screen and the Mail app will automatically attach it to your email. If you aren't satisfied, tap the Retake button to make a new scan.

Marking up an attachment

If you're attaching a photo or a PDF document, you can take advantage of iPadOS's Markup feature. With a picture attachment or PDF embedded in your outgoing message, double-tap the attachment, and tap Markup from the menu that appears.

You can summon the Markup feature also when you receive a PDF or picture attachment. Tap on the attachment and then tap the briefcase icon accompanied by the words Markup and Reply in the share sheet that appears.

Now that you're in markup mode, you can draw on that image or PDF, tapping the simple annotation tools just below. The tools, which are represented by icons, include several pens (your finger will be that pen unless you use an Apple Pencil or another optional stylus), a highlighter, and a pencil. You even have a ruler you can use to draw perfectly straight lines. Come on, how cool is that? To use the ruler, tap to select it from the palette of tools at the bottom of the Markup screen and drag it to where you want to draw your straight line. Then tap to choose the pen you want to use. Use your finger or a stylus to draw along the edge. Now, just pull your finger down the edge of the ruler and you'll have a perfectly straight line. It's great.

Tap + in the palette menu to access the text tool, a magnifier, or the signature tool, which lets you draw your signature. You'll also find an arrow tool for placing perfect arrows in your photo or document, and some other basic shape tools.

In markup mode, you have the option to change the color and thickness of the lines and symbols you draw and change the font and size of text.

Saving an email to send later

Sometimes you start an email message but don't have time to finish it. When that happens, you can save it as a draft and finish it some other time. Here's how:

1. **Start an email message, as described in one of the previous sections.**

2. **When you're ready to save the message as a draft, tap the Cancel button in the upper-left corner of the screen.**

3. **Tap the Save Draft button if you want to save this message as a draft and complete it another time.**

   If you tap the Delete Draft button, the message disappears immediately without a second chance. Don't tap Delete Draft unless you mean it!

To work on the message again, tap the Drafts mailbox. A list of all messages you saved as drafts appears. Tap the draft you want to work on, and it reappears on the screen. When you're finished, you can tap Send to send it or tap Cancel to save it as a draft again.

REMEMBER

The number of drafts appears to the right of the Drafts folder, the same way the number of unread messages appears to the right of other mail folders, such as your inbox.

Replying to, forwarding, or printing an email message

When you receive a message and want to reply to it, forward it, or print it, open the message and then tap the reply icon (the curved arrow at the lower-right corner of the screen, as shown in Figure 5-10). Then tap Reply, Reply All, Forward, or Print, as described next:

>> **Reply and Reply All:** The Reply button creates an email message addressed to the sender of the original message, with the content of the original message embedded in your reply. The Reply All button creates an email message addressed to the sender and all other recipients of the original message, plus anyone who was cc'd. (The Reply All option appears only if more than one recipient was on the original email.)

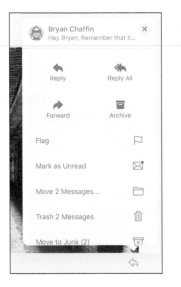

FIGURE 5-10:
Reading and managing an email message.

In both cases, the subject is retained with a *Re:* prefix added. So if the original subject were *iPad Tips,* the reply's subject would be *Re: iPad Tips.*

» **Forward:** Tapping the Forward button creates an unaddressed email message that contains the text of the original message. Add the email address(es) of the person or people you want to forward the message to, and then tap Send. In this case, rather than a *Re:* prefix, the subject is preceded by *Fwd:*. So this time, the subject would be *Fwd: iPad Tips.* If the email you're forwarding has an attachment, you'll be given the option to forward the attachment along with the message.

» **Print:** Tap Print if you want to print using an AirPrint-capable printer.

TIP

It's considered good form to leave the subject lines alone (with the *Re:* or *Fwd:* prefix intact), but you may want to change them sometimes. You can edit the subject line of a reply or a forwarded message or edit the body text of a forwarded message the same way you'd edit any other text. Worth noting: When the *Re:* is modified, a new email thread is created and the modified message won't be included in the old thread listing.

To send your reply or forwarded message, tap the Send button as usual.

Settings for sending email

You can customize the mail you send and receive in lots of ways. In this section, we explore settings for sending email. Later in this chapter, we show you settings that affect the way you receive and read messages. In each instance, start by tapping Settings on the Home screen.

You can customize your mail in the following ways:

» **To hear an alert when you successfully send a message:** From the main Settings screen, tap Sounds. Make sure the Sent Mail setting is turned on. You'll know because you'll see a sound type listed (among alert sounds and ringtones), Swoosh by default. Tap Sent Mail to select a different sound or choose None if going silent is your preference.

If you want to change other settings, tap the Sounds button at the top of the screen. If you're finished setting the settings, tap the Home button on the front of your iPad or swipe up from the bottom of your screen.

» **To add a signature line, phrase, or block of text to every email message you send:** Tap Settings ⇨ Mail, and then tap Signature at the bottom of the right pane. The default signature is *Sent from my iPad.* You can add text before or after it, or delete it and type something else. Your signature will be affixed to the end of all your outgoing email. You can choose a signature that is the same across all your accounts or select different signatures for each account.

» **To set the default email account for initiating email from outside the Mail application:** Go to Settings ⇨ Mail ⇨ Default Account. Note that if you have only one email account set up on your iPad, the Default Account setting will not be visible. If you have more than one email account on your iPad, tap the account you want to use as the default. The designated email account is the one that's used when you want to email a picture directly from the Photos app, for example. Also, if you choose one default account, you can dispatch mail from another account when you send your message.

Setting Your Message and Account Settings

Our final discussion of Mail involves more settings that deal with your various email accounts.

Checking and viewing email settings

Several settings affect the way you can check and view email. You might want to modify one or more, so we describe what they do and where to find them:

» **To specify how often the iPad checks for new messages:** Tap the Settings icon on the Home screen, and then tap Passwords & Accounts ⇨ Fetch New Data. You're entering the world of *fetching* or *pushing*. Check out Figure 5-11 to glance at your options. If your email account supports push and the Push setting is enabled on your iPad, fresh messages are sent to your iPad automatically as soon as they hit the server. If you turned off push or your email account doesn't support it, the iPad periodically fetches data instead. Choices for fetching are Every 15 Minutes, Every 30 Minutes, Hourly, Manually, and Automatically. Tap the one you prefer. With push email, messages can show up on the lock screen and in Notification Center.

» **To set the number of lines of each message to be displayed in the message list:** Go to Settings ⇨ Mail ⇨ Preview, and then choose a number. Your choices are 1, 2, 3, 4, and 5 lines of text or None. The more lines of text you display in the list, the fewer messages you can see at a time without scrolling, so think before you choose 4 or 5.

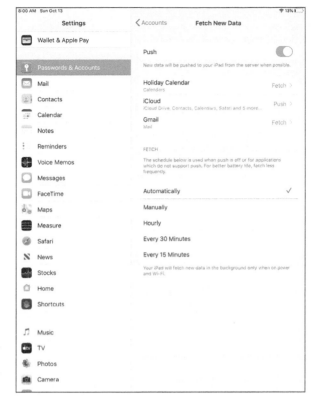

FIGURE 5-11:
Fetch or push?
It's your call.

>> **To specify whether the iPad shows the To and Cc labels in message lists:** From the main Settings screen, tap Mail, and then turn on or off the Show To/Cc Label setting.

>> **To turn on or off the Ask before Deleting warning:** Go to Settings ➪ Mail. Next, turn on or off the Ask before Deleting setting. If this setting is turned on, every time you want to delete an email, you must tap the trash (or archive) icon at the top of your email and then tap the red Delete button. When the setting is turned off, tapping the trash icon deletes the message, and you never see a red Delete button.

>> **To change swipe options:** Go to Go to Settings ➪ Mail ➪ Swipe Options. You can choose whether swiping left (on the preview pane) flags messages and whether swiping right marks messages as unread.

>> **To mark email addresses that originate or are received from a designated mail server:** Tap Settings ➪ Mail ➪ Mark Addresses and flip the switch on. Enter the email address from your company (or wherever) that you do *not* want marked. From then on, when you're composing a message, all email addresses sent to or from the specified address will appear in blue, while all

other mail addresses will be shaded red. Why do this? The idea is that you can more easily identify mail dispatched to addresses outside your organization, alerting you to a potential security risk if you're exchanging, say, sensitive information.

>> **To specify whether the iPad will automatically display images embedded in an email:** Tap Mail and then tap Load Remote Images in the right pane so the switch is on. If it's off, you can still manually load remote images. Security risks are associated with loading remote images, and they can also hog bandwidth.

>> **To organize your mail by thread:** Tap Organize by Thread so that the setting is on. Then, as mentioned, you can choose whether to show the most recent message on top and whether to show all messages in a thread, even those since moved to other mailboxes.

Altering account settings

The last group of email settings we explore in this chapter deals with your email accounts. You most likely will never need most of these settings, but we'd be remiss if we didn't at least mention them briefly. So here they are, whether you need 'em or not:

>> **To stop using an email account:** Tap the Settings icon on the Home screen, tap Passwords & Accounts ⇨ *account name,* and then flip the switch for Mail to off (gray).

TIP

This setting doesn't delete the account; it only hides it from view and stops it from sending or checking email until you turn it on again. (You can repeat this step to turn off calendars, contacts, reminders, and notes in a given account.)

>> **To delete an email account:** Tap the Settings icon on the Home screen; tap Passwords & Accounts ⇨ *account name* ⇨ Delete Account ⇨ Delete. Tap Cancel if you change your mind and don't want your account blown away, or tap Delete to proceed.

WARNING

Deleting an email account will also remove calendar entries, contact names, and notes from the given account.

You can find still more advanced Mail settings, reached the same way: Tap Settings ⇨ Passwords & Accounts ⇨ Account ⇨ Advanced. Your exact path may be different depending on the kind of account you're working with. For example, Gmail requires you to tap Account and iCloud requires you to tap Account ⇨ iCloud ⇨ Mail to get to the Advanced settings.

The settings you see under Advanced (sometimes shown as Advanced Settings under a specific email account) will vary by account. This list describes some of the settings you might see:

>> **Specify how long until deleted messages are removed permanently from your iPad:** In iCloud Mail, your choices are Never, After One Day, After One Week, and After One Month. Tap the choice you prefer. Other mail accounts may give you different time frame options or not present this setting.

>> **Choose whether drafts, sent messages, archived messages, and deleted messages are stored on your iPad or on your mail server:** Tap Advanced and then choose the setting under Mailbox Behaviors. You can decide for drafts, sent messages, and trash. If you choose to store any or all of them on the server, you can't see them unless you have an Internet connection (Wi-Fi or cellular). If you choose to store them on your iPad, they're always available, even if you don't have Internet access. In certain circumstances, you also get to determine whether to delete or archive discarded messages.

We strongly recommend you don't change the next two items unless you know exactly what you're doing and why. If you're having problems with sending or receiving mail, start by contacting your ISP (Internet service provider), email provider, or corporate IT person or tech department. Then change these settings only if they tell you to. Again, these settings and exactly where and how they appear vary by account.

>> **Reconfigure mail server settings:** In the Incoming Mail Server or Outgoing Mail Server section of the account settings screen, tap Host Name, User Name, or Password and make your changes.

>> **Adjust SSL, authentication, or IMAP path settings, or the server port:** Tap Advanced and then tap the appropriate item and make the necessary changes.

And that, as they say in baseball, retires the side. You're now fully qualified to set up email accounts and send and receive email on your iPad.

Chapter **6**

Getting Messages

M essages (formerly iMessage) is your one-stop shop for communicating with your friends, colleagues, and anyone who sends you an SMS text message. You can communicate with individuals or groups. You can share images, Maps directions, and files. You can customize your messages with stickers and memoji, a feature that lets you create a cartoon version of yourself. Apple even has apps for Messages that add all kinds of features, such as stickers, song lyrics, and games you can play with your friends. In addition, Messages uses end-to-end user encryption, which keeps prying eyes out of your conversations. We show you how to use all these great features in this chapter, so read on!

TIP

The Messages app used to be called iMessages. But individual messages sent through the Messages app are still called iMessages. Confused? Don't be, because no one is going to call the tech police on you if you use either word when talking about Apple's messaging system.

Sending iMessages

To start a new message, tap the Messages icon on the Home screen to launch the Messages app and then tap the compose new message icon, the little pencil-and-paper icon in the left pane of the screen (in the Messages list).

At this point, with the To field active and awaiting your input, you can do three things:

TIP

>> **If the recipient *is* in your contacts list, type the first few letters of the name.** A list of matching contacts appears. Scroll through it if necessary and tap the name of the contact.

The more letters you type, the shorter the list becomes. And after you've tapped the name of a contact, you can begin typing another name so you can send this message to multiple recipients at once.

>> **Tap the blue circled + icon on the right side of the To field to select a name from your contacts list.**

>> **If the recipient *isn't* in your contacts list, type his or her phone number or email address.**

You have a fourth option if you want to compose the message first and address it later. Tap inside the text-entry field labeled simply iMessage. When you've finished typing, tap the To field and use one of the preceding techniques to choose the person to send it to.

REMEMBER

You can communicate with people who don't have an Apple device, but messages will be exchanged through SMS text messages or MMS multimedia-type missives. If you're involved in an SMS schmooze-fest, your message bubbles will be green. If you're indeed exchanging iMessages with others, your bubbles will be blue. The distinction is important because most of the fancy multimedia tricks we tell you about in this chapter won't work unless you're exchanging iMessages.

Group messages

You aren't limited to sending iMessages to a single person. Group chats in Messages allow multiple people to carry on a conversation, including sharing images, directions, files, and all the other goodies in Messages.

REMEMBER

If even one member of a group chat is not using Messages — for instance that cousin who insists on using an Android device — all messages in the group chat are sent as SMS or MMS messages. You can tell because your outgoing chat bubbles will be green.

To initiate a group message, type in the To field the names or phone numbers of everyone you want to include. When you've finished addressing and composing, tap the Send button to send your message on its merry way. To name the group, tap the Group chat in the list of ongoing chats on the left side of the Messages screen. Then, at the top of the message history for the group chat, tap the bar containing the group chat's members. Three new icons appear: audio, FaceTime and the *i*-in-a-circle (info). Tap the info icon, and then tap the Name field and enter the name you want.

You can see all participants in a group chat by tapping the Group chat in your list of chats, and then tapping the *i*-in-a-circle (info) icon to reveal the Details pane. If any group members are sharing their location with you, you'll also see a Maps interface with their location in the Details pane. Scroll down to the bottom of the Details pane to see the images and links shared in the group chat and the files sent. To leave a group, tap Leave This Conversation in the info pane.

To add someone to the group, tap the + Add Contact button in the Details pane.

Adding voice to an iMessage

You can record an audio message and send it to a recipient. Apple calls this feature Tap to Talk, and here's how to take advantage of it. Tap and hold down on the sound wave icon to the right of the text-entry field, keeping your finger on the icon the entire time you're speaking. Your voice appears as a waveform at the bottom of the screen, as shown in Figure 6-1.

To send your recording immediately, keep your finger pressed down when you've finished recording and then swipe up to send the message. To listen to your recording before you send it, lift your finger from the sound wave icon to stop recording. Then tap the play icon that appears. If you're not thrilled with what you've just recorded, swipe left to cancel or tap the X to the left of the recorded message.

FIGURE 6-1:
Lending your voice to an iMessage.

TIP

Sometimes hearing someone's voice just makes a message clearer, easier to understand, or more meaningful. Sending voice recordings through Messages can be a powerful way to communicate, and we encourage you to try it!

The recipient of your recorded iMessage will be able to tap a play icon to listen to what you have to say.

WARNING

Listen right away because by default the iMessage expires in two minutes. You can go to Settings ⇨ Messages ⇨ Audio Messages to have audio messages never expire.

Keep in mind that the sound wave icon that lets you record your voice is enabled only if you're sending a Message to a chat partner. It won't be available if you're chatting with someone in SMS or MMS mode, which is when your chat bubbles are green.

Massive multimedia effects overhaul

iPadOS is chock-full of wonderful Messages effects, including the capability to draw and write using your finger, send Digital Touch effects, react to Messages, and use screen effects. You can also replace words with emojis lightning fast, and use the tapback feature to offer a quick reaction to the sender.

The Messages app in iPadOS also includes a built-in App Store for third-party stickers and emojis and full-blown apps that run in Messages.

Let's plunge right in. Follow the previous instructions in the "Sending iMessages" section and choose a recipient or group you want to engage with, and then tap the gray App Store button, between the camera icon and the iMessage text box. A new row of recent apps appears below the iMessage field, as shown in Figure 6-2.

The first icon is for Photos, which you can tap to cherry-pick images and videos from your Photos library.

The blue App Store icon accesses the Messages App Store for stickers and apps that run right inside Messages. Figure 6-3 shows the Messages App Store opened to a sampling of seasonal stickers. Tap the magnifying glass icon to browse other kinds of apps or to search for a specific Messages app.

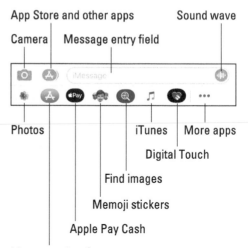

FIGURE 6-2:
When sending an iMessage, you can add a picture or a sketch, visit a dedicated App Store, choose from installed sticker packs, or add your memoji.

Stickers are fun and a great way to convey simple or complex thoughts and feelings. Try them out. We think you'll like them, too.

TIP

With Bitmoji, one of our favorite Messages apps, you can build a cartoon representation of yourself, kind of like Apple's memoji feature (which we describe later in the chapter). Bitmoji provides hundreds of funny, silly, and sometimes poignant stickers you can add to your cartoon. It seems like whatever you're trying to say, Bitmoji has a sticker for that. And it's free!

The other icons in the row are for Apple Pay, memoji, find images, Music, Digital Touch, and more apps, which displays other recent apps you've opened in Messages. Keep reading to learn more about these features, and other aspects of Messages.

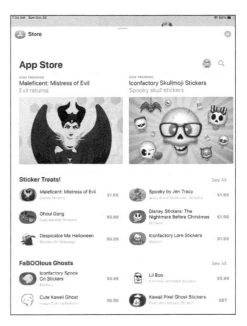

FIGURE 6-3:
The Messages App Store gives you fast access to stickers and apps just for Messages.

Let's start with some of the features that allow you to personalize and add to your Messages conversations:

>> **To comment on a message with a tapback:** Press and hold down on the message until the tapback bubble appears, as shown in Figure 6-4, and then tap the appropriate icon.

If you change your mind and want to dismiss the tapback bubble without adding a tapback icon to the message, just tap the screen anywhere *outside* the tapback bubble. Tapback is a great way to emphasize a message, to show your agreement or disagreement with a message, or to indicate that you like that message.

WARNING

Tapback works only with other devices running iPadOS, iOS 10 and above, or macOS Sierra and above. If the recipients are using any other operating system, they won't see any cute balloons, just plain old text that reads, "*Your-name-here* Loved/Liked/Disliked/ Laughed At/Emphasized/Questioned *item-name-here.*"

FIGURE 6-4:
Tap a tapback icon to send a quick reaction to the sender.

>> **To replace text with an emoji:**
You can add emoji to a message
any time by tapping the emoji key
on your keyboard.

iPadOS will also make quick (and
usually great) recommendations
for substituting written words with
emojis; simply check the space
between the iMessage input field
and your keyboard. These
recommendations shift and

FIGURE 6-5:
Choose from the suggested emojis to replace a
word with an emoji.

change depending on what you're typing. If more than one emoji is associated
with the word, as shown in Figure 6-5, you'll see multiple emojis suggested;
tap the emoji you want and it will replace the word you're typing. How
convenient!

>> **To add bubble or screen effects:** Prepare your message as usual, but rather
than tapping the little up-arrow-in-a-blue-circle to send it, press and hold it
until the Bubble and Screen Effects screen appears. Tap the Bubble tab at the
top to select Slam, Loud, Gentle, or Invisible Ink as the bubble effect for your
message. The Invisible Ink effect means your iMessage recipient will have to
swipe across the message or tap the message bubble to read it. Or tap the
Screen tab and swipe left or right to select Echo, Spotlight, Balloons, Confetti,
Send with Love, Lasers, Fireworks, Shooting Star, or Celebration as the screen
effect for this message. Try it, because you need to see it to believe it!

If you change your mind and don't want to add an effect, tap the *x*-in-a-circle
to dismiss the Bubble and Screen Effects screen.

>> **To send a handwritten message:** Sometimes nothing but a handwritten
note will do. Tap the handwriting icon in the lower-right corner of the keyboard (and shown in the margin). You'll be whisked off to a white area where
you can write your message using your finger, an Apple Pencil accessory (for
iPad Pro models), or a third-party stylus. Tap > if you need more space.

If you prefer a premade message
or one you previously created, tap
the tiny clock icon at the bottom-
left corner of the white writing
area to display a list to choose
from. Figure 6-6 shows premade
messages saying Thinking of You,
Congratulations, I'm Sorry, and
more.

FIGURE 6-6:
Choosing a handwritten preset.

TIP

You can use the handwriting icon to draw images, too, so let your imagination run when using this fun feature.

» **To send Digital Touch effects:** Digital Touch effects first appeared on Apple Watch, but are now found also in iPadOS. They allow you to send customized animations designed to convey emotions and other abstract thoughts. Tap the gray App Store icon to reveal the row of iMessage apps available to you. Tap the Digital Touch icon (the heart with two fingers laying across it) to reveal the Digital Touch interface shown in Figure 6-7.

Here's how Digital Touch works:

FIGURE 6-7:
We just sent a heartbeat through the Digital Touch interface.

- **To expand the Digital Touch interface to full screen:** Drag the short gray bar at the top of the Digital Touch interface towards the top of the screen.

- **To sketch:** Draw with one finger.

- **To send a pulsing circle:** Tap with one finger.

- **To send a fireball:** Tap and hold down with one finger.

- **To send a kiss:** Tap with two fingers.

- **To send a heartbeat:** Tap and hold down with two fingers.

- **To send a broken heart:** Tap and hold down with two fingers, and then drag down.

- **To switch ink colors:** Tap one of circles on the left. If you see only one hue option, tap the colored circle to reveal other choices.

- **To add a picture or video to your Digital Touch effect:** Tap the camera icon on the right.

WARNING

As soon as you lift your finger, heartbeat, fireball, and kiss Digital Touch messages are sent automatically. Don't tap or press the screen in Digital Touch mode unless you really mean it.

Next, let's look at the built-in App Store we mentioned, where you can buy (or download for free) sticker packs, new effects, lyric quoting apps, games you can play with your friends, apps for professional sports, and more. To get free stickers and see what other third-party apps are available, tap the gray App Store icon to the left of the text field, and then tap the blue App Store icon that appears below (refer to Figure 6-3).

After you've acquired apps, this is also where you access them. So, for example, to send a sticker from a sticker pack you've downloaded, you'd tap the gray App Store icon to display the row of installed and available apps. Then tap the icon for the sticker packs or app you want to use (or even just browse), and use the sticker pack or app as desired. When you're finished, tap another app icon to open a different app, or tap the iMessage input field to close the app interface.

Memoji, a mouthful, but worth it

Memojis are so much fun! You can use them to create a cartoon version of yourself to send in your iMessages as a sticker. Figure 6-8 shows some of the memojis Bryan has created, including an attempt to create Hank Hill on the far left, and some of Apple's stock characters on the right. Below the different memoji characters are stickers Apple created using these memojis. Every memoji you make will have these sticker options. Cool, right?

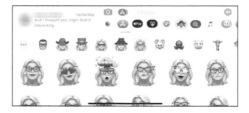

FIGURE 6-8:
Memojis give you personalized stickers for your iMessages.

Here's how to create your own memoji:

1. **Tap the gray App Store icon to the left of the iMessage input field, and then tap the memoji stickers icon (refer to Figure 6-2).**

2. **Tap the circle with three dots on the upper-left corner of the memoji pane.**

3. **Tap New Memoji.**

4. **Customize your memoji.**

   Tap to choose your skin color, hairstyle, brows, eyes, head, nose, mouth, ears, facial hair, eyewear, and headwear. Each of those categories of features has multiple options to choose from. Spend as much or as little time as you want to create the perfect memoji for you.

5. **Tap Done on the memoji creator pane.**

That's it! Your new memoji is now available in the list of available memojis. As noted, your new memoji will also have stickers based on what you created, premade and ready to go.

If you want to edit, duplicate, or delete a memoji, tap the memoji and then tap the circle with three dots on the left side of the memoji pane. A list of options appears: New Memoji, Edit, Duplicate, and Delete. Then do one of the following:

» Tap Edit to make changes to the memoji you already created.

» Tap Duplicate to use what you already created as the starting-off point for a new memoji. This option is useful if you want to change your hat, your glasses, or some other minor feature.

» Tap Delete to permanently delete the memoji you created. You'll be asked to tap Delete again to confirm the deletion. When you do so, the deleted memoji disappears, and the next memoji in your list takes its place.

Tap Done to go back to Messages.

Now that you've created a memoji and have a list of stickers, it's time to insert a memoji sticker in an iMessage. Tap the memoji sticker you want to use to add it to your iMessage input field. Then tap the blue send arrow on the right side of the iMessage input field to send your memoji to your recipient. Or, if you change your mind and want to delete the memoji from your iMessage input field before sending, tap the small gray x-in-a-circle.

Animoji, too!

Animojis are at least as much fun as memojis, but you'll need an iPad Pro with Face ID to use them. You can record an audio message and map it to an animoji or memoji character. That character will then move to match what your face did when you recorded the message. Here's how it works.

If you have an iPad Pro with Face ID, the row of available apps that appears below your iMessage input field when you tap the gray App Store icon will include an icon of a monkey with an open mouth. Tap the monkey icon to open the Animoji app in Messages, as shown in Figure 6-9.

FIGURE 6-9:
Animoji lets you send an animated message based on your emoji or Apple's premade characters.

Here's how to create and use an animoji:

1. **Choose an animoji character.**

   Tap one of the memojis you created, follow the steps in the preceding section to create one, or choose from Apple's premade characters. Your iPad Pro is now ready to map your facial movements and record a message.

2. **Position your iPad for recording by holding it so that it's upright and in front of your face.**

   The Face ID camera in your iPad Pro is now mapping your facial movements. If you look at your animoji, you'll see that it moves as you move. It opens its eyes with you, its mouth moves like yours, and even your head tilts are captured. Now you're ready to record!

3. **Record your animoji:**

   a. *Tap and hold the red record button that appears in the bottom-right corner of your iPad's screen.*

   b. *Say (or sing!) what you want.* You have up to 30 seconds to record whatever you want.

   c. *When you're finished, simply lift your finger from the red record button.* Your animoji will immediately play back, allowing you to preview what you recorded.

   d. *Tap the blue replay button on the left side of your screen as many times as you want to preview it.*

4. **When you're ready to send your animoji, tap the blue up-arrow-in-a-circle on the right side of your screen.**

   And with that, it's sent! Now all you have to do is wait for your chat recipient to send you back the LOLs and heart tapbacks.

Apple Pay Cash, right in Messages

Did you know you can send and receive money in your Messages app? It's part of Apple Pay Cash, which itself is part of Apple Pay. Although Apple limits the Wallet app to iPhone, Apple Pay is still part of iPadOS.

Outside Messages, you can use Apple Pay on your iPad on sites that have enabled support for Apple Pay. In Messages, you can both send and receive money that comes from or goes to your Apple Pay balance. You can then use that balance to pay for things, or to send money to someone using Apple Pay Cash. If you want to send more money to someone than you have in your Apple Pay Cash balance, Apple Pay Cash will pull from the bank account you've added to Apple Pay Cash. If you're paying for something that costs more than your Apple Pay Cash balance, you can do so using any of the credit cards attached to your Apple Pay account.

Here's how to send or request money via Apple Pay Cash:

1. **Tap the Apple Pay Cash icon (refer to Figure 6-2).**

   The Apple Pay Cash interface opens, as shown in Figure 6-10.

2. **Tap to choose how much money you want to send (or request).**

   Use the + and – button, or tap the $1 text to open a keypad where you can tap exactly how much money you want to send (or request).

FIGURE 6-10:
Sending money through Apple Pay Cash is easy and fast.

3. **Tap Request or Pay, depending on what you want to do:**

   - Tap Request to ask that person for money.

   - Tap Pay to have the money taken from your Apple Pay balance or your bank account and sent to your iMessage recipient.

   The amount you're sending or requesting will be added to a new message waiting to be sent.

4. **Complete the transaction by** tapping the up-arrow-in-a-circle in the iMessage input field.

To cancel an unsent Apple Pay Cash transaction, tap the gray x-in-a-circle in the upper-right corner of the transaction to cancel without sending. After you have sent a transaction, it cannot be unsent.

To view the details of an Apple Pay Cash transaction, tap the black Apple Pay square in your Messages chat. You see who sent you the money, when it was sent, the status of the transaction, how much you received, and a transaction ID.

Being a golden receiver: Receiving iMessages

When determining your settings for receiving iMessages, first things first. Decide whether you want to hear an alert when you receive a message:

>> **If you want to hear an alert sound when you receive a message:** Go to Settings ⇨ Sounds ⇨ Text Tone, and then tap an available sound. You can audition the sounds by tapping them. You can also create your own tones in GarageBand for iPad.

REMEMBER

You hear the sounds when you audition them in the Settings app, even if the ring/silent switch is set to Silent. After you exit the Settings app, however, you *won't* hear a sound when a message arrives if the ring/silent switch is set to Silent.

>> **If you *don't* want to hear an alert when a message arrives:** Instead of tapping one of the listed sounds, tap None, which is the first item in the list of alert tones. You can also turn off alerts for individual chats and group chats. To do so, tap the iMessage you want to silence, tap the bar above that chat with the name of the person your chatting with, tap the *i*-in-a-circle (info) icon to reveal the Details tab, and scroll down and tap the Hide Alerts button. When that button is green, you won't hear alerts or receive notifications just for that chat!

>> **If you don't want any messages:** Turn off iMessage by going to Settings ⇨ Messages ⇨ iMessage and tapping the toggle so that it goes from green to white. You'll still get SMS messages when you turn off iMessages, so if you don't want any text message notifications, consider the do not disturb feature. It lives up to its name. Go to Settings ⇨ Do Not Disturb to activate this feature, and you'll see a moon icon in the status bar. Even easier, turn on do not disturb in Control Center, and you won't be inundated with messages.

The following pointers explain what you can do with iMessages you receive:

>> **When your iPad is asleep:** All or part of the text and the name of the sender appear on the unlock screen. Slide to the right to reply to a specific message (you'll have to get past any passcodes first).

>> **When your iPad is awake and unlocked:** All or part of the message and the name of the sender appear at the top of the screen in front of whatever's already there.

TIP

These notifications are on by default; turn them off in the Settings app's Notifications pane if you don't care for them. You'll also see any notifications for messages you've received in Notification Center.

>> **Reading or replying to a message:** You can read a message or reply to a notification in three ways. Tap the Messages icon on your Home screen to simply go to the chat you want. You can also swipe downward from the middle-top of the screen to display Notification Center and choose a specific Messages notification, or tap the live notification when it appears if you can be quick (the notification fades away in a few seconds).

>> **Following the conversation:** When viewing an individual chat or group chat, your messages appear on the right side of the screen in blue bubbles (green bubbles if it's an SMS or MMS message with someone not using iMessage) and the other person's messages appear in light gray bubbles, whether it's an iMessage, SMS message, or MMS message. When your message has been delivered, that fact will be noted just below the last bubble in your exchange. If there was a problem delivering the message, you'll see Not Delivered instead. If at first you don't succeed, try again.

>> **Forwarding a conversation:** If you want to forward all or part of a conversation to another iMessage user, press against a text bubble in that chat and tap the More button, which shows up at the bottom of the screen along with a Copy option. (You'll also **see** the aforementioned tapback icons.) Tap additional text, photo, or video bubbles you want to forward (the one you pressed to summon the More button is already selected) so that a check mark appears in a circle to the left of each. Then tap the forward (curved arrow) icon at the lower right of the screen. The contents of the selected text bubbles are copied to a new text message; specify a recipient and then tap Send.

>> **Deleting part of a single conversation thread:** Press against a text bubble and tap More. Tap each text bubble you want to delete; a check mark appears in the circle next to each one. Then tap the delete (trash can) icon at the bottom of the pane, and tap Delete Message(s). Or, to delete the entire conversation in one fell swoop, tap the Delete All button at the top of the screen and then tap Delete Conversation.

>> **Deleting an entire conversation thread:** Tap the Edit button at the upper left of the Messages list, tap the circle that appears to the left of the person's name, and then tap the Delete button at the bottom of the pane. Or swipe from right to left on the message in the Messages pane and then tap the red Delete button.

Sending pix and vids in a message

To send a picture or video in a message, follow the instructions for sending a text message in the "Sending iMessages" section. Then tap the camera icon to the left of the text-entry field at the bottom of the screen and take a pic or video, or tap the gray App Store icon and then the Photos icon to select an image from your

Photos library. You can also add text to photos or videos. When you're finished, tap the Send button.

If you receive a picture or video in a message, it appears in a bubble just like text. You can view a still image or live photo in-line, or tap the image to have it go full screen. In the case of a live photo, you can tap and hold down on it to play the short recording. (See Chapter 9 for more info on live photos.) If someone sends you a video, you can tap the play icon on the video to play it right in Messages. Tap again to have the video take over the full screen.

In full-screen mode, tap the share icon in the upper-right corner of a received video or picture for additional options, such as sharing the image on Facebook or Twitter, and assigning it to a contact. If you don't see the icon, tap the picture or video once, and the icon will magically appear.

Meanwhile, in Settings ⇨ Messages, you can enable a Low Quality Image Mode switch. The setting applies to the images you send and will help you conserve data.

Smart messaging tricks

Here are some more things you can do with messages:

>> **Search your messages for a word or phrase.** Type the word or phrase in the search field at the top left of the Messages listing pane.

>> **Send read receipts to allow others to be notified when you have read their missives.** Tap Settings ⇨ Messages, and slide the switch so that Send Read Receipts is on.

TIP

In iMessages, you can see when your own message has been delivered and read, and when the other person is readying a response. You can also tap the *i*-in-a-circle (info) icon to reveal the Details pane and then tap Send Read Receipts. Read Receipts is turned on, but only for the person with whom you are chatting.

>> **Use a Bluetooth keyboard instead of the on-screen keyboard.** Follow the instructions in Chapter 15 to pair your Bluetooth keyboard with your iPad.

>> **Dictate a message (third-generation iPads or later).** Tap the microphone key on your keyboard and start talking. Tap the microphone key again when you're finished. Dictating text isn't as quick or as much fun as Tap to Talk, but it works.

>> **Open a URL included in an iMessage.** Tap the URL to open that web page in Safari.

>> **Call or FaceTime the person you're texting with right from iMessages.** Tap the circled picture or initials representing the person you're communicating with, and then tap the audio call icon or FaceTime icon to call them directly. If you tap the *i*-in-a-circle icon to open the Details pane, and then tap the person's name or icon again, you'll open up the person's full Contacts pane, where you can initiate an email or use other contact information.

>> **See an address included in an iMessage.** Tap the address to see it on a map in Maps.

>> **Choose how you can be reached via iMessage.** Tap Settings ⇨ Messages ⇨ Send & Receive. Then add another email address or remove existing addresses. You can also select the email address (or phone number) from which to start new conversations.

>> **Show the Subject field.** Flip the switch to show a Subject field with your messages.

>> **Filter unknown senders.** Flip this switch to turn off notifications for iMessages from folks who are not among your contacts. You can sort such unknown senders into a separate list.

>> **Block a sender.** Block someone who is harassing you or has left your good graces. Tap Settings ⇨ Messages ⇨ Blocked and select a name from your contacts. You will no longer receive messages or FaceTime calls from this person.

>> **Share your location.** Meeting a recipient in an unfamiliar place? In the middle of your conversation, you can share your location on a map. Tap the *i*-in-a-circle at the upper-right corner, and then tap either Send My Current Location or Share My Location. Choosing the latter gives you the option to share your whereabouts indefinitely, until the end of the day or for one hour. You can monitor how much time is left before your location will no longer be shared.

>> **See all the message attachments at once.** Tap the *i*-in-a-circle (info) icon to reveal the Details pane, where you can browse all the photos and videos from your conversation.

>> **Keep Messages history.** You can keep your entire Messages history on the iPad permanently, for one year, or for 30 days. Tap Settings ⇨ Messages ⇨ Keep Messages and make your choice.

You are now a certified iMessage maven.

3

The Multimedia iPad

Chapter **7**

Apple Music, Books, News, and TV+

The iPad is a great multimedia device. You can listen to music with the Music app, read e-books on the Books app, read news from all over the world with the News app, and watch some great new TV shows and movies with Apple TV+ using the Apple TV app. We show you all these apps and their corresponding services in this chapter.

Introducing Your iPad's Music Player

The Music app is the musical hub inside your iPad. In previous editions, we called it your iPad's inner iPod, but it's become a lot more. You can not only manage your music library and listen to songs in the Music app but also tap into a library of more than 55 million songs through the Apple Music subscription service. Read on to learn more!

The Music app has been organized with five icons at the bottom of the screen: Library, For You, Browse, Radio, and Search. This layout is a lot like the App Store, which you read more about in Chapter 10. In the following sections, we take a closer look at these sections.

< If you don't see these icons, tap the back icon in the upper-left corner of the screen (and shown in the margin).

For You, the Apple Music section of the Music app

We're going to start with the For You icon. Why not the Library? Because For You is where you find Apple Music, Apple's premium music subscription service. The vast majority of music is being consumed by streaming through services such as Apple Music, Spotify, and Pandora. This trend is a significant shift from the early days of the iPad, when everyone bought their music from the iTunes Store and managed it from their Macs and PCs in the iTunes app. Let's dig deeper into Apple Music so you can see what the fuss is about.

Apple Music gives you access to 55 million songs. That's right, 55 million songs, plus curated playlists, song recommendations, and Beats Radio, Apple's streaming music channel with human DJs, sort of like a legacy radio station. You get all this for $9.99 per month or $99 per year, $4.99 per month for college students, or $14.99 per month for a family sharing plan for up to six people. Your first three months are free, giving you plenty of time to get hooked on Apple Music before automatic billing kicks in.

REMEMBER

You'll be married to that subscription price for as long as you want to listen to Apple Music. If you ever stop subscribing, you lose access to music you used to stream and any music you downloaded to your devices through your Apple Music subscription.

If you haven't already subscribed to Apple Music, you'll be asked to subscribe the first time you open the Music app. You'll be asked also when you open the For You icon, because it's full of the curated content from Apple Music we mention earlier. In Figure 7-1, you see the subscription options offered to new Apple Music subscribers.

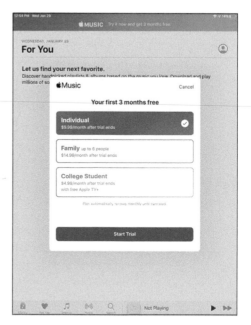

FIGURE 7-1:
Subscribe to Apple Music for access to 55 million songs.

To subscribe on your iPad, choose the option you want, confirm or sign in with your iCloud account, and you're done! If you're already subscribed and are signed into iCloud in Settings ⇨ Apple ID, you'll find Apple Music content in the For You section. In Figure 7-2, you see some of Bryan's recent plays in For You, along with music suggestions from Apple Music.

FIGURE 7-2:
For You offers
recently played
music and
Apple Music
suggestions.

After you subscribe to Apple Music, you can tap the For You or Browse icons, which we discuss in more detail later, and then tap to hear any artist, genre, playlist, or song. It's that simple! You can tap the iCloud download icon next to a song or album to download that music to your device for offline listening, or stream anything you want when you have a connection to the Internet, be it Wi-Fi or cellular. Note that streaming music counts against most cellular data plans; check with your provider if you're unsure.

Finding new music in Browse

The Browse icon in the Music app is all about finding new music, looking at music by genre, and viewing other recommended content from the Apple music team. While For You is centered on what Apple Music thinks you're interested in, Browse offers a more general look at music, especially new releases and other new additions to the Apple Music catalog. Just like with For You, when you have a subscription to Apple Music, you can tap any artist, playlist, genre, song, or other listing and play that music whenever you want.

But unlike For You, Browse also lets you see content whether or not you have a subscription to Apple Music, allowing you to preview songs and see new releases. If you try to play a song, however, you'll be asked to sign in with an Apple ID that has subscribed to Apple Music.

Listening to human DJs in the age of streaming music

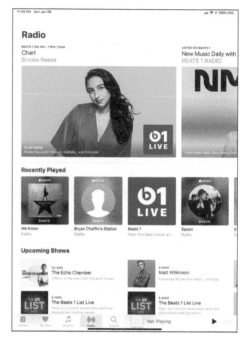

NEW

Tap the Radio icon to see a feature unique to Apple Music: Beats Radio. In Radio, you'll find several stations algorithmically designed around your music. For instance, Figure 7-3 shows the We Know radio station, which is designed around the Hamilton soundtrack, Bryan Chaffin's Station, which is based on other music Bryan has recently played, and Spoon Radio, which is based on one of Bryan's favorite bands, Spoon.

But the crown jewel in Apple Music's radio crown is Beats 1, an Internet radio station created by humans and with human DJs. The content is created hands-on by Apple's talented staff, with other content created by big and small artists. You can listen to individual shows with distinct flavors helmed by named DJs. In Figure 7-3, you can see a schedule of shows at the bottom of the page, as well as some flagship shows promoted in the large banner at the top of the screen.

FIGURE 7-3:
The Radio section features radio stations built around your music.

To listen to any of your radio stations or Beats 1, tap the show or station you want to enjoy. You can view content in the Radio section at any time, but you need an active subscription to Apple Music to listen to those shows.

Managing music in the Library

Now let's move on to your music, which you'll find in the Library icon at the bottom of the Music app screen. The Library is dedicated to songs you've ripped from CDs or downloaded from the iTunes Store or other online music stores. The songs in your library represent song files you've purchased and downloaded from the iTunes Store or downloaded from Apple Music for offline listening. You also find songs you've synced to your iPad from your Mac or PC.

If you have multiple Apple devices and want to keep your music library synced between all of them, use the Sync Library feature in Settings ⇨ Music by tapping the Sync Library button to turn it green. With Sync Library, changes to the music library on one device are synced automatically to your other Apple devices.

For more information on syncing music to your iPad from your Mac or PC, please see Chapter 3.

Figure 7-4 shows some of Bryan's library, sorted by album. Each album shows the album cover, the name of the album, and the artist. Tap Library in the upper-left corner of the screen to sort your library by Recently Added, Playlists, or Artists.

Working with playlists

As with individual songs, you can create and play playlists on your iPad, or play and manage playlists synced to your library through the Sync Library feature. To see your playlists, tap Library in the upper-left corner of the Library section in the Music app, and then tap Playlists. You see a list of any playlists you've created. You can tap any playlist to view its contents, and then tap the play icon on the Playlist page to play it.

FIGURE 7-4:
The Library shows all the music on your iPad.

To edit your playlist, tap Edit in the upper-right corner of your playlist screen. In edit mode, you can change the name of your playlist and add cover art. If it's a playlist you created, you can also rearrange the order of the songs by dragging the three lines next to a song. If the playlist is one of Apple's Smart playlists, such as My Top Rated, you can't change the order of the songs.

To create a playlist, tap Library ⇨ Playlists in the upper-left corner of the Library screen. Then tap New in the upper-right corner to bring up the New Playlist screen. Tap Playlist Name and enter a name for your playlist, and then tap the Add Music button to add new songs. You can choose from your library or the For You content, or you can browse for content. Add as many songs as you like.

When you're finished, tap the Done button in the upper-right corner of the Add Music sheet. You can tap Description to add an optional description, and can tap the camera icon on the left side to add cover art. Finally, tap the Done button in the upper-right corner. Your new playlist will be listed in the main playlist view, where you can tap and play it whenever you want.

Managing your own music with iTunes Match

iTunes Match is another music-related subscription service from Apple. Unlike Apple Music, however, iTunes Match helps you manage the song files in your own music library. It does so by taking the music in your iTunes (macOS Yosemite and earlier) or Music (macOS Mojave or later) library and uploading it to iCloud. You can then stream that music on your Apple devices or through iTunes on Windows, without having to sync or otherwise transfer the files. For offline listening on your other devices, you can download those uploaded files from iCloud.

Here's how it works: When you subscribe to iTunes Match, Apple goes through your music library and identifies every song. If Apple has one of those songs in its own massive library, it matches your file to its file and gives you access to that song in iCloud. If Apple doesn't have a song in your library — say a bootleg, a live recording, or something else obscure — it uploads the unknown song to your iCloud so you can access it.

TECHNICAL STUFF

As a bonus, all the music iTunes matches plays back from iCloud at 256-Kbps AAC quality even if your original copy was lower quality. You can even replace your lower bit-rate copies by downloading higher-quality versions after the matching process completes. On the other hand, if your original song file is higher quality than 256-Kbps AAC, you will be able to stream or download it from iCloud only at 256-Kbps AAC quality. Few people can hear a difference in quality at 256-Kbps or higher, but if you're an audiophile who can — and whose song files are of higher quality than Apple's 256-Kbps — think about this tradeoff before subscribing to iTunes Match.

TIP

If you don't have a bunch of obscure songs not found in Apple's extensive Music catalog, you probably don't need iTunes Match. On the other hand, if you're interested only in the music you own that's already in your library, iTunes Match is a less expensive way to stream your music from iCloud on all your devices than an Apple Music subscription.

You can store up to 100,000 songs in iCloud, and songs you purchased from the iTunes Store don't count against that limit. Only tracks or albums you specify are stored locally on your devices, saving gigabytes of precious storage space.

All this comes at a cost, $24.99 per year to be precise. To enable iTunes Match, go to iTunes (macOS Yosemite or earlier and Windows) or the Music app (macOS Catalina or later), and click iTunes Store in the sidebar or click Store at the top of iTunes in Windows. If you don't see iTunes Store in the sidebar of iTunes or the Music app on your Mac, go to iTunes ⇨ Preferences ⇨ General and enable iTunes Store. After you've clicked iTunes Store, scroll to the bottom of the screen on your Mac or Windows PC and click iTunes Match, and then click the Subscribe button. You'll be asked to sign in with your iCloud account and confirm your billing information.

Searching for music in the Music App

Search may be one of the most important parts of the Music app for many users because that's where you search both your own library and Apple Music for specific artists, songs, albums, and even lyrics. Tap the Search icon at the bottom of the Music app screen to go the search screen. As seen in Figure 7-5, Bryan has tapped in the search field and selected the option to search Apple Music.

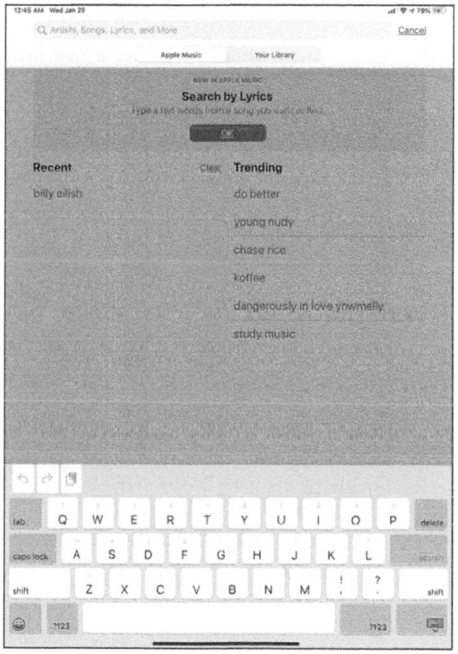

To search your Library, simply tap Your Library and enter your search term. When searching either Apple Music or your own library, your iPad will display live results that change the more characters you type.

Also shown in Figure 7-5 are recent searches — Billy Eilish in this case — as well as searches that were trending on Apple Music. Tap any search result in the Search section to get more information about that artist, song, album, or lyric.

FIGURE 7-5:
Search Apple Music or your own library in the Search section of the Music app.

What about the iTunes Store?

All this talk about Apple Music may have you wondering about Apple's venerable iTunes Store. Never fear, dear reader, because the iTunes Store is still on your iPad, but now it's a separate app from the Music app. If you prefer to own your music, you can use the iTunes Store to buy songs and download them to your iPad whenever you want. (You can also buy movies and TV shows in the iTunes Store app.)

Tap the iTunes Store icon on your Home screen. Figure 7-6 shows the home page of the iTunes Store, which defaults to the Music section. Tap an artist, album, or song to view more information, including price. Note that links to Apple Music content in the iTunes Store may take you back to the Music app. That may be a little confusing at first — at least we think it is — but it's not surprising considering how hard Apple is pushing its subscription service.

If you buy a song or album in the iTunes Store, it will be added to your music library, which is also back in the Music app. To play your newly purchased music, tap the Music app on your Home screen on the dock and then tap the Library icon at the bottom of the screen. If you don't immediately see your new music, you can tap Library in the upper-left corner and then tap Recently Added. Your new purchase will be at the top when it has finished downloading.

FIGURE 7-6:
Buy music from the iTunes Store.

Songs in the iTunes Store tend to be priced at $0.99 or $1.29, with most albums starting at $7.99. Songs purchased will be charged to your iCloud account, and you'll be asked to sign into your iCloud account if you aren't already when purchasing from the iTunes Store.

The iPad Is a Great E-Book Reader

We love reading books on our iPad, and big reasons are the Apple Books app and the Book Store in the Books app. With clear text, the ability to control fonts, accurate page numbers, and great page curling and turning effects that make it feel like you're reading a real book, Apple Books offers a terrific reading experience.

TIP

Amazon's popular Kindle platform is available also on the iPad through the Kindle app in the App Store. We prefer Apple Books, though, and even if you're already a Kindle user, we recommend checking out Books.

Open Books by tapping the Books icon on your Home screen. In earlier versions of iOS, you had to download the Books app from the App Store, but in iPadOS it's installed by default. The first time you open the Books app, you'll see the Get Started screen. Like the App Store, which we talk about in Chapter 10, and the Music app and iTunes Store app, which we talk about earlier in this chapter, the Books app has five icons at the bottom of the screen: Reading Now, Library, Book Store, Audiobooks, and Search. We walk through all five icons in this section.

TECHNICAL STUFF

The default file format for Apple Books is EPUB (.epub), an open format for e-books. You can add EPUB files to Books through file transfers or even by emailing them to yourself and using the Open With feature to send them to Books. We discuss syncing files to your iPad in more depth in Chapter 3. Books also supports Apple's own multitouch format for e-books created with the iBooks Author app on the Mac. Most of the books available through the Book Store are EPUB files, and the format of these books is transparent to you.

The Reading Now section offers quick access to the Books you have most recently opened, as well as books Apple is promoting. In Figure 7-7, you see the book Dryan is reading at the top of the screen, signified by the image of a physical open book. Other recent books can be viewed by swiping left to right in the Current section of the screen.

Below the list of Current books are books recommended to you based on what you've already read, and below that — not shown in Figure 7-7 — are Current Bestsellers. In our test iPad, which didn't have any books loaded onto it, we were shown lists, such as Oprah's Book Club, Customer Favorites, Popular Pre-Order, and Special Offers.

FIGURE 7-7:
The Reading Now section in Books offers recent book titles and recommendations for new books.

Your own personal library

Tap the Library icon to view all the books you have in your Books iCloud library, whether or not they've been downloaded to your iPad. Books that haven't been downloaded have an iCloud icon below the cover art for the book. Tap that icon to download the book from iCloud to your iPad. Tap a book's cover art to open the book to the last page you had open. If you haven't previously opened a particular book, tapping it will take you to the first page of the story's text.

To view the table of contents for a book, tap to open the book, and then tap the menu icon in the upper-left of the screen. If you don't see the menu icon, tap anywhere on the page to bring up hidden controls and buttons, including the menu icon. Tap Resume to leave the table of contents and go back to the page you were on.

As you're reading, you can turn the page in two ways. One way, which turns the page quickly, is to tap the page's right margin. The second way is more fun, and some will find it more natural. If you tap and drag the right margin, you slowly turn the page, just as if you were turning a real page on a real book. You'll even see the text of the page you're turning reversed and dimmed, as if you were seeing through a piece of paper. We love this effect not for its gee-whiz awesomeness but rather because it can make the reading experience more immersive, especially for those who grew up reading printed books. Indeed, the effect will disappear into the background and you'll cease to notice it because it feels so natural. To turn back a page, tap the left margin or tap and drag the left margin to the right.

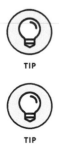

There's a third way to turn pages, too. Quickly tap and flick any page to the left (to advance it) or the right (to go back a page). In our experience, this technique quickly became second nature.

Let's take a second to jump to Settings ⇨ Books, where the Both Margins Advance setting allows you to advance the page by tapping either margin. To activate this feature, toggle the Both Margins Advance button on (green). You can still go back a page by tapping and dragging the left margin when this setting is active. Other settings allow you to toggle on and off full justification and auto-hyphenating. We recommend leaving those settings on, which is the way your iPad ships.

Font and layout controls in Books

Tap ᴀA at the top of any page in a book to reveal the font control panel for Books, as shown in Figure 7-8. In this control panel, tap the small *A* to make the font smaller or tap the large *A* to make the font larger. Any changes you make will carry over to your other books in the Books app. Above the font size control buttons is a screen brightness slider. Tap and drag this slider to adjust your screen brightness as you see fit.

Tap Fonts below the font size controls to change the font of your books. Some, but not all, books will list Original as the font, probably at the top of the list. If Original is listed and selected, you're reading your book in the font chosen by the publisher. You can also choose Athelas, Charter, Georgia, Iowan, Palatino, San Francisco, New York, Seravek, or Times New Roman, all standard publishing fonts. Fonts are subjective, so feel free to choose the one you like the best, or to just leave it set to Original.

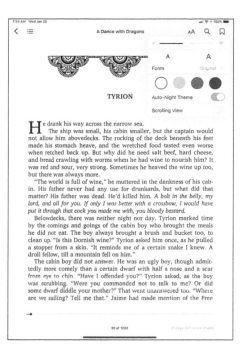

Next in the control panel are four circles that graduate from white to dark. These circles control the background color of the pages in your books, as well as the color of the text, which is optimized for each background color. Tap any circle to see how it affects your reading experience. The default is the white with the black outline, which gives you a white page with black text. The darkest circle on the right is the night theme, with black pages and a very light gray (almost white) text. This mode can help reduce eye strain at night.

FIGURE 7-8:
Control the look and feel of your e-books with the font control panel in Books.

Below the circles is a toggle for Auto-Night Theme. Tap this toggle on (green), and the iPad's sensors will determine when you're in a low-light environment and switch to Night Theme (and switch back when you're in a brighter environment). We read at night a lot and find that this setting does reduce eye strain.

The last control is Scrolling View, which is off by default. To activate it, tap the toggle on (green) and your book will now scroll up and down. Some people think scrolling up and down makes more sense on an iPad than flipping pages right to left. Try it. You might like it!

Searchable Books

Next, let's look at the search feature, another reason that makes e-books great. Tap the magnifying glass icon at the upper right of a Books page to pull down a search field. Type a word or page number in this field and you'll get results for every instance of your search term in the book. Tap a result and you jump straight to that page, with the word or phrase that matches your search highlighted.

At the bottom left of the screen, you'll also see a Back to Page *xx* button that will take you straight back to where you were. To be sure, this isn't a feature you'll use all the time, but when you need it, it's priceless. Imagine wanting to revisit a passage that has stuck in your mind or a character or event that you're sure has more meaning. Or if you're reading non-fiction, imagine wanting to find an instruction or a quote. As we've said, when you need this feature, you won't be able to imagine going back to printed books!

Book(mark) 'em, Danno!

Another great feature of Books is the bookmark feature. In the upper right of your screen is a banner icon. Tap this icon to bookmark the current page, turning the icon from white to red. It's kind of like dog-earing a page in a printed book, but without making the book lover in you cringe. You can bookmark as many pages as you want. To revisit your bookmarks, tap the table of contents icon in the upper left. You see three buttons at the top of the page: Contents, Bookmarks, and Notes.

Tap the Bookmarks button to see any bookmarks you've made in your current book. The Books app will list them, along with the chapter title and the date you made the bookmark. Bookmarks are a great way to revisit favorite passages or important bits. When you've finished looking at your bookmarks, tap Resume to go back to the page you were reading. To remove a bookmark, tap the bookmark icon on the bookmarked page to turn it from red to white.

Highlights and notes

Another great reason to embrace e-books and the Books app is the ability to highlight text and even attach a note to that highlight. To learn more about how this works, first turn to any page in any e-book. Now, tap and hold down on a word, which brings up the text selector tool. Drag the selector handles until the word or passage you want to highlight is selected.

In Figure 7-9, we selected the passage *savior come from across the sea* and then tapped Highlight, which added the yellow highlight mark, and then tapped the Note icon, which opened the yellow Note field. The highlighted text stands out if you flip through the pages, and you can tap the note icon in the margin to review your note. All notes are listed in the Notes section in the table of contents, allowing you to tap through to any of them. Not everyone needs this feature, but those who do will find it invaluable.

Buying books in the Book Store

If you're looking at a book now, tap the back arrow in the upper left to return to your library, because now it's time to go shopping in the Book Store. Tap the Book Store icon at the bottom of the page. Apple does a great job of presenting new releases, top charts (Apple's version of best sellers), and staff picks, and you can browse and read about books all you want.

At the top of Figure 7-10, you see a promo for 2019 bestsellers priced at $8 or less. You can swipe left in that section to see other promos. Not shown in the screenshot is Winters Biggest Books, several individual books being promoted, and another promo for Oprah's Book Club. Below the promo section is the For You section, which are books recommended for you based on the books you've already purchased and read. Not shown in the screenshot are New & Trending books, Top Charts, Coming Soon, Books We Love (by Apple staff),

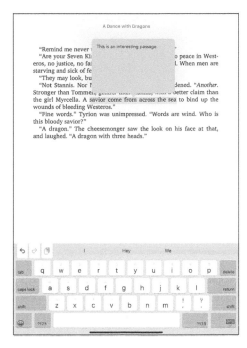

FIGURE 7-9:
Highlight passages and add Notes.

FIGURE 7-10:
Buy e-books in the Book Store.

special offers, and links to browsing by genre. These promotional areas are customized for you and may appear differently in your Book Store.

Tap any book to get a full screen page of information about that book. Figure 7-11 shows *The Philip K. Dick Anthology*, with a button for buying it for $0.99, a button for marking it Want to Read, and a button for downloading a free sample. Almost every book in the Book Store will allow you to download a free sample. You can also read the publisher's description of the book, and the preview section gives you an idea of what the book's pages look like.

Not shown in the screenshot are lists of More Books Like This, More Books by Philip K. Dick, More Audiobooks by Philip K. Dick, other books Customers Also Bought, and Top Books in Short Stories, and then a version history of this book along with any requirements the title might have. Tap the Buy button to purchase and download the book. Tap the x-in-a-gray-circle to close the book's promo page and go back to the Book Store. You can also swipe left and right to see other books the Books app thinks you might be interested in.

FIGURE 7-11:
Lots of information is available on the details pane.

After you purchase a book, you can view it in your library. Tap the book in your library to open it, and then read it as described earlier in this chapter.

Read books with your ears in the Audiobooks section

The Book Store also has a section for *audiobooks*, recorded books that have been read by a human narrator. Audiobooks can be listened to right in the Books app, and are listed in your library along with your e-books. You can view just your audiobooks by tapping Collections in your library at the top left and choosing

Audiobooks in the menu that opens. Audiobooks in your iCloud library that haven't been downloaded to your iPad will have an iCloud icon below them. Tap the iCloud icon to download the audiobook.

TIP The Book Store has fewer audiobooks than e-books in. That said, Apple has been adding more and more audiobooks to the Book Store in recent years, and many popular titles are available.

TIP Audiobooks tend to be more expensive than e-books.

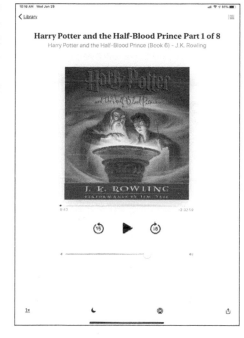

Tap the cover art for the audiobook to open it, as shown in Figure 7-12. Tap the play icon to play the audiobook and tap the pause icon to stop. Tap the 15 icon with an arrow going counterclockwise to back up the recording by 15 seconds, something that's useful if you missed something or were interrupted. You can tap that icon as many times as you want. Tap the 15 icon with an arrow going clockwise to advance the audiobook by 15 seconds.

Tap and drag the timeline below the cover art to advance or rewind the audiobook to a specific point in the recording. Tap and drag the volume button to change the volume.

FIGURE 7-12:
Audiobook playback controls are intuitive and easy to use.

At the bottom of the screen are four icons: 1x, a quarter moon, the AirPlay icon, and the share icon. The 1x button is a playback speed button. Tap 1x to cycle through different playback speeds. Your options are 1x, 1¼x, 1½x, 1¾x, 2x, down to ¾x, and back to 1x. What speed works for you is subjective, so feel free to try different options to find the speed you like.

The quarter moon icon is a way of playing your audiobook for a certain number of minutes before it automatically stops, a great tool for listening yourself to sleep. Tap the quarter moon icon and choose to end the playing at a time between 5 minutes and 1 hour, when the current track ends, or after a custom number of hours or minutes or both.

The AirPlay icon at the bottom of the screen allows you to choose your audio source. Tap the AirPlay icon to pick between any connected headphones, nearby HomePods, nearby Apple TVs, connected Bluetooth speakers, or any nearby AirPlay-capable speakers.

Tap the share icon to share information about your audiobook through the standard share sheet. Tap Library in the upper-left corner to return to your library view.

Searching the Book Store

The fifth icon at the bottom of the Books app is the search icon (magnifying glass). Tap the search icon to open the search page for the Books app. In addition to the search field, you'll see a list of your recent searches, if you've made any, as well as a list of trending searches that other Books customers have performed.

To perform a search, tap the search field and enter an author, a title, or even a genre. Tap any of the results to get more information. Search results include any relevant books in your library as well as in the Book Store.

We love the Books app and the Book Store, and we think you will, too. If you're already a fan of e-books, give the Books app a spin. If you're curious about e-books but haven't tried one, dive right into the Books app; you can download a sample for free.

Apple News and Apple News+

Apple got serious about its News app a few years ago, and it got even more serious with the release of iPadOS. The key to Apple's approach to presenting third-party news is human curation, a theme you may have noticed throughout this chapter. Apple uses human curation for many of its news selections, rather than relying solely on computer algorithms to make those decisions. In addition, Apple has focused on layout and presentation to make reading news stories in the News app pleasant and enjoyable. Some of the larger publications use tools that Apple provides to make News app versions of their stories visually stunning.

Tap the News app on your home screen to open it. You'll first be taken to the today view, as shown in Figure 7-13. The today view includes Top Stories and Trending Stories, a list of stories gaining momentum in the News app. Not shown in Figure 7-13 are other curated sections, such as Conversation Starters, a For You section based on what you tend to read, multiple articles from the publications you read the most, and Business.

Tap the navigation icon in the upper-left corner of the News app to find links to the home pages for specific publications, as shown in Figure 7-14. At the top of this menu is News+, which we discuss next, as well as links to Today View, Saved Stories, and History, a list of articles you have already read. You'll also see publications you're subscribed to. As shown in Figure 7-14, Bryan subscribes to *The Wall Street Journal* and *The Washington Post*. Below that are publications Bryan has chosen to follow for free. Not shown in Figure 7-14 is a link to Discover Channels & Topics, where you can choose additional publications and topics to follow.

To edit the publications you follow, tap the Edit button in the upper-right corner of the Navigation menu. You can remove publications from your follow list by tapping the red circle with a – sign, and then tapping the Unfollow button that is revealed. You can reorder an item by tapping its icon with three lines and dragging it to the new location.

REMEMBER

You can access a systemwide today view in iPadOS by swiping from the left side of any Home screen. One of the widgets in the iPadOS today view is the News widget, which includes headlines from the News app. What you read in the News app will help inform what the News widget shows you in the iPadOS today view.

FIGURE 7-13:
Today in Apple News.

FIGURE 7-14:
The Navigation menu in the News app.

When reading an article in the News app, you can tap the back arrow in the upper-left corner to return to the page that brought you to where you are now. You can also tap the navigation icon (shown in the margin) to jump to Today or another section of the News app, such as News+, which we describe next.

Apple News+ is yet another optional subscription service from Apple, and it gives you access to articles from top magazines and newspapers. Apple News+ is $9.99 per month, and your first month is free.

Tap the Navigation icon and tap News+ to go to the News+ section of the News app, as shown in Figure 7-15. If you haven't already subscribed, you'll be presented with a large advertisement for subscribing to the service at the top. Below that advertisement are buttons that allow you to navigate the different publications that are part of your subscription.

Tap the Browse the Catalog button to see a list of every magazine and newspaper — there are hundreds. The other buttons break down that catalog into specific genres, such as Business & Finance, Cars, and Entertainment. If you haven't subscribed, you can tap through to individual articles, but you'll be able to read only the publication, title, author, date, and any sort of title image the article may have.

FIGURE 7-15:
 News+ in the News app.

Tap the navigation icon and then tap another section to leave Apple News+.

Apple TV+

NEW

We talk about the Apple TV app in Chapter 8, but we want to talk about Apple TV+ now. Apple TV+ is Apple's new original content subscription service. Apple TV+ offers subscribers TV shows and movies developed for and available exclusively through Apple TV+. As of this writing, Apple TV+ is just $4.99 per month, with a one-week free trial when you first subscribe. For a limited time — Apple hasn't said when it will end — people who buy a new iPhone, iPad, iPod touch, Apple TV, or Mac get an entire year for free.

We don't expect Apple to offer that free year forever, but it makes sense to do it now, while the service is new. That's because Apple is rolling out new shows as they go, and while we think many of those shows are great, there's not yet a deep catalog to justify the price. This is especially true when you consider Apple TV+'s competition is Disney+, Amazon Prime, Hulu, Netflix, and other services with more extensive catalogs of original and sometimes third-party legacy content.

As of this writing, Apple TV+ has launched shows such as *See, The Morning Show, For All Mankind, Servant, Truth Be Told,* and *Little America,* as well as documentary movies such as *The Elephant Queen* and kids shows such as *Ghost Writer* and *Helpsters.* We know of dozens of other shows that have been signed by Apple and are in development, and Apple adds new shows every few weeks.

To watch Apple TV+ shows, tap the Apple TV app on your Home screen, and then tap the Watch Now icon at the bottom of the screen. Scroll down and tap one of the Apple TV+ buttons. You see a landing page dedicated to Apple TV+ content, as shown in Figure 7-16.

FIGURE 7-16:
Apple Originals on Apple TV+ in the TV app.

If you haven't already subscribed to Apple TV+, you'll be able to browse the content with frequent opportunities to start a 7-day free trial. During that trial, you can watch as many shows or movies as you want. If you don't cancel your subscription before the 7 days is up, you'll be automatically billed $4.99 per month. If you have a free year because you purchased one of the devices we mentioned earlier, you won't start paying until that year is up.

To view a movie or episodes of a show, tap the cover art for that movie or show. Then tap the Play First Episode button to start a new show, or Play Next Episode for a show you've already started. Scroll down on the show's information page to see a list of seasons and episodes. You can download any show to your iPad by tapping the iCloud download icon below the episode. By downloading, you can watch shows offline, say on an airplane, a long car ride, or anywhere else you may not have Internet access. You will, of course, need a Wi-Fi or cellular data connection to stream shows. As we say throughout the book, streaming video can use a lot of bandwidth, so be mindful of your cellular data caps if you're watching a show over your cellular connection.

To leave the Apple TV+ section of the TV app, tap the Watch Now button in the upper-left corner, or tap one of the icons at the bottom of the TV app screen.

And that concludes our look at Apple's content delivery apps and services. All these apps and services are great experiences on the iPad, and we think you're going to like them.

Chapter **8**

iPad Videography

Video streaming on mobile devices has become incredibly popular, with many people watching more video on their iPads and iPhones than on TV. That might be hard for some of us to believe, but the combination of Apple's gorgeous Retina display and massive proliferation of video-subscription services such as Netflix, Disney+, Hulu, Amazon Prime Video, and Apple's own Apple TV+ — not to mention YouTube — make mobile devices such as the iPad a go-to destination for watching video.

Although the iPad isn't going to replace the TV set in your living room, watching movies and other videos on Apple's prized tablet is a cinematic treat. What's more, the iPad's cameras can help turn you into a filmmaker.

And video on the iPad ventures into another area: video chat. You can keep in touch with friends and loved ones by gazing into each other's pupils. You do it all through *FaceTime,* a clever video chat program that comes with your iPad. In the interest of equal time, we'd also like to point out that you can do video chats on your iPad by downloading a popular third-party app such as Skype, among others.

We get to FaceTime later in this chapter. For now, and without any further ado, let's get on with the show!

Finding Stuff to Watch

With iPadOS, Apple has brought all its video offerings, even shows you're watching through third-party services, under the umbrella of the TV app. In the TV app, you can find almost all of the streaming content available on your iPad, as well as movies and TV shows from the iTunes Store and anything shared from iTunes on your Mac or PC. (If you haven't done so yet, now is as good a time as any to read Chapter 3 for all the details on syncing.)

You can still go to dedicated apps from third party-services, too. So if Netflix is the only subscription service you have, want, or need, you're covered.

Watching shows with the TV app

When you first launch the TV app, it opens on the Watch Now tab, alongside tabs for Library and Search. All of these tabs are designed for content from iTunes, third-party services, and videos you've loaded onto your iPad through iTunes (or shared from iTunes). Videos you've made on your iPad are in the Photos app, which we get to later.

From the Watch Now tab, you can find TV shows and movies, no matter where they are. It's almost like having an Apple TV set-top box inside your iPad.

For instance, as of this writing, Seth McFarland's comedy *The Orville* is being offered under the What to Watch section of the TV app. Tap that show, and you get a new page with a description, an episode list, and an Open In button. Tap the Open In button, and an overlay pane appears with all the places where you can watch *The Orville,* specifically, Hulu, Fox Now, and AT&T TV, as shown in Figure 8-1. You can tap whichever app you want. If the app you tapped is not installed, you'll get a new screen inviting you to download it. A quick download later, and you have your new show!

FIGURE 8-1:
Want to watch *The Orville?*

And that's the secret of the TV app. You don't need to know which network or service a given TV show is on to find it. The TV app acts as a centralized location for finding shows available in your region, be they on Netflix, ABC, NBC, CBS, Fox, HBO, iTunes, and many other services, including streaming services in other markets. When a show is available in two places, say iTunes and Netflix, you can choose which source you want to get it from.

TIP

Some streaming services, such as Netflix and HBO NOW, require subscriptions. Others, such as the ABC app, show commercials during streams. Still others, such as HBO GO, are part of a cable or satellite subscription.

You can browse the TV app by genre, hits, trending movies, trending TV shows, and a list of recently watched shows.

Tap the Library tab at the bottom of the app, and you find all the shows you've purchased or rented from iTunes as well as other videos. On the left side of the screen are organizational tabs, such as Recent Purchases, TV Shows, Movies, and Genres, as shown in Figure 8-2.

FIGURE 8-2:
The Library tab in the TV app Is the home for movies, TV shows, and downloaded videos.

Apple's TV app is a one-stop shop for all your streaming needs. You can still choose to use any given streaming app on its own — you don't have to go through the TV app — but the TV app can be a great way of finding shows you're looking for and discovering new shows you didn't even know you wanted to watch.

Renting and buying at the iTunes Store

Although you can use the TV app to find all movies and TV shows on iTunes, you can also browse in iTunes itself. iTunes features dedicated sections for purchasing or renting episodes of TV shows and for buying or renting movies, as shown in Figure 8-3.

Pricing varies, but it's not atypical (as of this writing) to fork over $1.99 to pick up an episode of a popular TV show in standard definition or $2.99 for a high-def version. And a few shows are free. You can also purchase a complete season of a favorite show — prices are usually about $24.99 for standard-def and $29.99 to $39.99 for high-def or 4K, when available.

A new release feature film typically costs $19.99 in high definition or $14.99 in standard def, but you'll see prices higher and lower.

You can also rent many movies, typically for $2.99, $3.99, or $4.99, though Apple sometimes serves up a juicy 99-cent rental as well, and we've seen rentals as high as $6.99. Not all movies can be rented, and we're not wild about current rental restrictions — you have 30 days to begin watching a rented flick and 48 hours to finish watching after you've started.

FIGURE 8-3:
Bone up on a movie before buying or renting it.

In some instances, *Rocketman* is one example, purchasing a movie in HD also gets you iTunes Extras, featuring the kind of bonus content sometimes reserved for DVDs or Blu-rays.

Tap a movie listing in iTunes, and you can generally preview a trailer before buying (or renting) and check out additional tidbits: the plot summary, credits, reviews, and customer ratings, as well as other movies that appealed to people who bought the movie you're looking at. And you can search films by genre or top charts (the ones other people are buying or renting), or rely on the Apple Genius feature for recommendations based on stuff you've already watched. (Genius works for movies and TV much the way it works for music, as we explain in Chapter 7.) Apple also groups movies by various themes — Kids Movies and Notable Indies are two examples.

Perusing podcasts and courseware

In iPadOS, Apple features both podcasts and content in a dedicated iTunes U app (see Figure 8-4). Lots of audio podcasts and courses are available, but the focus here is on video. You can watch free courses that cover *Sesame Street*, sports, investing, political shows, news, technology, and much more. iTunes U now has content for younger students too, from K-12.

Some teachers even add homework and grade you (though that's not necessarily typical). You might also have private discussions with your professor through the app, which is amazing. And here's unqualified good news: There's no tuition.

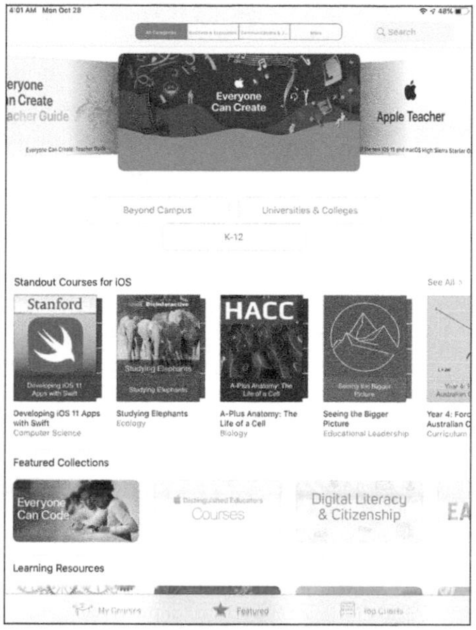

Watching your own videos

You can find videos you've created in your Photos library, whether they're raw videos you filmed with your iPad or edited videos you created in iMovie.

FIGURE 8-4:
Get smart. iTunes U offers a slew of lectures on diverse topics.

Check out the "Shooting Your Own Videos" section, later in this chapter, for directions on creating movies with the iPad.

Are we compatible?

The iPad works with many popular Internet video standards, such as HTML 5, CSS 3, and JavaScript. (Note that the iPad does not support Flash.) On increasingly rare occasions, you may run into a snag if you're trying to watch AVI, DivX, MKV, or other videos formats.

TIP

For a somewhat technical work-around for video formats not supported on iPad — without potential conversion hassles — try the $5.99 Air Video HD app from Bit Cave Ltd. Air Video HD can deliver AVI, DivX, MKV, and other videos stored on your Mac or PC that wouldn't ordinarily play on your iPad. You have to download the free Air Video Server software to your Mac or PC to stream content to your iPad. Or, for converting from a broader range of formats, try the excellent (and free) HandBrake app at http://handbrake.fr/.

A moment for HEVC

One of iPadOS's big under-the-hood features is the High-Efficiency Video Codec (HEVC) for storing video. HEVC's claim to fame is smaller video files with the same or higher quality as before.

So far, the file format is used only internally by the Photos app on your Mac and the Camera and Photos apps on your iPad running iPadOS. You can't currently export files in the HEVC format, and iPadOS intelligently exports using more common file formats. In other words, you don't need to worry about HEVC; it's just something Apple is using to make videos take up less space. We expect this to change over time, because HEVC is an industry standard like its predecessor, H.264.

Playing Video

Now that you know what you want to watch, it's time to find out how to watch it. For these steps, we walk you through watching a movie, but the steps for TV shows and downloaded videos are similar:

1. **On the Home screen, tap the TV icon.**

   You see a tabbed interface for Watch Now, Library, and Search.

2. **Tap the Library tab.**

   You see poster thumbnails for any movies you previously purchased through iTunes — even for those movies you haven't downloaded yet (refer to Figure 8-2).

3. **Tap the poster that represents the movie or other video you want to watch.**

   You're taken to a movie summary page that reveals a larger movie poster, a description, the genre, the run time, and a play icon, as shown in Figure 8-5.

4. **To start playing a movie (or resume playing from where you left off), tap the play icon. Or to download the movie to your iPad for later playback, tap the iCloud icon.**

5. **(Optional) Rotate your iPad to landscape mode to maximize the video's view.**

FIGURE 8-5:
The movie info
screen.

Finding and Working the Video Controls

While a video is playing, tap the screen to display the controls shown in Figure 8-6. Here's how to work the controls:

» **Play or pause the video:** Tap the play/pause icon.

» **Adjust the volume:** Drag the volume slider to the right to raise the volume and to the left to lower it.

» **Restart, skip back, or skip forward:** Tap and drag the playhead to where you want the video to start. You can use the rewind 15 seconds icon to go back 15 seconds, or the fast-forward 15 seconds icon to move ahead 15 seconds.

» **Set how the video fills the screen:** Tap the scale icon, which toggles between filling the entire screen with video and fitting the video to the screen. Alternatively, you can double-tap the video to go back and forth between fitting and filling the screen.

Fitting the video to the screen displays the film in its theatrical aspect ratio. *Filling* the entire screen with the video may crop or trim the sides or top of the picture, so you don't see the complete scene the director shot.

» **Select subtitle settings:** Tap the audio and subtitles icon. You see options to select a different language, turn on or hide subtitles, and turn on or hide closed captioning. The control appears only if the movie supports one or more of these features. You can change certain subtitle styles by choosing Settings ➪ Accessibility ➪ Subtitles & Captioning and then turning on the Closed Captions + SDH switch.

>> **Use picture-in-picture:** Tap the picture-in-picture icon to continue to watch the video in a small window, which you can drag around the screen while using a separate app on your tablet. Alternately, if you're watching a video when you close the TV app, the movie will automatically go into picture-in-picture mode.

>> **Hide the controls:** Tap the screen again (or just wait for them to go away on their own).

>> **Access bonus features:** Tap the Extras button. You won't see this button in every movie.

>> **Tell your iPad you've finished watching a video:** Tap the X in the top-left corner. You return to the last video screen that was visible before you started watching the movie.

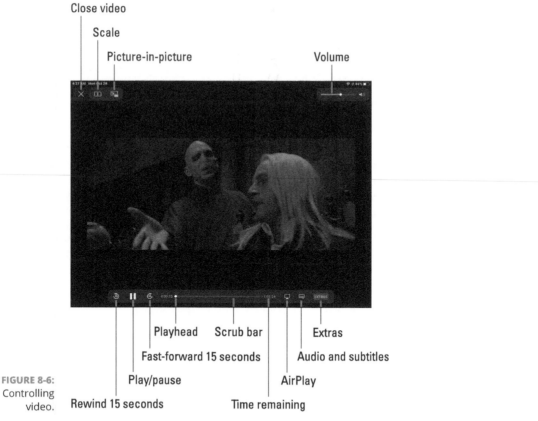

FIGURE 8-6: Controlling video.

Watching Video on a Big TV

We love watching movies on the iPad, but we also recognize the limitations of a smaller screen, even one as stunning as the Retina display. Friends won't crowd around to watch with you, so Apple offers two ways to display video from your iPad to a TV:

>> **AirPlay:** Through AirPlay, you can wirelessly stream videos as well as photos and music from the iPad to an Apple TV set-top box connected to an HDTV or a 4K TV. Start watching the movie on the iPad, summon Control Center by swiping down from the upper-right corner of the screen, and then tap the Screen Mirroring button. Apple TVs on the same Wi-Fi network will be listed as options. Tap the Apple TV you want, and your iPad's screen will be shown on that Apple TV. When you're finished, open Control Center on your iPad and tap Stop Mirroring.

You can multitask while streaming a video. Therefore, while the kids are watching a flick on the TV, you can surf the web or catch up on email.

REMEMBER

Although you can stream from an iPad to an Apple TV and switch screens between the two, you can't stream to the iPad a rented movie that you started watching on Apple TV.

>> **AV adapter cables:** Apple and others sell a variety of adapters and cables for connecting the iPad to a TV. For instance, Apple sells a Lightning–to–digital AV adapter for $49 that lets you connect an HDMI cable (which you'll have to supply) from the tablet to the TV. If you have an iPad Pro with a USB-C port, you can use a similar adapter from Apple called the USB-C Digital AV Multiport Adapter for $69. Both adapters also let you *mirror* the iPad screen on the connected TV or projector. So you can not only watch a movie or video but also view anything else that's on the iPad's screen: your Home screens, web pages, games, other apps, you name it. You can also mirror what's on the screen through AirPlay.

Restricting Video Usage

If you've given an iPad to your kid or someone who works for you, you may not want that person spending time watching movies or television. You might want him or her to do something more productive, such as homework or the quarterly budget. That's where parental restrictions come in. Please note that the use of this iron-fist tool can make you unpopular.

Tap Settings ⇨ Screen Time. The first time you open this setting, you'll be asked whether the iPad is yours or your child's. If it's your child's iPad, choose This Is My Child's iPad, tap Use Screen Time Passcode, and set up a four-digit passcode that will be required to make changes to Screen Time settings. Next, tap Content & Privacy Restrictions, and then tap the toggle next to Content & Privacy Restrictions so that it turns green. Tap Content Restrictions to view all the different ways you can limit content, including movies and TV shows.

Tap Movies to restrict movie ratings (G, PG, PG-13, and so on), or choose Don't Allow Movies to block movies altogether. Tap Content Restrictions at the top of the screen to go back to the previous screen, and tap TV Shows to block based on rating or Don't Allow TV Shows to block all TV shows. For more on restrictions, flip to Chapter 15, where we explain the settings for controlling (and loosening) access to iPad features.

Deleting Video from Your iPad

REMEMBER

Video takes up space — lots of space. After the closing credits roll and you no longer want to keep a video on your iPad, here's what you need to know about deleting it.

To remove a downloaded video you purchased from Apple in the iTunes Store — the flick remains in iCloud — open up the TV app, tap the Library tab at the bottom of the screen, and then tap the Downloaded tab. The Library tab displays the TV shows and movies you've downloaded to your iPad. Tap Edit in the upper-right corner of the screen, and a circle will appear next to each movie or TV show in your list. Select the show you want to delete by tapping its circle, then tap the Delete button that is now in the upper-right corner of your screen. When your iPad asks if you're sure you want to delete the video, tap Delete Download. (If you change your mind, tap outside the Delete button.) You can also swipe left on any given title, and tap the red Delete button that appears.

Shooting Your Own Videos

Your iPad has a great camera on the back, plus the FaceTime camera in the front. Let's take a look at the resolutions you can shoot with the camera on the back of your iPad:

>> To 1080p: Every iPad that can run iPadOS can shoot 1080p — or HD — video with the back camera. They all have video stabilization, too.

>> 4K video at 30fps (frames per second): iPad Pro 10.5-inch, iPad Pro 2nd generation 12.9-inch (2017).

>> 4K video at 30fps or 60fps: iPad Pro 12.9-inch 3rd generation (2018) and iPad Pro 11-inch (2019).

TIP

4K video image quality is astounding but is also a memory hog that claims roughly 350MB for just one minute of video, and that's at 30fps.

You can shoot video with the front-facing FaceTime camera as well, which includes a sensor that permits *HDR*, or *high dynamic range*, video. (Read Chapter 9 for more on HDR.)

Now that we've dispensed with that little piece of business, here's how to shoot video on the iPad:

1. **On the Home screen, tap the Camera icon.**

2. **Scroll through the list of images (Photo, Square, Pano, and so on) until Video is selected.**

   When *Video* appears in yellow instead of white, it's selected. On some models you can also choose Time Lapse or Slo-Mo.

TIP

   You can't switch from the front to the rear camera (or vice versa) while you're capturing a scene. So before shooting anything, think about which camera you want to use, and then tap the front/rear camera icon in the top-right corner of the screen when you've made your choice.

3. **Tap the red record button (labeled in Figure 8-7) to begin shooting a scene.**

   When you choose a non-video shooting format — Photo or Square — the round shutter button is white. In any case, while you're shooting a scene, the counter will tick off the seconds.

4. **Tap the red record button again to stop recording.**

   Your video is automatically saved to the All Photos album, alongside any other saved videos and digital stills that land in the Photos app.

TIP

   As of this writing, not every iPad model offers a flash. If yours doesn't, you'll need good lighting to capture the best footage.

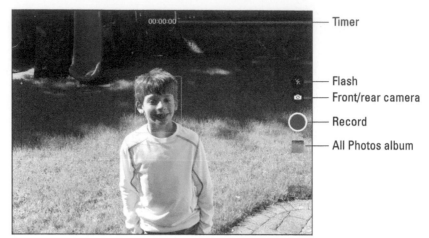

Timer

Flash

Front/rear camera

Record

All Photos album

FIGURE 8-7:
Lights, camera,
action.

Going slow

If you have an iPad model that runs iPadOS, you get another shooting benefit: the capability to capture video in slow motion, which we think is truly nifty. Now you can play back in slow motion your kid's amazing catch in the varsity football game.

Depending on your iPad, you'll be able to shoot at 120 frames per second (fps) at 720p or 1080p, or even 240fps at 720p or 1080p. However, the frame rate and resolution you're using to record your slow-motion video won't matter unless you're a professional videographer. And remember that the best camera to use is always the camera you have with you, so set your camera to Slo-Mo and grab the action!

But first things first: To shoot in slow motion, launch the Camera app and select Slo-Mo as your shooting format of choice. Shoot your slow-motion footage the same way you shoot at regular speeds. Note that the white circle surrounding the red shutter icon has teeny-tiny lines around it.

To check out your handiwork, tap the All Photos album (labeled in Figure 8-7), and then tap the slow-motion video you want to watch. The video starts playing at normal speed, and then slows at a point determined by the iPad. To change when slow-motion begins and ends, tap Edit and slide the vertical bars just above the frame viewer, as shown in Figure 8-8. (When the vertical lines are close, the video plays at a normal speed; when the lines are spread apart, the video plays slowly.) Note that when you play back a segment in slow motion, any accompanying audio is slowed too. Tap Revert to go back to the point at which the iPad arranged for the video to start going slow.

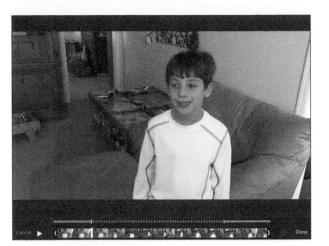

FIGURE 8-8:
Adjusting your
slow motion
playback.

Going fast

The time-lapse camera feature on your iPad has the opposite effect of slo-mo, enabling you to capture a scene and play it back at a warped speed. Even better, every iPad covered in this book sports the Time-Lapse option! To make a time-lapse video, choose the Time-Lapse option the same way you select other shooting modes, and then tap the record icon. The app captures photos at dynamically selected intervals. When you're ready to watch the sped up sequence, tap play as you do with any other video.

Editing what you shot

We assume you captured some really great footage, but you probably shot some stuff that belongs on the cutting room floor as well. No big whoop — you can perform simple edits right on your iPad. Tap the All Photos album just below the shutter button in the Camera app to find your recordings. Or tap the Camera app, tap the Albums tab at the bottom of the screen, and then tap the Videos section on the left side of the screen. When you record slo-mo or time-lapse videos, iPadOS creates an album for them so you can find them quickly. Select your video, and then:

1. **If the on-screen controls are not visible, tap the video recording.**

2. **Tap the Edit button.**

3. **Drag the start and end points along the frame viewer at the bottom of the screen to select only the video you want to keep.**

   The lines turn yellow.

4. **Tap Done and then tap either Trim Original or Save as New Clip (as shown in Figure 8-9).**

   If you choose Trim Original, Photos will alter the original file — be careful when choosing this option. Save as New Clip creates a newly trimmed video clip; the original video remains intact. The new clip is stored in the All Photos, Videos, Slo-Mo, or Time-Lapse album.

5. **To discard your changes, tap Cancel.**

FIGURE 8-9:
Getting a trim.

TIP

For more ambitious editing on the iPad, consider iMovie for iPad, a free app closely related to iMovie for Mac computers. Among its tricks: You can produce Hollywood-style movie trailers, just like on a Mac.

WARNING

Any video edited with the iPadOS version of iMovie must have originated on an iOS or iPadOS device. You can't mix in footage shot with a digital camera or obtained elsewhere.

Sharing video

You can play back in portrait or landscape mode what you've just shot. And if the video is any good, you'll likely want to share it with a wider audience. To do so, open the All Photos album, Videos album, or another album, and tap the thumbnail for the video in question. Tap the share icon, and you can email the video (if the video file isn't too large), send it as a Message (see Chapter 5), or keep a copy in Notes.

And you have many other options: You can save the video to iCloud or share it in numerous other places, including Twitter, Facebook, Flickr, YouTube, Vimeo, and (if a Chinese keyboard was enabled) the Chinese services Youku and Tudou. You can also view your video as part of a slideshow (see Chapter 9) or, if you have an Apple TV box, dispatch it to a big-screen television via AirPlay.

Seeing Is Believing with FaceTime

We bet you can come up with a lengthy list of people you'd love to be able to eyeball in real time from afar. Maybe the list includes your old college roommate or your grandparents, who've long since retired to a warm climate. That's the beauty of *FaceTime*, the video chat app. FaceTime exploits the two cameras built into the iPad, each serving a different purpose. The front camera — the FaceTime camera as it's called — lets you talk face to face. The back camera shows what you're seeing to the person you're talking to.

To take advantage of FaceTime, here's what you need:

WARNING

>> **Access to Wi-Fi or cellular:** The people you're talking to need Internet access, too. On an iOS or iPadOS device, you need Wi-Fi or a cellular connection and an Internet connection on your iPad. You also need at least a 1Mbps upstream and downstream connection for HD-quality video calls; faster is always going to be better.

Using FaceTime over a cellular connection can quickly run through your monthly data allotment and prove hazardous to your budget. However, you can do an audio-only FaceTime call, which can cut down significantly on your data usage.

>> **FaceTime on recipient's device:** Of course you can do FaceTime video only with someone capable of receiving a FaceTime video call. That person must have an iPad 2 or later, an Intel-based Mac computer (OS X 10.6.6 or later), a recent-model iPod touch, or an iPhone 4 or later.

Getting started with FaceTime

Now, let's get started with FaceTime by tapping the FaceTime app on the Home screen to launch the app. If you haven't signed in with your Apple ID, head to Settings➪Apple ID and sign in. If you need to create an account, tap Don't Have an Apple ID or Forgot It?

REMEMBER

If this is the first time you've used a particular email address for FaceTime, Apple sends an email to that address to verify the account. Tap (or click) Verify Now and enter your Apple ID and password to complete the FaceTime setup. If the email address resides in Mail on the iPad, you're already good to go.

If you have multiple email addresses, callers can use any of them for Face-Time. To add an email address after the initial setup in iPadOS, tap Settings ⇨ *yourname* ⇨ Name, Phone, Numbers, Email ⇨ Reachable At, and tap Edit. Tap Add Email or Phone Number to add or delete email addresses or phone numbers. Apple will send confirmation messages to both.

You can turn FaceTime on or off by going to Settings ⇨ FaceTime. Tap the Face-Time toggle so it displays green to turn it on or white to turn it off. If you leave FaceTime activated, however, you don't have to sign in every time you launch the app.

Making a FaceTime call

Now the real fun begins — making a video call. (We say "video call" because you can also make FaceTime audio calls.) Follow these steps:

1. **Tap the FaceTime app from the Home screen or by asking Siri to open the app on your behalf.**

   You can check out what you look like before making a FaceTime call because the front FaceTime camera activates and puts what it sees on the screen. So put on a happy face, because you're about to been seen and heard by a loved one!

   Any recent calls you've made or received are displayed in a list on the left side of the screen.

2. **Choose someone to call:**

   - *Your recent calls list:* If you've already made or received a call, tap anyone in your recent calls list to FaceTime that person again. Below the name of each person in the list is the method you used to call the person before (FaceTime or a cellular call). Tapping an entry in this list will duplicate that method of calling.

     Or tap the *i*-in-a-circle to access the full entry in your contacts. At the top of the contacts list you'll see several ways to contact the person: message, call (as in cellular phone call), FaceTime, mail, and Apple Pay.

- *Your contacts:* Tap the + icon and the list of recent calls will become the New FaceTime pane. You have two ways to find someone.

  One, start typing a name in the To field, and iPadOS will display all potential matches from your contacts. The more of the person's name you type, the more accurate those suggestions will be. Tap the name you want, and two green buttons appear on the screen. Tap the Audio button to make an audio-only FaceTime call to that person, or tap the Video button to make a video call.

  Two, you can tap the circle with a plus sign in it to show all your contacts, where you can choose the specific person you want. Tap a name in your contacts list, and you will get the person's entry in your contacts, including multiple ways to contact him or her: message, cellular phone call, FaceTime, mail, and Apple Pay.

How you look to the other person

Whom you're talking to

Switch cameras   Mute

End call

FIGURE 8-10:
Bob can see Ed, and Ed can see Bob (and Zeke the dog) in FaceTime.

3. **If necessary, move the picture-in-picture window.**

   When a call is underway, you can see what you look like to the other person through a small picture-in-picture window, which you can drag to any corner of the video call window. The small window lets you know if your mug has dropped out of sight.

4. **(Optional) To toggle between the front and rear cameras, tap the camera icon (labeled in Figure 8-10).**

5. **Tap the End Call button when you're ready to hang up.**

While you're on a FaceTime call, the following tips will be handy:

>> **Rotate the iPad to its side to change the orientation.** In landscape mode, you're more likely to see everybody at once.

>> **Silence or mute a call by tapping the microphone icon.** Be aware that you can still be seen even though you're not heard (and you can still see and hear the other person).

TIP

>> **Momentarily check out another iPad app by pressing the Home button and then tapping the icon for the app.** At this juncture, you can still talk over FaceTime, but you can no longer see the person. You also won't be visible to them, which lets them know you're not currently in the FaceTime app. Tap the green bar at the top of the iPad screen to bring the person and the FaceTime app back in front of you.

Through the split view feature in iPadOS, you can conduct and view a FaceTime video call while engaged in other activities on the iPad.

TIP

Caller ID on FaceTime works just like caller ID on a regular phone call. You can choose the email address or phone number you want displayed when you call that person via FaceTime. To set your caller ID info, go to Settings ➪ FaceTime and, under Caller ID, tap the phone number or email address you want to use.

Receiving a FaceTime call

Of course, you can get FaceTime calls as well as make them. FaceTime doesn't have to be open for you to receive a video call. Here's how incoming calls work:

>> **Hearing the call:** When a call comes in, the caller's name, phone number, or email address is prominently displayed on the iPad's screen, as shown in Figure 8-11, and the iPad rings.

>> **Accepting or declining the call:** Tap the green Accept button to answer the call or Decline if you'd rather not. If your iPad is locked when a FaceTime call comes in, answer by sliding the Slide to Answer button to the right, or decline by doing nothing and waiting for the caller to give up. You can also tap Message to send a canned iMessage *(Sorry, I can't talk right now; I'm on my way; Can I call you later?)* or a custom message. Or you can tap Remind Me to be reminded in one hour that you may want to call the person back.

>> **Silencing the ring:** You can press the sleep/wake button at the top of the iPad to silence the incoming ring. If you know you don't want to be disturbed by FaceTime calls before you even hear a ring, visit Control Center (see Chapter 14) to put your iPad on mute. You can also turn on the do not disturb feature in Control Center to silence incoming FaceTime calls.

>> **Blocking unwanted callers:** If a person who keeps trying to FaceTime you becomes bothersome, you can block him or her. Go to Settings ➪ FaceTime ➪ Blocked Contacts ➪ Add New, and choose the person's name from your contacts. In the FaceTime app, you can block a caller who shows up on your caller list by tapping the *i*-in-a-circle next to the caller's name and then tapping Block This Caller.

FIGURE 8-11:
Tap the green button to accept the call.

>> **Removing people from the call list:** If you don't want to block a caller but don't want the person clogging up your call list, tap Edit, tap the circle next to the person's name so that a check mark appears, and then tap Delete.

TIP

You can also receive calls to your iPhone on your iPad, as long as they're on the same Wi-Fi network. Go to Settings ➪ FaceTime ➪ Calls from iPhone and change the option so the button turns to green.

Although we heavily endorse the use of FaceTime, we'd be remiss if we didn't acknowledge other video-calling services you can easily take advantage of on your iPad. These include Microsoft-owned Skype, Google's Hangout, Facebook Messenger, Whatsapp, LINE, and Snapchat.

With that, we hereby silence this chapter. But you can do more with the cameras on your iPad, and we get to that in Chapter 9.

Chapter **9**

Photography on a Larger Scale

Throughout this book, we sing the praises of the iPad's vibrant multitouch display. You'd be hard-pressed to find a more appealing portable screen for watching movies or playing games. As you might imagine, the iPad you have recently purchased (or are lusting after) is also a spectacular photo viewer. Images are crisp and vivid, at least those you shot properly. (C'mon, we know Ansel Adams is a distant cousin.)

What's more, you can shoot some of those pictures directly with your prized tablet. The reasons, of course, are the front and rear cameras built into the device. If you read Chapter 8, you already know you can put those cameras to work capturing video. In this chapter, you get the big picture on shooting still images.

Okay, we need to get a couple of things out of the way: The iPad may never be the most comfortable substitute for a point-and-shoot digital camera, much less a pricey digital SLR. As critics, we can quibble about the fact that some models have no flash and shooting can be awkward.

But we're here, friends, to focus on the positive. And having cameras on your iPad may prove to be a godsend.

In this chapter, we point out other optical enhancements in the most recent iPads. The 11-inch iPad Pro and third-generation 12.9-inch iPad Pro have a 12-megapixel camera with backside illumination, an impressive f/1.8 aperture, and a multi-element lens. The iPad mini 4, iPad mini 5, iPad 9.7 inch, and iPad 10.2 inch have an 8-megapixel camera with an f/2.4 aperture. All these models have a hybrid infrared filter (like that on an SLR), for more uniform colors. And face detection makes sure the balance and focus are just right for up to ten faces on the screen.

Such features are photographer-speak for potentially snapping darn sweet pictures. And we can think of certain circumstances — selling real estate, say, or shopping for a home — where tablet cameras are quite convenient.

Apple has made finding pictures in your stash an easier task, too, with an organizational structure that arranges photos in the Photos app by days, months, and years. And iPadOS automatically gathers collections that are meant to trigger precious memories.

Meanwhile, you're in for a treat if you're new to *Photo Booth*, a yuk-it-up Mac program that is also on the iPad. Photo Booth may be the most fun use of the cameras yet. We get to Photo Booth at the end of this chapter. Over the next few pages, you discover the best ways to make the digital photos on the iPad come alive, no matter how they arrived on your tablet.

Shooting Pictures

You can start shooting pictures on the iPad in a few ways. So we're going to cut to the chase immediately:

1. **Fire up the camera itself. Choose one of the following:**

   - On the Home screen, tap the Camera app icon.

   - On the lock screen, swipe from right to left.

   - Drag Control Center down from the top-right corner of the screen and tap the Camera app icon.

   - Ask Siri (read Chapter 14) to open the Camera app for you.

   However you get here, your iPad has turned into the tablet equivalent of a Kodak Instamatic, minus the film and in a much bigger form factor. You're also effectively peering through one of the largest viewfinders imaginable!

2. **Keep your eyes peeled on the iPad display, and use the viewfinder to frame your image.**

3. **Select a shooting format:**

   - *Photo:* Think snapshot.

   - *Square:* This gives you a picture formatted to make nice with the popular Instagram photo-sharing app.

   - *Pano:* Short for panorama, Pano shooting mode lets you capture epic vistas.

   - *Video, Slo-Mo,* or *Time Lapse:* We kindly refer you to Chapter 8.

   You move from one format to another by swiping up or down along the right edge of the screen so that the format you've chosen is highlighted in yellow.

4. **Snap your image by tapping the white round camera button.**

   The button is at the middle-right edge of the screen whether you're holding the iPad in portrait mode or landscape mode (see Figure 9-1).

   The image you shot lands in the All Photos album, labeled in Figure 9-1. We explain what you can do with the images on the iPad later in this chapter.

Live photos

HDR

Timer

Flash (on compatible iPads only)

Front/rear camera

Camera button

All Photos album

Shooting formats

FIGURE 9-1:
Using the iPad
as a camera.   Zoom slider

Here are some tips for working with the Camera app:

>> **Adjust the focal point.** Tap the portion of the screen in which you see the face or object you want as the image's focal point. A small rectangle surrounds your selection, and the iPad adjusts the exposure and focus for that part of the image. (The rectangle is not visible in Figure 9-1). Your iPad can detect up to ten faces in a picture. Behind the scenes, the camera is balancing the exposure across each face. If you want to lock the focus and exposure settings while taking a picture, press and hold your finger against the screen until the rectangle pulses. AE/AF Lock will appear. Tap the screen again to make AE/AF Lock disappear.

TIP

Next to the focus box is a sun icon. When the sunny exposure icon is visible, drag your finger up or down against the screen to increase or decrease the brightness in a scene. And you can lighten or darken scenes for both still photos and video.

>> **Zoom in or out.** Tap the screen with two fingers and spread (unpinch) to zoom in or pinch to zoom out, or drag the slider up or down on the left side of the screen. The iPad has a 5X digital zoom, which basically crops and resizes an image. Such zooms are lower quality than optical zooms on many digital cameras. Be aware that zooming works only with the rear camera.

>> **See grid lines to help you compose your picture.** Tap Settings ⇨ Camera and tap the Grid switch to turn it on (the switch turns green). Grid lines can help you frame a shot using the photographic principle known as the rule of thirds.

TIP

>> **Toggle between the front and rear cameras.** Tap the front/rear camera icon (see Figure 9-1). The front camera is of lower quality than its rear cousin but is more than adequate for most things, including FaceTime and Photo Booth.

>> **Shoot in HDR.** To exploit *HDR (high dynamic range)* photography, tap the HDR icon. The HDR feature takes three separate exposures (long, normal, short) and blends the best parts of the three shots into a single image. In Settings (under Photos & Camera), you can choose to keep the normal photo along with your HDR result or just hang on to the latter.

>> **Burst out.** In the blink of an eye, burst mode on the iPad can capture a burst of pictures — up to ten continuous images per second. Just keep your finger pressed against the camera button to keep on capturing those images. This feature works with the front FaceTime camera and the rear camera.

>> **Capture panoramas.** If you're traveling to San Francisco, you'll want a picture of the magnificent span that is the Golden Gate Bridge. At a family reunion, you want that epic image of your entire extended clan. We recommend the panorama feature, which lets you shoot up to 240 degrees and stitch together a high-resolution image of up to 43 megapixels.

To get going, drag the screen so that Pano becomes your shooting mode of choice. The word *Pano* will be in yellow. Position the tablet so it's where you want your pano to begin and tap the camera button when you're ready. Steadily pan in the direction of the arrow. (Tap the arrow if you prefer panning in the opposite direction.) Try to keep the arrow just above the yellow horizontal line. When you've finished shooting your pano, tap the camera button again to stop.

» **Geotag your photos.** The iPad is pretty smart when it comes to geography. Turn on Location Services (in Settings ⇨ Privacy ⇨ Location Services) and the specific location settings for the camera appear in Settings. Pictures you take with the iPad cameras will now be *geotagged,* or identified by where they were shot.

Think long and hard before permitting images to be geotagged if you plan on sharing them with people from whom you want to keep your address and other locations private — especially if you plan on sharing the photos online.

» **Use the self-timer.** Many physical cameras have a self-timer that lets you be part of a picture. The self-timer built into the Camera app adds this functionality to your iPad, whether you're using the front or rear camera.

Tap the timer icon and choose 3 seconds or 10 seconds as the time interval between when you press the camera button and when the picture is captured. You'll see a countdown on the screen leading up to that moment. To turn off the self-timer, tap the Off button.

You can also add pictures to your iPad in several other ways. Alas, one of these methods involves buying an accessory. We zoom in in the following sections.

Syncing pix

We devote an entire chapter (see Chapter 3) to synchronizing data with the iPad, so we don't dwell on it here. But we'd be remiss if we didn't mention it in this chapter. (The assumption in this section is that you already know how to get pictures onto your computer.)

When the iPad is connected to your computer, click the Photos tab on the iPad Device page in iTunes on the Mac or PC. Then select a source from the Sync Photos From pop-up menu.

Connecting a digital camera or memory card

Almost all the digital cameras we're aware of come with a USB cable you can use to transfer images to a computer. Of course, the iPad isn't a regular computer, isn't equipped with a USB port, and doesn't have a memory card slot. So, you'll need an adapter.

For its part, Apple sells an optional Lightning–to–USB camera adapter ($29), as well as Lightning–to–SD card camera reader cables (also $29) for iPad models with the Lightning connector. The SD card reader connector accommodates the SD memory cards common to many digital camera models. You can also buy a USB-C–to–USB adapter for $19 for iPad Pro models with USB-C.

TECHNICAL STUFF

The camera connection kit and the Lightning connectors support many common photo formats, including JPEG and RAW. The latter is a format favored by photo enthusiasts.

Saving images from emails and the web

You can save many of the pictures that arrive in emails or you come across on the web: Just tap and hold down on an image, and then tap Add to Photos when the menu pops up. Pictures are stored in the All Photos album, which we get to shortly. You can also tap Copy to paste said image into another app on your device.

Tracking Down Your Pictures

So where exactly do your pictures live on the iPad? We just gave some of the answer away; the images you snap on your iPad first land in a photo album appropriately dubbed All Photos in your Photos app.

In the Photos or Camera app — you can get to the former by tapping a thumbnail image in the latter — you'll also find pictures you've shared with friends and they've shared with you through the iCloud photo-sharing feature. The photos you imported are readily available, and are grouped in the same albums they were in on the computer.

Moreover, every picture you take with your iPad (and other iOS devices) can be stored in an iCloud photo library. You can access any of these pics if you have a Wi-Fi or cellular connection to the Internet. No more fretting about images hogging too much storage space on your tablet. What's more, the pictures are stored in the cloud at their full resolution in their original formats. (Apple will leave behind versions ideally sized for your tablet.)

You can still download to the iPad images that you want available when you're not connected to cyberspace.

In this section, we show you not only where to find these pictures but also how to display them and share them with others — and how to dispose of the duds that don't measure up to your lofty photographic standards.

Get ready to literally get your fingers on the pics (without having to worry about smudging them). Open the Photos app by tapping its icon either on the Home screen or in Camera app. Then take a gander at the buttons at the bottom of the screen: Photos, For You, Albums, and Search. We describe these options, and several more, in this information-packed section.

Choosing albums

Tap Albums to pull up a list all the albums you've created on your iPad, with a premade album called Recents at the upper left, as shown in Figure 9-2. Apple has kindly supplied additional premade albums: Panoramas, Bursts, Selfies, Screenshots, Videos (shooting videos is described in Chapter 8), Live Photos, Portrait, Time-Lapse, Slo-mo, Animated, Hidden, Imports, and Recently Deleted, which gives you a chance to recover any images accidentally given the heave-ho. The Recently Deleted album also displays the number of days before each picture is permanently gone.

Tap an album listing to open it. You'll see the minimalistic interface shown in Figure 9-3, which reveals the by-now-familiar Recents album.

FIGURE 9-2:
Recents is a premade album at the top of your list of photos on the Albums tab.

Browse the thumbnails to find the picture or video you want and then tap it. We show you all the cool things you can do from there.

REMEMBER

You'll know when a thumbnail represents a video rather than a still image because the thumbnail includes the length of the video.

Meanwhile, you can tell whether a photo is part of a burst binge in several ways. The first is exposed here in All Photos. The thumbnail that represents this sequence of shots will appear as though it's sitting on a stack of photos. Tap the thumbnail now. In the second way, the word *Burst* appears in the upper left of an image you've opened, with a numerical count of burst photos in parentheses. You can keep any burst images you've captured. Third, there's the aforementioned premade Bursts album.

If you can't locate the thumbnail for a photo you have in mind, flick up or down to scroll through the pictures rapidly, or use a slower dragging motion to pore through the images more deliberately.

To return to the list of albums, tap Albums at the upper-left corner or bottom of the screen. After backing out, you can create an album from the albums view by tapping the + in the upper-left corner (refer to Figure 9-2), typing a name for the album, and tapping Save. To select pictures (or videos) to add to your newly minted album, tap their thumbnails.

FIGURE 9-3:
Digging into the Recents album.

Shortly, we show you how to add pictures to an *existing* album.

Albums you create on the iPad reside only on the iPad. They can't be synced or copied to your PC or Mac, at least without work-arounds through a third-party app such as Dropbox.

Categorizing your pics

Placing pictures into photo albums has been the way of the world forever. But albums *per se* are not the only organizing structure that makes sense. Apple has cooked up a simple but ingenious interface for presenting pictures that is essentially a timeline grouped by years, months, days, and of course, all photos.

This timeline breakdown is designed to help you drill down to the photos you want. When you tap on a given year, Photos shifts over to the Months tab. If, say, you're viewing your photos in October 2020 and you tap 2018, the Photos app will take you to October 2018 as a starting point. If you were viewing photos in January, the Photos app would take you straight to January for the year you tapped. Tapping a month shifts you over to the Days tab, where you can scroll through the photos you took in that month.

To scroll through your photos with a focus on visuals, you'll want to use the All Photos tab, where everything is laid out chronologically.

Figure 9-4 shows side-by-side-by-side views of years, months, and days.

FIGURE 9-4:
View your photos by years (left), months (center), and days (right).

Through all these views, you'll see location information headings that get more specific as you move from years to days, assuming your iPad knows where the pictures were taken. (Go to Settings ➪ Privacy ➪ Location Services ➪ Camera and tap While Using the App to have the location of your photos saved when you take them.)

Tap the Albums tab at the bottom of the Photos app, and then tap the Places album. Apple will fire up a map and show you how many pictures were taken in that location, as shown in Figure 9-5.

To quickly skim all the pictures in the years view, press and drag your finger across the grid — as you do so, the thumbnails swell in size, one by one. Lift your finger and that last thumbnail takes over a chunk of the screen, ready for you to admire it, edit it, or share it.

FIGURE 9-5:
Finding pictures on a map.

You can also tap a thumbnail in days or all photos view to see icons for sharing the picture, making it a favorite, discarding it, and editing it, as shown in Figure 9-6. Tap again and those picture controls disappear and the picture is bordered on the top and bottom by black bars.

Making memories

Hidden within everyone's photo collection are the crown jewels, those images that trigger the most precious memories. The Photos app in iPadOS has a Memories feature that can help gather such memories automatically. Tap the For You tab to take a photographic trip down memory lane.

How does it work? The Photos app scans your picture library and collects images of vacations and birthday parties, as well as whatever the app deems are the best pictures you took during a given year or shorter time frame.

FIGURE 9-6:
You can share, discard, or edit a photo.

In Bryan's Photos app, for example, the Memories feature built memories based on trips he took to the California coast and Texas, as shown in Figure 9-7. Within such memories, you can play a Memories movie that the app automatically generates, complete with theme music, titles, and transitions. You can edit those movies too, by changing the title, music, duration, and photos in the movies. Apple promises to deliver up to three new memories daily if you're actively adding photos to your library.

Inside a memory, you can view pictures the app thinks are related, as well as by the people in them or by place (with photos plotted on a map).

In grouping photos into albums and such, Apple exploits advanced computer machine learning using facial, object, and scene recognition along with location data to make intelligent choices.

If you cherish any of the memories that Apple has kindly put together on your behalf, tap Add to Favorite Memories at the bottom so you can easily access it whenever you choose. If you change your mind, tap Remove from Favorite Memories. And if you don't like a memory from the start — perhaps it's too bittersweet — tap Delete Memory to get rid of it, though the individual pictures remain in your collection.

TIP

Want to see memories built around holiday events in your home country? Go to Settings ⇨ Photos and tap Show Holiday Events so that it's green.

FIGURE 9-7:
Thanks for the Photos memories.

Live Photos

Did you know photos can come alive? It's true. A Live Photo looks like a normal photo, but if you tap and hold down on one, it turns into a 3-second video. It's practically magic, just like the books about the kid with the lightning bolt scar on his forehead.

Live Photos require an iPad Pro or iPad 9.7-inch or newer model. To put the camera app in Live Photo mode, tap the icon just above HDR (labeled in Figure 9-1). The Live Photos feature is active when the icon is yellow. When you take a photo, your iPad will capture 1.5 seconds before you press the button and 1.5 seconds after you press the button and make your photo live! It's a terrific effect, and we're confident you'll be delighted and amazed by it. When you want to stop taking Live Photos, just tap that icon again.

A moment for HEIF

iPadOS includes a big under-the-hood feature called High Efficiency Image File Format (HEIF) for still images. HEIF's calling card is smaller photos with the same or higher quality as before. Plus, they support editing Live Photos in new and unique ways.

HEIF is used internally by the Photos app on Macs and by the Camera and Photos apps on iPads running iPadOS. You can't currently export files in the HEIF format, and iPadOS intelligently exports more common file formats. In other words, you don't need to worry about HEIF; it's just something Apple is using to make photos take up less space. We expect this to change over time, because HEIF is an industry standard like its predecessor, JPEG.

Searching for pictures

Your iPad has one more feature to help you find a given photo among the thousands or tens of thousands you've shot. You can search your entire photo library. From the Photos app, tap the search icon, the one that resembles a magnifying glass.

Apple has kindly grouped some of your pictures into potentially helpful search categories: Moments, People, Places, and Categories. What you see may be different, depending on the kinds of photos you have on your iPad. To perform a search for particular photos, just type a search term with the on-screen keyboard, perhaps the date or the time a photo was taken or the location where it was shot.

But the big breakthrough comes with the capability to search pictures by what's in them: mountains, beaches, lakes, cats, whatever.

TECHNICAL STUFF

When your iPad is locked and plugged in to power (in other words, when you aren't otherwise using it), it uses some impressive machine learning to identify these elements in your photos. The process happens in the background, essentially invisible to you, and the work is performed locally, on your iPad, rather than on Apple's servers.

TIP

You can also enlist Siri to search for specific photos. For example, tell your obedient voice assistant something like, "Show me all the pictures I took at the baby shower."

Sharing your photos

Apple recognizes that you might want to share your best images with friends and family and have those pictures automatically appear on their devices.

An impressive and aptly named solution called Shared Photo Streams arrived on the iPad, iPod touch, and iPhone way back with iOS 6 (and a bit earlier on Macs running macOS Mountain Lion). The feature is now referred to as iCloud photo sharing, and it enables you to create albums of pictures and videos for sharing and to receive photo streams other people make available to you. Here's how:

1. **On the Home screen, tap Settings.**

2. **Tap Photos.**

3. **If the iCloud Photos option isn't on (green), tap it to turn it on.**

4. **Open the Photos app and tap the Albums tab.**

5. **Tap the + at the upper-left corner of the screen, tap New Shared Album, and then type a name for your stream in the iCloud dialog that appears.**

   The name is your call, but we recommend something descriptive, along the lines of *My Trip to Paris* (and you should be so lucky).

6. **Tap Next and choose who will receive your stream.**

   You can type a phone number, a text address, or an email address, or choose one of your contacts by tapping the +-in-a-circle in the To field of the iCloud pop-up window.

7. **Above the To field, tap Create.**

8. **Add photos as follows:**

   a. *Make sure the Shared icon is selected, and then tap the selected stream.*

   b. *Tap the +-in-a-square. Your Photos Library appears. Tap each photo you want to include. You can choose from All Photos or Albums.*

   c. *Tap Done.*

9. **(Optional) Enter a comment.**

10. **Tap Post.**

    The recipient will receive an email and can choose to subscribe to your shared album by tapping the button shown.

TIP

We recommend checking out the activity view at the top of the Shared tab. It provides a nice summary of photos you and your pals posted.

Admiring Your Pictures

Photographs are meant to be seen, not buried in the digital equivalent of a shoebox. The iPad affords you some neat ways to manipulate, view, and share your best photos.

Maneuvering and manipulating photos

You've already found out how to find individual pictures in albums, via iCloud, and in years, months, days, and memories. You may already know (from previous sections in this chapter) how to display picture controls. But you can do a lot of picture maneuvering without summoning those controls. Here are some options:

» **Skip ahead or view the preceding picture:** Flick your finger left or right.

» **Switch from landscape or portrait mode:** When you turn the iPad sideways, the picture automatically reorients itself from portrait to landscape mode. Rotate the device back to portrait mode and the picture readjusts accordingly.

» **Zoom:** Double-tap to zoom in on an image and make it larger. Do so again to zoom out and make it smaller. Alternatively, on the photo, spread your thumb and index finger apart to zoom in and pinch them to zoom out.

» **Pan and scroll:** This cool little feature was once practically guaranteed to make you the life of the party. Now it's commonplace, if no less cool. After you zoom in on a picture, drag it around the screen with your finger, bringing the part of the image you most care about front and center. In this way, you can zoom in on Fido's adorable face as opposed to, say, the unflattering picture of the person holding the dog in his lap.

Launching slideshows

Those of us who store a lot of photographs on computers are familiar with running slideshows of those images. It's a breeze to replicate the experience on the iPad:

1. **Tap the Photos icon from the Home screen or tap the Recently Added button in the Camera app.**

2. **Do one of the following to select photos for your slideshow:**

   - *In the Photos app:* Select an album and tap Slideshow in the upper-right corner. You've designated every photo and video in that album to be part of the slideshow. To cherry-pick the pictures in the slideshow, tap Select and then tap each image you want to include so that a check mark appears. If you want to save the selected pics in a new album, tap the share icon and then tap Add to Album to make a new album.

   - *In the Camera app:* Tap the All Photos button to see recent images you have taken, then tap the All Photos button at the top right of the screen.

3. **Tap Slideshow to start the slideshow, tap the screen, and then tap Options.**

4. **Choose a theme and the music (if any) you'd like to accompany the slideshow.**

   You have five theme choices (Origami, Magazine, Dissolve, Ken Burns, and Push). Why not try them all, to see what you like? You can go with Apple's theme music or choose from your iTunes stash.

5. **Choose whether the slideshow should repeat rather than end automatically, and determine the length between slides.**

   How long each slide plays is determined by how far you drag the slider in Options: all the way to the left (a tortoise icon) to all the way to the right (a hare).

6. **Choose where you get to see the slideshow.**

   You can view the slideshow on the iPad or have it beamed wirelessly to an Apple TV on your network. Tap the icon in the upper right to make that selection.

7. **Tap the play icon to start the slideshow.**

Press Done when you've finished watching. That's it! Enjoy the show.

Storing pictures in the (i)Cloud

As mentioned, through the iCloud service, any photo you take with the iPad or with an iOS 8 or later device can be automatically stored in the cloud and pushed to another iPad or to your PC, Mac, iPhone, iPod touch, or Apple TV (third generation or later). Pictures are uploaded when your iCloud devices are connected to Wi-Fi.

WARNING

Using the iCloud photo library has a catch: You have to pay for storage. You get 5GB of iCloud storage gratis, but shutterbugs will use that up in a flash. So you'll likely spring for one of the following monthly plans: 50GB of storage for 99¢, 200GB for $2.99, 1TB for $2.99, or 2TB for $9.99 a month.

Photos taken on the iPad aren't whisked to iCloud until you leave the Camera app. That way, you get a chance to delete pictures you'd rather not have turn up everywhere. But after you leave the Camera app, all the photos there are saved in the All Photos album (in the list of Albums in the Photos app), including pictures that arrived as email attachments you saved as well as screen captures taken on the iPad.

You can save pictures in the All Photos album to any other album on the tablet. Start by tapping the Select button at the upper-right corner of the screen. Next, tap each photo you want to move. Tap the Add To button that shows up at the top of the screen and choose the new album destination for your chosen images.

TIP

If for some reason the pictures you snap on the iPad are not uploaded, go to Settings ⇨ Photos, and make sure My Photo Stream is turned on.

Editing and Deleting Photos

The Photos app is never going to serve as an editing substitute for, say, Adobe Photoshop. But you can dramatically (and simply) apply touch-ups and alter the composition of your pictures right from the Photos app.

In iPadOS, Apple has simplified access to the editing controls, displaying them as soon as you tap Edit. As shown in Figure 9-8, you're taken immediately to the Adjust controls. Tap whichever control you want, such as contrast, exposure, or brightness, and then drag the slider for that control until you reach a level you're satisfied with — you see the effect on the image as you drag the slider. Tap Done when you're finished or Cancel to start over.

FIGURE 9-8: Who says you can't improve the quality of the picture?

To start, choose an image and tap Edit. You'll see the Adjust screen, as Figure 9–8 reveals.

The screen sports the following icons:

- **Live Photo:** Edit the key frame of your Live Photo. Tap Done when you're satisfied with your choice.

- **Adjust light, color, B&W:** Apple provides numerous editing controls to adjust brilliance, exposure, highlights, shadows, brightness, contrast, and black point (light); saturation, vibrance, warmth, tint, sharpness, definition, noise reduction, and vignette.

- **Add a filter:** Choose from Vivid, Dramatic, Mono, Silvertone, and Noir filters. Some, such as Vivid and Dramatic, have Warm and Cool variations. In Figure 9-9, we chose Dramatic Warm. Better yet, you can apply these after the fact. If you're not satisfied after applying a filter, tap Original or Cancel to go back to the original.

- **Rotate, straighten and crop:** Summon three additional icons that allow you to rotate the image, change the perspective of the image, or skew the image.

- **Auto-enhance:** Tapping the auto-enhance icon lets the iPad take a stab at making your image look better. Apple lightens or darkens the picture, tweaks color saturation, and more. Tap Done if you like the result.

- **Exposure:** Adjust your photo's light exposure. All the way up and you'll wash out your photo. All the way down, and your photo becomes much darker. Tap Done when you've adjusted it to your liking, or move to another adjustment.

- **Brilliance:** Adjust the vibrancy of your photo. Tap Done if you like the result, or move to another adjustment.

- **Highlights:** Adjust tonal range of just the highlights in your photo. Tap Done if you like the result, or move to another adjustment.

- **Shadows:** Adjust the tonal range of just the shadows in your photo. Tap Done if you like the result, or move to another adjustment.

TIP

If you aren't satisfied with any of the edits you've applied to your pictures, you can always tap Cancel followed by Discard Changes to restore the original. If you tap Done instead and apply the changes, you can still change your mind later. Open the image, tap the Edit icon, tap Revert, and then tap Revert to Original, which will remove all edits made to the pic.

FIGURE 9-9:
From straightening to cropping, you can make a good picture better.

Editing Live Photos

With some simple controls that look a lot like the editing tools discussed in the preceding section, you can trim the length of a Live Photo, set the keyframe, apply effects, turn off sound, and more.

The biggest difference in editing a Live Photo and a regular photo is setting the *keyframe,* which is the still you see when you're not tapping and holding down on a Live Photo. To change the keyframe, tap your Live Photo, and then tap the Edit button in the upper right of the screen. In addition to the familiar editing and filter options at the bottom of the screen, you'll see a Live photo icon on the left side of the screen. Tap that icon to get a video timeline that will look familiar if you read Chapter 8, which covers video features of the iPad.

One of the frames in that timeline will have a white square around it. Just tap and drag that square along the timeline until you get a frame you like. When you've finished editing, tap the Make Key Photo link, which appears above the timeline. Then tap Done in the upper-right corner, and your Live Photo will be represented by its new keyframe.

To mute sound in your Live Photo, tap the volume button, as shown at the top of Figure 9-10. To convert your Live Photo to a boring old regular photo, tap the Live button on the left side of the screen. To trim the length of your Live Photo, grab the handles at either end of the timeline and move them where you want. Otherwise, the editing tools are the same as described previously.

FIGURE 9-10:
Set the keyframe in a Live Photo by sliding the box on the timeline.

Okay, so we told a tiny fib by intimating that photographs are meant to be seen. We should have amended that statement by saying that *some* pictures are meant to be seen. Others, you can't get rid of fast enough. Fortunately, the iPad makes it a cinch to bury the evidence:

1. **Tap the objectionable photograph.**

2. **Tap to display the picture controls, if they're not already displayed.**

3. **Tap the trash icon.**

4. **Tap Delete Photo (or tap anywhere else to cancel, if you change your mind).**

   In an instant, the photo is mercifully disposed of. It's also deleted from the iCloud photo library across all your devices.

More (Not So) Stupid Picture Tricks

You can take advantage of the photos on the iPad in a few more ways. In each case, you tap the picture and make sure the picture controls are displayed. Then tap the share icon (shown in the margin) to display the choices shown in Figure 9-11. (Not all the options are visible in the figure.)

FIGURE 9-11:
Look at what
else we can do!

Here's a rundown of each choice:

>> **AirDrop:** AirDrop is a neat wireless method for sharing photos, videos, or other files with folks who happen to be nearby and also have an iOS 7 or later device or a Mac running macOS High Sierra or later. You turn on the feature in Control Center (see Chapter 2) and choose whether to make your iPad discoverable to everyone or just contacts who are in the vicinity. Tap a photo to select it and then tap the photo or icon representing the person and the device with whom you're trying to share the image (see 5K Stack, which happens to be Bryan's Mac, in Figure 9-11). That person will receive an invitation to accept the photograph or reject it on his or her device. If the photo is accepted, the picture lands on the person's device almost immediately.

>> **Messages:** Apple and your provider support picture messaging through MMS (Multimedia Messaging Service). Tap the Messages option, and the picture is embedded in your outgoing message; you need to enter the phone number, email address, or name of the person to whom you're sending the picture. iPadOS also suggests people you might want to share your image with based on past history and recent iMessage chats. In Figure 9-11, Bryan's iPad thinks Bryan might want to send that image to in the line of contacts just below the selection preview.

>> **Mail:** Some photos are so precious that you just have to share them with family members and friends. When you tap Mail, the picture is embedded in the body of an outgoing email message. Use the virtual keyboard to enter the email addresses, subject line, and any comments you want to add — you know, something profound, such as "Isn't this a great photo?" After tapping Send, you have the option to change the image size (small, medium, or large) or keep the actual size. Consider the trade-offs: A smaller-sized image may get

through any limits imposed by your or the recipient's Internet service provider or company. But if you can get the largest image through, you'll give the recipient the full picture (forgive the pun) in all its glory. (Check out Chapter 5 for more info on using email.)

>> **Notes:** You can add your chosen image to the Notes app.

>> **Reminders:** Send your image to the Reminders app to create a new reminder with that image embedded in it.

>> **Books:** Tap the Books app icon to add your image to the Books library.

>> **iCloud Photo Sharing:** You can post pics to a shared album.

>> **Twitter:** Lots of people send pictures with their tweets these days. The iPad makes it a breeze. Tap Twitter and your picture is embedded in an outgoing tweet. Just add your words, sticking to Twitter's character limit of 280, and tap Post.

>> **Facebook:** Lots (and we mean lots) of people also share photos on the world's largest social network. After your Facebook account is configured, you too can post there from your iPad.

>> **Sina Weibo** and **Tencent Weibo:** If you've enabled a Chinese keyboard, you'll see options for China's own social networks.

>> **Flickr:** The Yahoo!-owned service is another popular photo-sharing destination.

>> **Save PDF to Books:** You can turn the image into a PDF you can stash in the Books app.

>> **Copy:** Tap to copy the image and then paste it into an email or elsewhere.

>> **Duplicate:** You may want to duplicate a photo so that you can edit it while also keeping an original.

>> **Slideshow:** We discuss slideshows earlier in this chapter. Here is another starting point for a slideshow, which as you know, can be accompanied by an optional musical soundtrack.

>> **AirPlay:** Own an Apple TV set-top box? You can use AirPlay to stream photos from your iPad to the TV.

>> **Save Image:** If you didn't shoot the image in question on your iPad but want to add it to the device, tap the Save Image option.

>> **Hide:** Don't want the image to be seen (but don't want to delete it either)? Tap Hide and then tap Hide Photo. The selected pic will be hidden from the days, months, and years views but still visible in albums view.

>> **Assign to Contact:** If you assign a picture to someone in your contacts list, the picture you assign pops up whenever you receive a FaceTime call or iMessage from that person. Tap Assign to Contact. Your list of contacts appears on the screen. Scroll through the list to find the person who matches the picture of the moment. As with the Use as Wallpaper option (described next), you can drag and resize the picture to get it just right. Then tap Set Photo.

You can also assign a photo to a contact by starting out in Contacts. To change the picture you assigned to a person, tap his or her name in the contacts list, tap Edit, and then tap the person's thumbnail picture, which also carries the label Edit. From there, you can take another photo with the iPad's digital camera, select another photo from one of your albums, edit the photo you're already using (by resizing and dragging it to a new position), or delete the photo you no longer want.

>> **Use as Wallpaper:** The Apple-supplied background images on the iPad can't measure up to pictures of your spouse, kids, or pet. When you tap Use as Wallpaper, you see what the present image looks like as the iPad's background picture. You're given the opportunity to move the picture around and resize it, through the now-familiar action of dragging or pinching against the screen with your fingers. You can even see how the picture looks against the time and date that appear on the lock screen. Another option is to take advantage of the Perspective Zoom setting, which lets you exploit a parallax animation effect in which the picture moves as you move the iPad. Tap the screen to toggle the setting on or off. When you're satisfied with what the wallpaper looks like, tap the Set button. Options appear that let you use the photo as wallpaper for the lock screen, the Home screen, or both, as shown in Figure 9-12. Per usual, you can also tap Cancel. (You find out more about wallpaper in Chapter 15.)

FIGURE 9-12:
Beautifying the iPad with wallpaper.

>> **Print:** If you have an AirPrint-capable printer, tap Print to print the photo. You can choose how many copies of the print you want to duplicate.

>> **More:** Tapping here lets you post pictures to other sites with sharing plug-ins or extensions.

Sometimes you want to make decisions about multiple pictures at the same time, whether you're sharing them online, copying or printing them, adding them to a new album, or deleting them in bulk. Here's a convenient way to do so. Launch the Photos app and either tap a specific album in the app or open a days view or all photos view so that you see thumbnails of your pictures. Next, tap Select at the upper right, and then tap each thumbnail on which you're planning to take action, so that a check mark appears. As you do, the count for each picture you select increases. From here, you can delete them, or you can tap the share icon to share pictures on a social network in bulk, email them, send them via a message, or copy or print them, as discussed previously. The options that appear may vary depending on how many pictures you've selected — for example, the number of photos you can email is limited.

Entering the Photo Booth

Remember the old-fashioned photo booths at the local Five and Dime? Remember the Five and Dime? Okay, if you don't remember such variety stores, your parents probably do, and if they don't, their parents no doubt do. The point is that photo booths (which do still exist) are fun places to ham it up solo or with a friend as the machine captures and spits out wallet-size pictures.

With the Photo Booth app, Apple has cooked up a modern alternative to a real photo booth. The app is a close cousin to a similar application on the Mac. Here's how Photo Booth works:

1. **Tap the Photo Booth icon on the Home screen.**

    You get the tic-tac-toe-style grid shown in Figure 9-13.

2. **Point the front-facing camera at your face.**

    You see your mug through a prism of eight rather wacky special effects: Thermal Camera, Mirror, X-Ray, Kaleidoscope, Light Tunnel, Squeeze, Twirl, and Stretch. The center square (what is this, *Hollywood Squares?*) is the only one in which you come off looking normal — or, as we like to kid, like you're supposed to look. Some of the effects make you look scary; some, merely goofy.

You can also use the rear camera in Photo Booth to subject your friends to this form of, um, visual abuse.

3. **Choose one of the special effects (or stick with Normal) by tapping one of the thumbnails.**

Ed chose Mirror for the example shown in Figure 9-14 because, after all, two Eds are better than one. (Sorry, couldn't resist.) You can pinch or unpinch the image to further doctor the effect.

TIP

If you're not satisfied with the effect you've chosen, tap the icon at the lower-left corner of the app to return to the Photo Booth grid and select another.

4. **When you have your bizarre look just right, tap the camera button on the screen to snap the picture.**

Your pic lands (as do other pictures taken with the iPad cameras) in the All Photos album.

From the All Photos album or from right here in Photo Booth, pictures can be shared in all the usual places or deleted, which you might want to seriously consider, given the distortions you've just applied to your face.

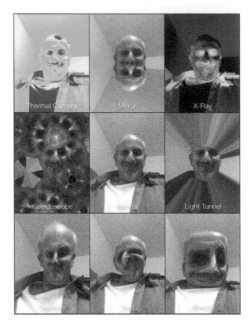

FIGURE 9-13:
Photo booths of yesteryear weren't like this.

FIGURE 9-14:
When one coauthor just isn't enough.

Nah, we're only kidding. Keep the image and take a lot more. Photo Booth may be a blast from the past, but we think it's just a blast.

TIP

Before leaving this photography section, we want to steer you to the App Store, which we explore in greater depth in Chapter 10. Hundreds, probably thousands, of photography-related apps are available there, a whole host of them free. That's too many to mention here, but we know you'll find terrific photo apps just by wandering around the place. Head to the Photo & Video category to get started.

And there you have it. You have just passed Photography 101 on the iPad. We trust that the coursework was, forgive another pun, a snap.

The iPad at Work

4

Learn how to shop 'til you drop in the App Store, an emporium replete with a gaggle of neat little programs and applications. Best of all, unlike most of the stores you frequent, a good number of the items can be had for free.

Get down to business and explore staying on top of your appointments and people with Calendar and Contacts.

Discover time- and effort-saving utilities such as Reminders, Notes, and Clock.

Take control of your iPad with Notifications and Control Center.

Find out how powerful your iPad really is, and learn about all the multitasking features you have at your fingertips.

Get to know Siri, your (mostly) intelligent assistant. She responds to your voice and can do some amazing tasks, including sending messages, scheduling appointments and reminders, searching the web, and playing a specific song or artist.

Chapter **10**

Apply Here (to Find Out about iPad Apps)

O ne of the best things about the iPad is that you can download and install apps created by third parties, which is to say not created by Apple (the first party) or you (the second party). At the time of this writing, our best guess is that there are more than 4 million apps available and over 200 billion apps downloaded to date. Some apps are free, and other apps cost money; some apps are useful, and other apps are lame; some apps are perfectly well behaved, and other apps quit unexpectedly (or worse). The point is that of the many apps out there, some are better than others.

In this chapter, we take a broad look at apps you can use with your iPad. You discover how to find and download apps on your iPad, and you find some basics for managing your apps. Don't worry: We have plenty to say about specific third-party apps in Chapters 18 and 19.

Tapping the Magic of Apps

Apps enable you to use your iPad as a game console, a streaming Netflix player, a recipe finder, a sketchbook, and much, much more. You can run three categories of apps on your iPad:

>> **Apps made exclusively for the iPad:** This is the rarest kind, so you find fewer of these than the other two types. These apps won't run on an iPhone or iPod touch, so you can't even install them on either device.

>> **Apps made to work properly on an iPad, iPhone, or iPod touch:** These so-called *universal apps* can run on any of the three device types at native resolution.

>> **Apps made for the iPhone and iPod touch:** These apps run on your iPad but only at iPhone/iPod touch resolution rather than the full resolution of your iPad, as demonstrated in Figure 10-1.

TIP

You can double the size of an iPhone/iPod touch app by tapping the little 2x button in the lower-right corner of the screen; to return it to its native size, tap the 1x button. Figure 10-1 shows you what an iPhone/iPod touch app looks like on an iPad screen.

FIGURE 10-1: iPhone and iPod touch apps run at a smaller size (left), but can be increased to double size (right).

You can obtain and install apps for your iPad in two ways:

>> The App Store app on your iPad

>> Via automatic download

To switch on automatic downloads on the iPad, tap Settings ⇨ iTunes & App Store. Then tap the Automatic Downloads switch for Apps so that it turns green (on). After you do so, all apps you buy on other iPadOS and iOS devices will automagically appear on your iPad.

TIP

Consider also enabling automatic downloads for Music, Books, and Updates while you have the iTunes & App Store settings on your screen.

After you've obtained an app from the App Store, you can download it to up to ten iOS devices (as long as you log in with the same iCloud account or use Family Sharing).

TIP

But before you can use the App Store on your iPad, you first need an iTunes Store account.

If you don't have an iTunes Store account, you can't download a single cool app — not even the free ones — for your iPad.

REMEMBER

So, if you don't have an iTunes Store account, might we suggest that you get one now? Just tap Settings ⇨ iTunes & App Store ⇨ Sign In ⇨ Create New Account and follow the on-screen instructions.

Finding Apps in the App Store

Finding apps with your iPad is easy. The only requirement is that you have an Internet connection of some sort — Wi-Fi or wireless data network — so that you can access the App Store and browse, search, download, and install apps.

Browsing the App Store

To get started, tap the App Store icon (shown in the margin) on your iPad's Home screen. After you launch the App Store, you see five icons at the bottom of the screen, representing five ways to interact with the store, as shown in Figure 10-2. The first three icons — Today, Games, and Apps — offer three ways to browse the virtual shelves of the App Store. (We get to the fourth and fifth icons, Arcade and Search, shortly.)

The Today section, shown in Figure 10-2, highlights curated selections from the App Store, including Game of the Day and App of the Day, themed collections such as Top Games of the Week, and staff favorites (not shown in the figure).

The Games section lets you browse games in categories such as AR Games, New Games We Love, and Essential Game Picks, to name a few. Scroll down and you'll find sections for Top Paid Games, Top Free Games, Top Game Categories, and more.

The Apps section is like déjà vu all over again if you've already visited the Games section. It also contains categories such as Great on iPad, Our Favorites, and Apple Pencil Starter Kit, as shown in Figure 10-3. Scroll down a little farther and you'll find Top Paid Apps, Top Free Apps, Top App Categories, and more.

Most pages in the App Store display more apps than can fit on the screen at once. For example, the New to iPad section in Figure 10-3 contains more than the four apps you can see. A few tools help you navigate the Games, Apps, and other sections of the App Store:

>> **Swipe from right to left** to see more apps in most categories.

>> **Swipe up the screen** to scroll down and see additional categories.

>> **Tap the See All link** at the top right of most sections to (what else?) see all the apps in that section on one screen at the same time.

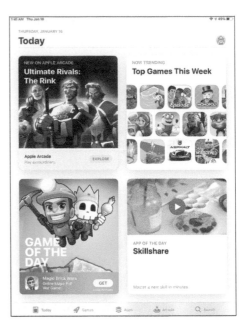

FIGURE 10-2:
The icons across the bottom represent different ways to browse the App Store.

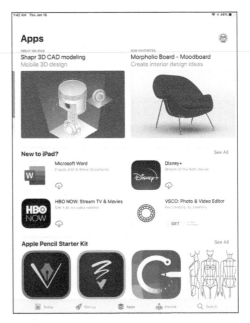

FIGURE 10-3:
The Apps section displays apps organized by themes, such as New to iPad.

Arcade

NEW

Apple introduced Arcade, a subscription game service, with iPadOS. It's the fourth icon at the bottom of the App Store. And it's really cool — let us tell you why!

With Arcade, you get on-demand access to more than 100 games, with Apple adding more every week. These are high-quality, top-tier games. Even better, none of them have in-app purchases, which means you can play the entire game without having to spend a penny outside the Arcade subscription itself. You'll find racing games, fighting games, strategy games, simulations, puzzles, mysteries, and so much more. These games are original, with most produced exclusively for Arcade.

But here's the best part. Arcade is just $4.99 per month, and that includes everything. To subscribe, tap the Try It Free button in the Arcade section to start a 30-day free trial. If you unsubscribe before the trial ends, you won't be charged. Otherwise, you'll begin paying $4.99 per month through your Apple ID. If you love playing great games, that price makes Arcade a no-brainer. Some of our favorites so far include Red Reign, Mini Motorways, and LEGO Brawls.

Searching for apps

Finally, the last option at the bottom of the screen is Search, the magnifying glass icon. If you know exactly what you're looking for (or even approximately what you're looking for), just tap Search to bring up the virtual keyboard, and then type a word or phrase. Then tap the Search key to initiate the search.

That's all there is to it.

Updating apps

NEW

Every so often the developer of an iPad app releases an update, but for some reason Apple made it harder to see your updates in the App Store in iPadOS. The Arcade icon on the Home screen replaced the Updates icon, so now you need to tap your profile button in the upper-right corner of any of the five main sections of the App Store. An account sheet will appear with your Apple ID, tabs for seeing previously purchased apps, managing subscriptions, redeeming gift cards and gift card codes, sending gift cards by email, and adding funds to your Apple ID.

At the bottom of the screen are recent and pending updates, with app icons, the name of each app, and update notes for the newest update. If an update has already been applied by the App Store, you'll see an Open button, which allows you to launch the app. If the app is waiting to be updated, you'll see an Update button. Tap the Update button to update the app. When the update is complete, the button changes to an Open button.

If you try to update an app purchased from any iTunes Store account except your own, you're prompted for that account's ID and password. If you can't provide them, you can't download the update. This doesn't apply, of course, if you've enabled Family Sharing (see Chapter 15).

One last tip: If you download an app and it doesn't work properly, try deleting and redownloading it from the App Store. Doing so fixes the problem as often as not.

Finding details about an app

Now that you know how to browse and search for apps in the App Store, the following sections show you how to find out more about a particular app. After tapping an app icon as you browse the store or in a search result, your iPad displays a details screen like the one shown in Figure 10-4.

Note the blue More link in the Preview section in Figure 10-4; click More to see a longer description of the app.

Bear in mind that the app description on this screen was written by the app's developer and may be biased. Never fear, gentle reader: In an upcoming section, we show you how to find app reviews written by people who have used the app (and, unfortunately, sometimes people who haven't).

TIP

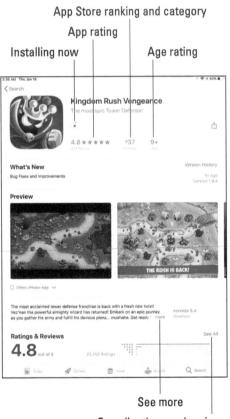

App Store ranking and category

App rating

Installing now

Age rating

See more

See all ratings and reviews

FIGURE 10-4:
Kingdom Rush Vengeance is the newest version of a great tower defense franchise.

Understanding the age rating

The Kingdom Rush Vengeance app is rated for age 9+, as you can see to the far right of the 4.8 user rating (labeled in Figure 10-4). The rating means that the app may contain content that is unsuitable for children under 9. Other age ratings are 4+, 12+, and 17+, each designed to help parents manage what games and apps their kids are using.

Checking requirements and device support for the app

One more thing: Remember the three categories of apps we mention at the beginning of the chapter, in the "Tapping the Magic of Apps" section? Scroll down the page to the Information section (not shown in Figure 10-4), and you'll find that this app *Requires iOS 9.0 or later. Compatible with iPhone, iPad, and iPod touch.*

Reading reviews

The Ratings & Reviews section of the details screen offers reviews written by users of this app. Each review includes a star rating, from zero to five. If an app is rated four stars or higher, you can safely assume that most users are happy with the app.

In Figure 10-4, you can see that this app has a rating of 4.8 stars based on 23K user ratings. That means it's a great app. Finally, Tap See All to read more user reviews.

REMEMBER

Don't believe everything you read in reviews. In our experience, people find some amazingly bad reasons to give apps bad — and sometimes good — ratings. Take App Store ratings and reviews with a grain of salt, and learn how to look for the reviews that resonate with you. We also like to look for a preponderance of opinions to help weigh the ones to take seriously. Lastly, make sure the review you're reading is for the current version — reviews of older versions may be inaccurate.

To read reviews from your iPad, tap the See All link in the Reviews section of an app's details page.

Downloading an app

To download an app to your iPad from the App Store, follow these steps:

1. **To start the download process, tap the blue price button (or the word *Get* or the download from iCloud icon) near the top of the app's details screen.**

   For apps with a price, the price button will morph into a blue Buy button. You may be prompted to sign in to your iTunes account, or to use Touch ID or Face ID to authorize the purchase. In Figure 10-4, you see the installing icon instead of a price because Bryan got too excited when he saw this app and paid for it before taking a screenshot.

2. **Tap the blue Buy button.**

   When the app is finished downloading and is installed on your iPad, the installing icon changes to an Open button.

DOWNLOADING OTHER CONTENT ON YOUR IPAD

You may have noticed that the App Store app on your iPad offers nothing but apps.

To obtain music, movies, and TV shows, you use the iTunes Store app; to read stories from newspapers and magazines, you use either the News app or the Safari app (both are included with your iPad).

But to download books and podcasts, you'll need the Books and Podcasts apps, respectively. For what it's worth, these apps work pretty much the same as the App Store. So, now that you understand how to navigate the App Store app, you also know how to use these other Store apps.

3. **Tap the Open button to launch the app.**

    If you close the App Store before the app finishes installing, you see your new app's icon on the Home screen. (Depending on how many apps you have installed on your iPad, you may need to swipe to another Home screen to find the new app.) The new app's icon is slightly dimmed and has the word *Loading* below it, with a pie chart to indicate how much of the app remains to be downloaded (about one third, as shown in the margin).

4. **If the app is rated 17+, click OK on the warning screen that appears after you type your password to confirm that you're 17 or older before the app downloads.**

The app is now on your iPad. If your iPad suddenly loses its memory (unlikely) or you delete the app from your iPad, you can download it again later from the App Store at no charge.

Working with Apps

Most of what you need to know about apps involves simply installing third-party apps on your iPad. However, you might find it helpful to know how to delete and review an app.

Deleting an app

Many of the preinstalled apps that came on your iPad — Photos, Camera, Contacts, Clock, Settings, and Messages, to name a few — can't be removed. But you can delete other apps.

TIP

You can, however, hide some of Apple's preinstalled apps by choosing Settings ⇨ Screen Time ⇨ Content & Privacy Restrictions ⇨ Allowed Apps. For any of the Apple apps listed, toggle the switch for the app you want to hide so that it goes from green to white.

Here's how to delete an app on your iPad:

1. **Press and hold any app icon until all the icons begin to wiggle.**

2. **Tap the little *x* in the upper-left corner of the app you want to delete.**

   A dialog appears, informing you that deleting this app also deletes all its data, as shown in Figure 10-5.

3. **Tap the Delete button.**

4. **To stop the icons from wiggling, press the Home or sleep/wake button, or swipe up from the bottom of your screen.**

> **Delete "FOX NOW"?**
> Deleting this app will also delete its data.
>
> Cancel | Delete

FIGURE 10-5:
Tap an app's little *x* and then tap Delete to remove the app from your iPad.

TIP

You also make icons wiggle to move them around on the screen or move them from page to page. To rearrange wiggling icons, press and drag them one at a time. If you drag an icon to the left or right edge of the screen, it moves to the next or previous Home screen. You can also drag additional icons to the dock (where Safari, Mail, Photos, and Music live) to make them available on every Home screen.

Writing an app review

Sometimes you love or hate an app so much that you want to tell the world about it. In that case, you should write a review. You can do this directly from your iPad.

To write a review from your iPad, follow these steps:

1. **Tap the App Store icon to launch the App Store.**

2. **Navigate to the details screen for the app.**

3. **Tap one to five of the stars at the top of the screen to rate the app.**

   You might have to type your iTunes Store password.

4. **In the Title field, type a title for your review, and in the Review field, type your review.**

5. **Tap the Send button in the upper-right corner of the screen.**

    Whichever way you submit your review, Apple reviews your submission. As long as the review doesn't violate the (unpublished) rules of conduct for app reviews, it appears in a day or two in the App Store in the Reviews section for the particular app.

TIP

You can configure the behavior of many apps in the Settings app. Scroll all the way down the list of settings and you'll find an alphabetical list of apps that have settings; tap an app in the list to see its settings.

Chapter **11**

People and Appointments

We hate to break the news to you, but your iPad isn't only for fun and games; it also has a serious side. The iPad can remind you of appointments and help you keep all your contacts straight.

Working with the Calendar

The Calendar program lets you keep on top of your appointments and events (birthdays, anniversaries, and the like). You open it by tapping the Calendar icon on the Home screen. The icon is smart in its own right because it changes daily, displaying the day of the week and the date right in the app icon on your home screen.

You can display five calendar views: year, month, day, week, and a searchable list view, which shows current and future appointments.

Tap one of the four tabs at the top of the screen — Day, Week, Month, or Year — to choose a view. A Today button in the lower-left corner of the screen returns you to the current date in any view. (Also at the bottom of the screen are the Calendars button and Inbox button, which we get to shortly.)

To get to list view, tap the search icon — a little magnifying glass — in the upper-right corner of the screen.

We take a closer look at these views in the following sections.

Year view

There's not much to the yearly view, but it does let you see the current calendar year with today's date circled in red. You can scroll up or down to see prior or future years, but that's about it; unfortunately, you can't tell on which days you have appointments in year view. Boo. Hiss.

Month view

Tap any of the months visible in year view to jump to that specific month, as shown in Figure 11-1. When your iPad is in month view, you can see which days have appointments or scheduled events. Tap a day to see the list of activities on the agenda for that day, which leads nicely into the next section.

FIGURE 11-1:
Month view.

Day view

As we just mentioned, you have to tap a date with an entry to see what you have going on in a 24-hour period — though to see an entire day's worth of entries, you might have to scroll up or down depending on how many entries you have. You can swipe to the left to advance to the next day of the week and beyond; swipe to the right to retreat one or more days; or tap a day near the top of the screen to jump to it.

In the day view, all-day events, birthdays, and events pulled from your Facebook account (if you provide your Facebook credentials) appear in a narrow strip above the timeline for the day.

Your daily appointments span the entire time in which they've been scheduled on your calendar. For example, if an appointment runs from 12:00 p.m. to 1:00 p.m., that hour will be blocked off on the calendar like the *Meeting with Editor* entry shown in Figure 11-2.

You find out how to create calendar entries in a moment, but for now know that you can press on an event and drag it to a new time slot should your plans change. If you have overlapping appointments, you'll see more than a single entry claim a given time slot.

Finally, calendars are color-coded according to the calendar in which you scheduled the appointment. These color codes will help you distinguish an appointment you made on your travel calendar versus, say, a work, family, or Facebook calendar.

FIGURE 11-2:
Day view.

Week view

In week view, shown in Figure 11-3, you can see an entire week at a glance. The current date is circled in red.

TIP

You can arrange to start your weekly view on any day of the week. Tap Settings ⇨ Calendars ⇨ Start Week On, and then tap the day on which you want to start your week. (Sunday is the default in the United States.)

List view

List view isn't complicated. You can get to this view by tapping the

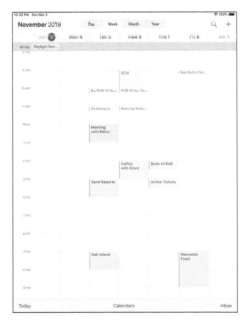

FIGURE 11-3:
Week view.

search icon (magnifying glass) in the upper-right corner of the screen. As you would expect, all your calendar appointments are listed chronologically, as shown in Figure 11-4. If you have a lengthy list, drag up or down with your finger or flick to rapidly scroll through your appointments. If you're looking for a specific calendar entry, you can search for appointments by typing the title, invitee names, location, or note in the search box above your list of entries.

Tap any of the listings to get meeting or appointment details for that entry. If you tap a person's birthday, you see his or her contact information. Sorry, but you just ran out of excuses for not sending a card.

FIGURE 11-4:
List view.

SYNCING CALENDARS WITH YOUR DESKTOP

The iPad can display the color-coding you assigned in Calendar on a Mac. Cool, huh? If you're a Mac user who uses Calendar, you can create multiple calendars and choose which ones to sync with your iPad. What's more, you can choose to display any or all of your calendars on your iPad. Calendar entries you create on your iPad are synchronized with the calendar(s) you specified in the iTunes (macOS Mojave and earlier) or Music (macOS Catalina) app Info pane. You can also sync calendars with Microsoft Outlook on a Mac or PC.

The best solution we've found is to use iCloud to keep calendars updated and in sync across all your iOS and iPadOS devices and computers. On the iPad, tap Settings ⇨ *yourname* ⇨ iCloud and make sure the Calendars switch is turned on (green).

One last thing: If you're a Mac user running OS X 10.9 Mavericks or later, iCloud is the *only* way you can sync calendar data.

Adding Calendar Entries

In Chapter 3, you discover pretty much everything there is to know about syncing your iPad, including syncing calendar entries from your Windows machine (using the likes of Microsoft Outlook) or Mac (using Calendar or Outlook) or Google Calendar. If you're syncing your calendar entries with iCloud, you can also manage your calendars at `https://www.icloud.com/` from any computer or device with a web browser.

In plenty of situations, you can enter appointments on the fly. Adding appointments directly to the iPad is easy:

1. **On the Home screen, tap the Calendar icon, and then (optionally) tap the Year, Month, Week, or Day view.**

2. **Tap the + icon in the upper-right corner of the screen.**

   The New Event overlay appears, as shown in Figure 11-5.

3. **Tap the Title and Location fields in turn and type as much or as little information as you feel is necessary.**

   Tapping displays the virtual keyboard (if it's not already shown).

TIP

   Don't forget you can use dictation or Siri to add a calendar entry. See Chapter 14 for more on dictation and Siri.

FIGURE 11-5: The screen looks like this just before you add an event to your iPad.

4. **To add start and end times:**

   a. *Tap the Starts field.* A carousel wheel, like the one shown for the Ends time in Figure 11-6, appears below the field you tapped.

   b. *Choose the time the event starts.* Use your finger to roll separate carousel controls for the date, hour, and minute (in 1-minute intervals) and to specify AM or PM. The process is a little like manipulating a combination bicycle lock or an old-fashioned date stamp used with an inkpad.

   c. *Tap the Ends field and choose the time the event ends.*

   To enter an all-day milestone (such as a birthday), tap the All-Day switch to turn it on (green). Because the time is no longer relevant for an all-day entry, you won't see Starts, Ends, or Time Zone options.

FIGURE 11-6: Controlling the Starts and Ends fields is like manipulating a bike lock.

TIP

5. **When you're finished, tap Add.**

TIP

We can't think of any easier way to add an entry than to instruct Siri along the lines of "Set a lunch appointment for tomorrow at noon with the Smiths." Siri will be pleased to comply.

That's the minimum you have to do to set up an event. But we bet you want to do more. The Calendar app makes it easy:

>> **Change the time zone.** If the correct location isn't already present, tap the Time Zone field and type the name of the city where the appointment is taking place.

>> **Set up a recurring entry.** Tap the Repeat field. Tap to indicate how often the event in question recurs. This setting is good for everything from a weekly appointment, such as an allergy shot, to a yearly event, such as an anniversary.

The options are Every Day, Every Week, Every 2 Weeks, Every Month, and Every Year. Tap the Custom field if you want to further refine those options. Tap Never if you are planning to never repeat this entry again.

>> **Add travel time to and from events.** Tap the Travel Time field and enable the Travel Time switch. A list of durations appears, ranging from five minutes to two hours. Tap a duration to specify your travel time.

>> **Assign the entry to a particular calendar.** Tap Calendar, and then tap the calendar you have in mind (Home or Work, for example).

>> **Invite people to join you.** Tap Invitees to specify who among your contacts will be attending the event.

>> **Set a reminder or alert for the entry.** Tap Alert and tap a time.

Alerts can be set so that you arrive at the time of an event, or 1 week before, 2 days before, 1 day before, 2 hours before, 1 hour before, 30 minutes before, 15 minutes before, or 5 minutes before the event. If it's an all-day entry, you can request alerts 1 day before (at 9:00 a.m.), 2 days before (at 9:00 a.m.), or 1 week before.

When the appointment time rolls around, you hear a sound and see a message like the one shown in Figure 11-7.

TIP

If you're the kind of person who needs an extra nudge, set another reminder by tapping the Second Alert field (which you'll see only if a first alert is already set).

FIGURE 11-7:
Alerts make it hard to forget.

- **Indicate whether you're busy or free by tapping Show As.** If you're invited to an event, you can tap Availability and then tap Free (if it's shown on your iPad).

- **Enter a web address.** Tap the URL field (at the bottom of the New Event screen) and type or copy and paste the web address.

- **Enter notes about the appointment or event.** Tap the Notes field (at the bottom of the screen) and type your note.

Tap Done after you finish entering everything.

Managing your calendars

When you have the hang of creating calendar entries, you can make the task much easier with these tips:

- **Choose a default calendar.** Tap Settings ➪ Calendar ➪ Default Calendar and select the calendar you want to use as the default for new events.

- **Make events appear according to whichever time zone you selected for your calendars.** In the Calendar settings, tap Time Zone Override to turn it on, and then tap Time Zone. Type the time zone's location, using the keyboard that appears. If you travel long distances for your job, this setting comes in handy.

  When Time Zone Override is turned off, events are displayed according to the time zone of your current location.

REMEMBER

- **Turn off calendar alert sounds.** Tap Settings ➪ Sounds ➪ Calendar Alerts, and then make sure the selected alert tone is set to None.

- **Set default alert times for birthdays, all-day events, or certain other events.** Tap Settings ➪ Calendar, and scroll down to Default Alert Times. For birthdays or other all-day events, you can choose to be alerted at 9:00 a.m. on the day of the event, at 9:00 a.m. one day before, at 9:00 a.m. two days before, or a week before. For other alerts, you can choose a default alert time at the time of event, 5, 10 15, or 30 minutes before, 1 hour before, 2 hours before, 1 day before, 2 days before, or 1 week before the event.

- **Modify an existing calendar entry.** Tap the entry, tap Edit, and then make whichever changes need to be made.

- **Wipe out a calendar entry.** Scroll down to the bottom of the event (if necessary) and then tap Delete Event. You have a chance to confirm your choice by tapping either Delete Event (again) or Cancel. If it's a repeating event, you can choose to Delete This Event Only or Delete All Future Events.

Letting your calendar push you around

If you work for a company that uses Microsoft Exchange ActiveSync, calendar entries and meeting invitations from coworkers can be *pushed* to your device so they show up on the screen moments after they're entered, even if they're entered on computers at work. Setting up an account to facilitate this pushing of calendar entries to your iPad is a breeze, although you should check with your company's tech or IT department to make sure your employer allows it. Then follow these steps:

1. **Tap Settings ⇨ Passwords & Accounts ⇨ Add Account.**

2. **From the Add Account list, tap Microsoft Exchange.**

3. **Fill in the email address and account description, and then tap Next.**

4. **Fill in your password and tap Next.**

5. **If required, enter your server address on the next screen that appears.**

   The iPad supports the Microsoft Autodiscovery service, which uses your name and password to automatically determine the address of the Exchange server. The rest of the fields should be filled in with the email address, username, password, and description you just entered.

6. **Tap Next.**

7. **Tap the switch to turn on each information type you want to synchronize using Microsoft Exchange.**

   The options are Mail, Contacts, Calendars, and Reminders. You should be good to go now, although some employers may require you to add passcodes to safeguard company secrets.

REMEMBER

If you have a business-issued iPad and it's lost or stolen — or you're a double agent working for a rival company — your employer's IT administrators can remotely wipe your device clean after you set up Microsoft Exchange.

One more thing: If you sync via iCloud, Google, or Microsoft Exchange, your calendar entries are automatically pushed to your iPad by the server when received.

Displaying multiple calendars

By tapping the Calendars button at the bottom of the yearly, monthly, weekly, or daily view, you can choose the calendar or calendars to display on your iPad. Merely tap each calendar you want to include so that a check mark appears next to it, as shown in Figure 11-8. To remove the check mark, tap again.

You can tap the Show All button (upper right) when you want your entire schedule to be an open book.

From the Calendars list, tap the *i*-in-a-circle for even more tricks. You can assign a color to your calendar, share the calendar with a given individual (tap Add Person to do so), make a calendar public (by flipping a switch), or delete the calendar.

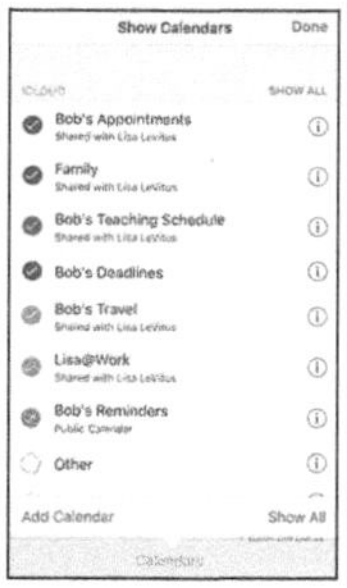

FIGURE 11-8:
Choosing the calendars to display.

Responding to meeting invitations

The iPad has one more important button in the Calendar app. It's the Inbox button, located at the bottom-right corner of the yearly, monthly, weekly, and daily views. If you partake in iCloud, have a Microsoft Exchange account, or have a calendar that adheres to the CalDAV Internet standard, you can send and receive a meeting invitation.

If you have any pending invitations, you'll see them when you tap the Inbox, which is separated into new invitations and invitations to which you've already replied. You can tap any of the items in the list to see more details about the event to which you've been invited. (Note that the Calendar's Inbox is not the same as your email inbox.)

Suppose a meeting invitation arrives from your boss. You can see who else is attending the shindig, check scheduling conflicts, and more. Tap Accept to let the meeting organizer know you're attending, tap Decline if you have something better to do (and aren't worried about upsetting the person who signs your paycheck), or tap Maybe if you're waiting for a better offer.

And as we point out previously, you can also invite other folks to attend an event you yourself are putting together.

Meantime, if you run into a conflict, why not ask Siri to change your schedule? For that matter, you can also call upon Siri to remind you when you have your next appointment. Visit Chapter 14 for more on this clever feature.

You can choose to receive an alert every time someone sends you an invitation. Tap Settings ⇨ Notifications ⇨ Calendar ⇨ Invitations and tap Allow Notifications to turn notifications on (green).

As mentioned, if you take advantage of iCloud, Google, or Microsoft Exchange, you can keep calendar entries synchronized between your iPhone, iPad, iPod touch and your Mac or PC. When you make a scheduling change on your iPad, it's automatically updated on your computer and other devices, and vice versa.

Subscribing to calendars

You can subscribe to calendars that adhere to the CalDAV and iCalendar (.ics) standards, which are supported by the popular Google and Yahoo! calendars and by the Mac's Calendar app. Although you can read entries on the iPad from the calendars you subscribe to, you can't create entries from the iPad or edit the entries that are already present.

To subscribe to one of these calendars, tap Settings ⇨ Passwords & Accounts ⇨ add Account. Tap Other and then choose Add CalDAV Account, Add Subscribed Calendar, Add LDAP Account, or Add CardDAV account. Next, enter the server where the iPad can find the calendar you have in mind, and if need be, a username, a password, and an optional description.

Finally, some apps, websites, and email messages will offer to add calendar events and subscriptions.

Sifting through Contacts

If you read the chapter on syncing (see Chapter 3), you know how to get the snail-mail addresses, email addresses, and phone numbers that reside on your Mac or PC into your iPad. Assuming you went through that drill already, all those addresses and phone numbers are hanging out in one place. Their not-so-secret hiding place is revealed when you tap the Contacts icon on the Home screen. The following sections guide you from the main screen to whatever you want to do with your contacts' information.

Adding and viewing contacts

To add contacts to your Contacts app, tap the + icon at the top of the screen and type as much or as little profile information as you have for the person. Tap Add Photo to add a picture from your photo albums or collections (or to take a snapshot with your iPad camera). You can edit the information later by tapping the Edit button when a contact's name is highlighted.

A list of your contacts appears on the left panel of the screen, with the one you're currently viewing shown in gray; see Figure 11-9. At the top on the right, you can see a mug shot of your contact — if you added one — with his or her address. Below that you'll see the contact's phone number, email address, home and another address, and birthday (all blurred in Figure 11-9 to protect Jacob's privacy). You also find an area to scribble notes about a contact.

You have three ways to land on a specific contact:

>> **Flick your finger so that the list of contacts on the left side scrolls rapidly up or down,** loosely reminiscent of the spinning Lucky 7s and other pictures on a Las Vegas slot machine. Think of the payout you'd get with that kind of power on a one-armed bandit.

>> **Slide your thumb or another finger along the alphabet on the right edge of the contacts list** or tap one of the teeny-tiny letters to jump to names that begin with that letter.

>> **Start to type the name of a contact in the search field near the top of the contacts list.** Or type the name of the place where your contact works. When you're at or near the appropriate contact name, stop the scrolling by tapping the screen.

FIGURE 11-9:
A view of all contacts.

When you tap to stop the scrolling, that tap doesn't select an item in the list. This may seem counterintuitive the first few times you try it, but we got used to it and now we really like it this way. Just think of that first tap as applying the brakes to the scrolling list.

You can change the way your contacts are displayed. Tap Settings ⟴ Contacts. Tap Sort Order or Display Order, and for each one, choose the First, Last option or Last, First option to indicate whether you want to sort or display entries by a contact's first or last name. You can also choose First Name & Last Initial or First Initial & Last Name.

Searching contacts

You can search contacts by entering a first or last name in the search field or by entering a company name.

You can locate people on your iPad without opening the Contacts app. Swipe down from the middle of the Home screen to pull down your iPad's Siri Search field. Type a name in the Search field, and then tap the name in the search results. You can also ask Siri to find people for you, and even have her compose and send them an email or iMessage, or call them via FaceTime video or audio chat.

If you're searching contacts with a Microsoft Exchange account, you may be able to search your employer's *global address list* (GAL for short). This search typically works in one of two ways:

>> Tap the Groups button in the upper-left corner of the All Contacts screen and then tap the appropriate Exchange server name to find folks. Groups on your computer might reflect, say, different departments in your company, friends from work, friends from school, and so on.

>> You can search an LDAP *(Lightweight Directory Access Protocol)* server. It strikes us that nothing is "lightweight" about something called an LDAP server, but we digress. Similarly, if you have a CardDAV account, you can search for any contacts that have been synced to the iPad.

Contacting and sharing your contacts

You can initiate an email from Contacts by tapping an email address under a contact's listings. Doing so fires up the Mail program on the iPad, with the person's name already in the To field. For more on the Mail app, we direct you to Chapter 5.

You can also share a contact's profile with another person. Tap the Share Contact button (you may have to scroll down to see it), and use the Mail or Messages app to send the contact's vCard, which is embedded in the body of a new Mail or Messages message. Just add an address and send it on its merry way. A *vCard,* in case you were wondering, is kind of like an electronic business card. You can identify it by its .vcf file format.

You can also share a contact's vCard with iPadOS's drag-and-drop feature. Just press and hold down on a contact in the list, and then drag it to another app (such as Messages or Mail).

Finally, you can tap a contact's snail-mail address to launch the Maps app and see it pinned to a map.

Linking contacts

The people you know most likely have contact entries in more than one account, meaning you might end up with redundant entries for the same person. The iPad solution is to *link* contacts. Find the contact in question, tap Edit, scroll to the bottom of the Edit screen, and tap Link Contact. Choose the related contact entry and then tap Link. It's worth noting that the linked contacts in each account remain separate and aren't merged.

Removing a contact

Hey, it happens. A person falls out of favor. Maybe he's a jilted lover. Or maybe you just moved cross-country and will no longer call on the services of your old gardener.

Removing a contact is easy, if unfortunate. Tap a contact and then tap Edit. Scroll to the bottom of the Edit screen and tap Delete Contact. You get one more chance to change your mind.

And that, gentle reader, should be pretty much all you need to work with Contacts. Onward!

IN THIS CHAPTER

» Noting Notes

» Remembering with Reminders

» Making your home smarter with the Home app

» Measuring things in thin air with the Measure app

» Punching the Clock app

» Getting the drop on AirDrop

Chapter **12**

Indispensable iPad Utilities

Notes, Clock, and Reminders are often overlooked, but we think they're the bee's knees. And managing your HomeKit smart devices with the Home app on your iPad has never been easier. And then there's Apple's new Measure app — we show you how it's practically magic.

In addition to describing some indispensable apps in this chapter, we also demonstrate how to create a Wi-Fi hotspot no matter where you are and how to share with AirDrop.

Taking Note of Notes

Notes creates notes that you can save or send through email. Over the years, it's gained many useful features, including "sketch with your finger" mode, checklists, and enclosures. In addition, many apps now allow you to save data directly to the Notes app (after tapping the share icon). Finally, all your notes can be synced across all your enabled Apple devices via iCloud.

To create a note, follow these steps:

1. **On the Home screen, tap the Notes icon.**

2. **Tap the note icon (shown in the margin) in the upper-right corner to start a new note.**

   The virtual keyboard appears.

3. **Type a note, such as the one shown in Figure 12-1.**

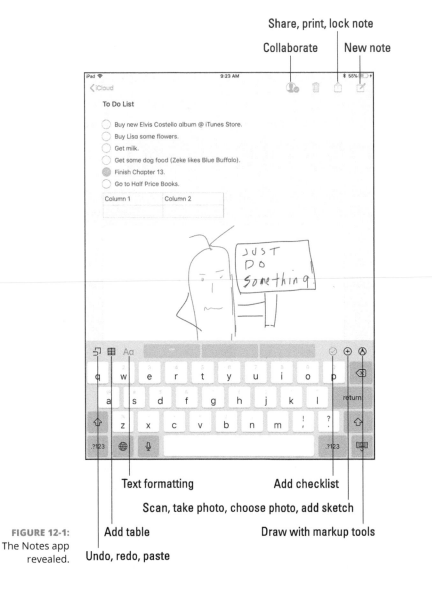

FIGURE 12-1:
The Notes app revealed.

Figure 12-1 shows off a few of the features in Notes: The list is formatted as a checklist, followed by a table with two columns and two rows, and then a crudely drawn sketch at the bottom.

Other things you can do before you quit the Notes app include the following:

>> Tap the back button in the upper-left corner of the screen (which says iCloud in Figure 12-1, but might say something else depending on how you've used Notes) to see either a list of all your notes or — if you sync Notes with more than one account, such as iCloud, Google, or Yahoo! — folders for each service you sync with.

>> When a list of notes is on-screen, tap a folder to see its contents, or tap a note to open and view, edit, or modify it. (**Hint:** The list is always visible when you hold your iPad in landscape mode.)

>> Tap the share icon at the top-right corner (and shown in the margin) to send the note using the Mail or Messages app (see Chapter 5 for more on Mail and Messages), copy the note to the Clipboard (see Chapter 2 for the scoop on copy and paste), post it to social media, assign it to a contact, lock it, print it (see Chapter 2 for more about printing), and more.

>> Collaborate with others by tapping the collaborate icon near the top-right corner (and shown in the margin) and sending them an invitation to collaborate.

>> Tap the trash icon near the top-right corner to delete the note.

When the keyboard is displayed, you can

>> Tap the check mark icon above the top row of keys to create a checklist; select text before you tap it to change existing text into a checklist.

>> Tap the Aa icon above the top row of keys to format text as Title, Heading, Body, Bulleted List, Dashed List, or Numbered List. Select the text before you tap it to change its format. Depending on the cursor's location in the note, you may see other options.

>> Tap the camera icon above the top row of keys to take a picture with the camera, select a picture from your Photos library, or scan a document to add to the note you're writing. The Document Scanner automatically senses and scans a document into the Notes app, crops its edges, and removes any skewing or glare. If you have iPad Pro and Apple Pencil, you can then use Apple Pencil to fill in the blanks or sign the document.

>> Tap the pen icon above the top row of keys to create a new finger sketch.

TIP

You can also use Siri to set up and dictate your note by speaking. (You hear more about Siri in Chapter 14.)

As with most iPad apps, your notes are saved automatically while you type them so you can quit Notes at any time without losing a single character.

We'd be remiss if we didn't remind you one last time that you can sync Notes with your Mac and other devices via iCloud. You enable Notes syncing in Settings ⇨ *your name* ⇨ iCloud on your iPad and System Preferences ⇨ Apple ID ⇨ iCloud on your Mac.

TIP

Enable the Notes widget to access your Notes from today view, as described in Chapter 15.

Finally, one of our favorite iPadOS features for those with an Apple Pencil and a compatible iPad is the ability to tap the lock screen with your Apple Pencil to launch Notes to a blank page so you can begin taking notes instantly. If this doesn't work for you, tap Settings ⇨ Notes and enable Access Notes from Lock Screen.

And that's all she wrote. You now know what you need to know about creating and managing notes with Notes.

Remembering with Reminders

You can find lots of good to-do list apps in the App Store; if you don't believe us, search for *to-do list.* You'll find more than 200 offerings for the iPad. Many are free, but others sell (and sell briskly, we might add) at prices up to $30 or $40.

What you get for free is Reminders, a simple to-do list app for making and organizing lists, with optional reminders available for items in your lists.

Tap the Reminders icon on your Home screen, and you'll see something that looks like Figure 12-2. Reminders on the right side of the screen belong to a default list called All, as indicated by the list name highlighted on the left side of the screen.

Working with lists

To create a new list, tap Add List at the bottom of the screen, type a name for the list on the virtual keyboard, and then tap Done. You can add an optional icon for each list, too, as shown in Figure 12-2, by tapping the Edit button at the top of the screen and then tapping the *i*-in-a-circle icon to bring up color and icon.

To manage the lists you create, tap the Edit button at the top of the edit list, shown in Figure 12-2. When you do, the left side of the screen goes into what we like to think of as edit mode, as shown in Figure 12-3.

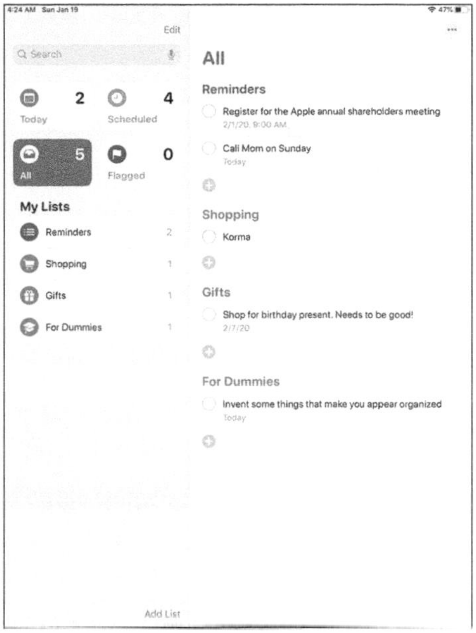

From this screen, you can

TIP

>> **Delete a list:** Tap the red minus sign for the list. The list's name slides to the left, revealing a red Delete button.

You can also delete a list without first tapping the Edit button by swiping the list's name from right to left. The red Delete button appears on the right; tap it to delete the list or tap anywhere else to cancel.

>> **Reorder (move up or down) lists:** Tap and drag your finger on the three horizontal lines (shown in the margin) to the right of a list's name in edit mode, and then drag the name up or down. When the list's name is where you want it, lift your finger.

FIGURE 12-2:
The Reminders app.

Setting up reminders

Reminders is a simple app, and the steps for managing reminders are equally simple. Here's how to remind yourself of something:

1. **On the Home screen, tap the Reminders app.**

2. **On the left side of the screen, tap the list to which you want to attach the reminder.**

   If you haven't created your own lists, you'll see the two default lists: All and Scheduled. Otherwise, you'll see a list of all the reminder lists you've created.

   The virtual keyboard appears.

3. **Tap + New Reminder at the bottom of the list to start a new reminder.**

4. **Type your new reminder.**

   Or just ask Siri to remind you. (See Chapter 14 for more about Siri.)

   The item appears in the current reminders list. At this point, your reminder is bare-bones; its date, repeat, and priority options have not been activated. To use those features, continue.

5. **Tap the reminder and then tap the little *i*-in-a-circle to set the following options in the details overlay, as shown in Figure 12-4 (not all options are visible):**

   - *Notes:* If you have anything else to add, tap the Notes field and type away.

   - *Remind Me on a Day:* Tap to specify a day for this reminder.

   - *Alarm:* Tap to specify a day and time for this reminder.

   - *Remind Me at a Time:* Tap to set a specific time of day.

   - *Repeat:* After you specify a day and time for a reminder, a Repeat button appears. Tap it if you want to set a second reminder for a different day or time.

   - *Remind Me at a Location:* Tap to set a location-based reminder. Just enable the At a Location switch, specify the location, and then choose When I Arrive or When I Leave.

   - *Priority:* Tap to specify a priority for this reminder. You can select None, Low, Medium, or High.

   - *List:* Tap if you want this reminder to appear in a different list. Then tap the list to which you want to move this reminder.

6. **After you've set your options, tap the Done button in the upper-right corner of the details overlay.**

TIP

Choose the list you want your new reminder to appear in *before* you create the reminder. But if you forget, you can always tap the *i*-in-a-circle icon and choose a different list.

FIGURE 12-3:
Tap the Edit button to create, delete, or reorder your lists.

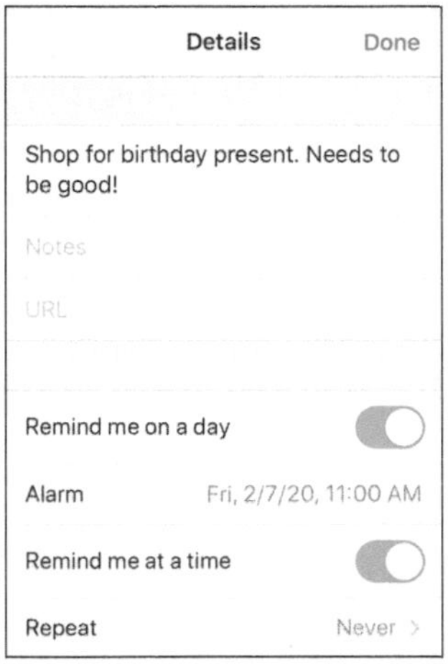

FIGURE 12-4:
Details for Our Shiny New Reminder.

Viewing and checking off reminders

After you create reminders, the app helps you see what you have and haven't done and enables you to do the following tasks:

>> **Check off reminders.** You probably noticed that every reminder you create includes a hollow circle to its left. Tap the circle to indicate that a task has been completed. When you do, Today, Scheduled, and All Numbers will adjust.

>> **Search reminders.** To search for a word or phrase in all your reminders, completed or not, tap the search field at the upper left, type your word or phrase, and then tap the search icon (magnifying glass). Or swipe down from the middle of any Home screen to search for it with Search.

>> **Keep reminders on your Mac or PC.** You can create reminders on your Mac or PC with Reminders (macOS Mountain Lion or later), or Tasks in Outlook. And if you're using iCloud, your reminders will always be up to date on all your devices.

That's about it. The Reminders app isn't a bad effort. If it lacks a feature or two that you desire, check out the myriad third-party to-do list apps in the App Store.

Loving the Lock Screen and Navigating Notifications

The lock screen is what you see when you first turn on or wake your iPad. You can quickly access the features and information you need most from the lock screen, even while the iPad is locked.

From the lock screen, you can do the following without unlocking your iPad first:

>> Swipe left to open the camera.

>> Swipe right to see today view (shown in Figure 12-5).

>> Drag down from the upper-right corner of the screen to open Control Center.

>> Swipe up from the center of the screen to see older notifications.

To fine-tune what you see on your lock screen, tap Settings ➪ Touch ID & Passcode. Here you can change settings for Today View, Recent Notifications, Control Center, and more.

When your iPad is locked, notifications appear on the lock screen; when it's unlocked, they appear at the top of the screen.

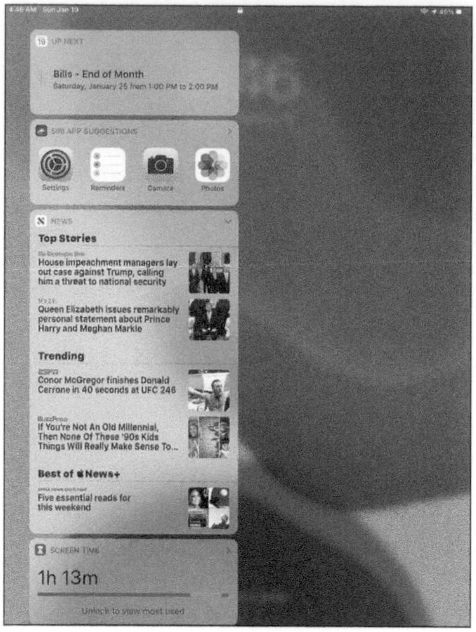

To summon older notifications to the forefront of your iPad screen when it's unlocked, all you need is the magical incantation — that is, a swipe from the top of the screen downward. Go ahead and give it a try. We'll wait.

Here's the rest of what you need to know about navigating notifications:

FIGURE 12-5:
The today view in all its splendor.

» **Open a notification on the lock screen.** Swipe right to open a notification with the appropriate app after authenticating with Touch ID, Face ID, or your passcode.

» **Open a notification on an unlocked iPad.** Tap the notification to open it in the appropriate program.

» **Edit or rearrange the widgets on the Today screen.** Tap the Edit button at the bottom of the screen (not shown in Figure 12-5).

» **Clear a single notification.** Swipe from right to left and then tap the Clear button.

» **Clear all notifications.** Swipe right to left to get to the Notification screen and then tap the little *x*-in-a-circle to the right of the section heading. The *x* turns into a Clear button; tap the Clear button and all notifications are cleared. If you have notifications from previous days, repeat this procedure for each one.

That's how to summon and use notifications. There's still a bit more to know — including how to change the notification settings for individual apps — but you have to wait until the chapter on settings (which happens to be Chapter 15).

Punching the Clock

Well, yes, most tablets do have a clock. But not every tablet has a *world clock* that lets you display the time in multiple cities on multiple continents. And not every device also has an alarm, a stopwatch, and a timer to boot.

So tap the Clock icon on your Home screen or in Control Center and see what the Clock app is all about.

World clock

Want to know the time in Beijing or Bogota? Tapping World Clock (in the Clock app) lets you display the time in numerous cities around the globe, as shown in Figure 12-6. When the clock face is dark, it's nighttime in the city you chose; if the face is white, it's daytime outside.

To add a city to the world clock, tap + in the upper-right corner and then use the virtual keyboard to start typing a city name.

The moment you press the first letter, the iPad displays a list of cities or countries that begin with that letter. Typing *v* brings up Andorra la Vella, Andora; Bantam Village, Cocos (Keeling) Islands; and Boa Vista, Brazil, among a myriad of other possibilities. You can create clocks for as many cities as you like, though only six cities at a time appear on-screen.

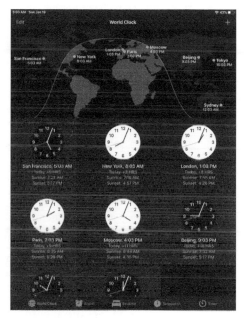

FIGURE 12-6:
What time is it in London?

To remove a city from the list, tap Edit and then tap the red circle with the white horizontal line that appears to the left of the city.

Alarm

Ever try to set the alarm in a hotel room? It's remarkable how complicated setting an alarm can be, on even the most inexpensive clock radio. Like almost everything else, the procedure is dirt-simple on the iPad:

1. **Tap Clock on the Home screen or Control Center to display the Clock app.**

2. **Tap the Alarm icon at the bottom of the screen.**

3. **Tap the + button in the upper-right corner of the screen.**

4. **Choose the time of the alarm by rotating the wheel in the Add Alarm overlay.**

   This step is similar to the action required to set the time that an event starts or ends on your calendar.

5. **Tap Save when the alarm settings are to your liking.**

That's what you can do with a regular alarm clock. What's the big deal, you say? Well, you can do even more with your iPad alarm:

>> **Set the alarm to go off on other days.** Tap Repeat and then tell the iPad the days you want the alarm to be repeated, as in Every Monday, Every Tuesday, Every Wednesday, and so on.

>> **Choose your own sound.** Tap Sound to choose the tone that will wake you up. You can even use songs from your Music library and any custom tones stored on your iPad.

   Your choice is a matter of personal preference, but we can tell you that the ringtone for the appropriately named Alarm managed to wake Ed from a deep sleep.

>> **Set the snooze to sleep in.** Tap Snooze on (showing green) to display a Snooze button along with the alarm. When your alarm goes off, you can tap the Snooze button to shut down the alarm for nine minutes.

>> **Name your alarm.** If you want to call the alarm something other than, um, Alarm, tap the Label field and use the virtual keyboard to type another descriptor.

TIP

Simple stuff, really. But if you want really simple, you can ask Siri to set the alarm for you. See Chapter 14 for how to use Siri.

You know that an alarm has been set and activated because of the tiny status icon (surprise, surprise — it looks like a clock) that appears on the status bar in the upper-right corner of the screen.

An alarm takes precedence over any tracks you're listening to on your iPad. Songs or videos with sound pause when an alarm goes off and resume when you turn off the alarm (or press the Snooze button).

WARNING

When your ring/silent switch is set to Silent, *your iPad still plays alarms from the Clock app.* It stays silent for FaceTime calls, alert sounds, or audio from apps. But it *will* play alarms from the Clock app.

Although it seems obvious, if you want to actually *hear* an alarm, you have to make sure that the iPad volume is turned up loud enough for you to hear.

Bedtime

The aptly named Bedtime feature in the Clock app is all about you getting a healthy and consistent night's sleep. To get started, you're asked a few simple questions, such as what time you would like to wake up, which days of the week the alarm should go off (the default is every day), and how many hours of sleep you need each night. You get to choose when to receive a bedtime reminder and which tone to hear when you wake up.

You can also get a good grasp on your sleep history by displaying data from your wakeup alarm, sleep trackers, and any other sleep data accumulated in HealthKit.

Stopwatch

If you're helping a loved one train for a marathon, the iPad Stopwatch function can provide an assist. Open it by tapping Stopwatch in the Clock app.

Just tap Start to begin the count, and then tap Stop when your trainee arrives at the finish line. You can also tap the Lap button to monitor the times of individual laps.

Timer

Cooking a hard-boiled egg or Thanksgiving turkey? Again, the iPad comes to the rescue. Tap Timer (in the Clock app) and then rotate the hour and minute wheels until the length of time you desire is highlighted. Tap the When Timer Ends button to choose the ringtone that will signify time's up.

After you set the length of the timer, tap Start when you're ready to begin. You can watch the minutes and seconds wind down on the screen. Or tap Pause to pause the countdown temporarily.

If you're doing anything else on the iPad — admiring photos, say — you hear the ringtone and see a *Timer Done* message on the screen at the appropriate moment. Tap OK to silence the ringtone.

Controlling Smart Appliances with Home

The Home app is all about managing HomeKit accessories, which fit into a broader tech trend of connecting devices known as the *Internet of Things (IoT)*. HomeKit is Apple's framework for IoT accessories in and around the house. We're talking door locks, lightbulbs, thermostats, and various other products you might like to control with your iPad.

Just launch the Home app on your Home screen, and tap the Add Accessory button in the middle of your screen to get started. If you already have an accessory added to your Home app, tap + at the top of the screen and then tap Add Accessory to add more.

If the device has a HomeKit setup code, you can scan it from the Add Device screen. You can also enter the device's HomeKit code by hand. Be sure to set which room the device is in so you can control your devices by room. Figure 12-7 shows Bryan's Home setup, with several devices and scenes, which we talk more about shortly.

If you have an Apple TV or Home-Pod, you can use it as a hub for your HomeKit accessories and access and control most devices from anywhere with Internet access. Without Apple TV or HomePod, you can control your accessories only when you're iPad is connected to the same Wi-Fi network.

Home scenes allow you to control multiple devices, set timers, or even add geolocation data to your controls.

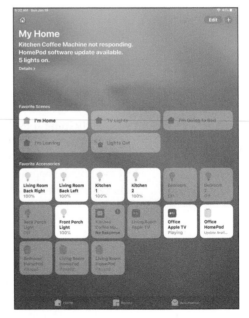

FIGURE 12-7:
The Home app lets you control HomeKit smart devices.

For example, Bryan set up the I'm Going to Bed scene to turn on his bedroom lights and turn off all other lights in the house. His I'm Leaving scene turns on the porch lights and turns off all other lights in his home. You can use Siri to activate any scene or device by name, such as "Hey Siri, I'm going to bed."

To create a scene, tap + at the top right of the screen, and then tap Add Scene. Then choose which devices and other parameters you want for your scene.

At the bottom of the Home app are three tabs, Home, Rooms, and Automation:

>> **Home:** Displays all scenes and devices (refer to Figure 12-7).

>> **Rooms:** Shows scenes and devices by room. Tap the menu icon in the upper-left to change the displayed room.

>> **Automation:** Offers a more exciting way to control your smart devices. With Home app automation, you can set devices or scenes to occur based on time; people arriving or leaving; or info from a sensor (if a HomeKit-enabled sensor is installed). To create an automation, tap + in the upper right, and then set the devices and parameters you want to control.

Measuring with the Measure App

NEW

We think the Measure app is nothing short of magical. You can use it and your iPad's camera to make very accurate measurements. Seriously!

Tap the Measure app icon on the Home screen. The screen is taken over by a view from your iPad's camera with instructions to Move iPad to Start. As you do so, your iPad is getting a fix on its surroundings. The Measure app will draw dotted lines around certain shapes. You can tap within those dotted lines to get measurements, as shown in Figure 12-8. In the middle of those measurements, the app even provides the area of the shape, 11 square inches in this case. We think that's pretty darned cool.

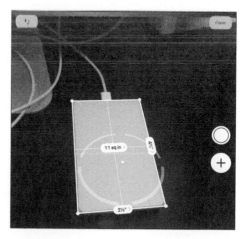

FIGURE 12-8:
Measure things with just your iPad and the Measure app.

You can also plot your own points by tapping the +-in-a-circle on the right side of the screen. Add additional points, and the Measure app will give you those measurements. Think about all those times when you wished you had a ruler or measuring tape with you. With the Measure app, now you do!

Sharing your connection (Personal Hotspot)

The personal hotspot is a feature that lets your iPad with Wi-Fi + Cellular share its cellular high-speed data connection with other devices, including computers, iPod touches, and other iPads.

REMEMBER

If your iPad is Wi-Fi only, feel free to skip this section — the Personal Hotspot option is available only on cellular iPads.

To enable your personal hotspot and share your cellular data connection with others, do the following:

1. **On the Home screen, tap Settings ⇨ Personal Hotspot.**
2. **Tap the Allow Others to Join switch to enable it (it will turn green).**
3. **Tap Wi-Fi Password and create or change the password for the Wi-Fi network you create.**

Now Wi-Fi, Bluetooth, or USB-enabled devices can join your hotspot network and share your iPad's cellular data connection.

REMEMBER

Your personal hotspot network adopts your iPad's name, which is *Bryan's iPad Pro* in Figure 12-9.

Most carriers offer support for personal hotspots in some or all of their data plans in the United States. Some don't, so check with your carrier if you don't see a Personal Hotspot option in the Settings app (and, of course, if your iPad has cellular capabilities).

WARNING

Some carriers don't charge extra for this feature, but the data used by connected devices counts against your monthly data plan allotment.

FIGURE 12-9:
Devices can
join this
network
via Wi-Fi,
Bluetooth,
or USB.

To see how much cellular data you're using, tap Settings ⇨ Cellular Data and scroll down until you see Cellular Data Usage, which displays your cellular usage for the current period as well as data used while roaming.

Dropping In on AirDrop

At various points when you're using your iPad, you encounter AirDrop, a fast, safe, and secure (through encryption) wireless method of sharing photos, videos, contacts, documents, and more with people you are close to physically.

You just tap the share icon (shown in the margin) in any app that offers one. AirDrop exploits both Wi-Fi and Bluetooth. No advanced setup is required.

REMEMBER

To be part of an AirDrop exchange, you and the recipient must be using an iPhone or iPad running iOS 7 or later, including iPadOS, or a Mac running macOS Yosemite or later.

Taking advantage of this clever feature involves three simple steps:

1. **Turn on the AirDrop feature (if it's not on already) in Settings ⇨ General ⇨ AirDrop.**

You have the option to make your device visible to Everyone (within the vicinity) or just to your contacts.

2. **Tap the share icon when it presents itself in an app, and then choose the file or files you want to share.**

NEW

3. **Choose someone who has the AirDrop icon added to his or her avatar.**

   In Figure 12-10, Bryan's iMac, which he named The Core, is first in his list. To see all nearby unlocked Apple devices with AirDrop activated, tap the AirDrop icon below the row of possible recipients.

Yes, you can choose more than one person. People in range who are eligible to receive the file are represented on your iPad by a circle.

The AirDrop process hath begun. The people on the receiving end will get a prompt asking them to accept the picture, video, or whatever it is you're offering them, as shown in Figure 12-11.

FIGURE 12-10:
Tap someone sporting an AirDrop icon to send him or her an item.

Assuming they take kindly to your offer and grant permission (by tapping Accept rather than Decline), the file lands on their devices in short order, where it is routed to its proper location. That is, a picture or video ends up in the Photos app, a contact in the Contacts app, and the Passbook pass in the Passbook app.

FIGURE 12-11:
Bob is about to receive a photo via AirDrop.

Chapter **13**

iPad: Your Multitasking and Productivity Powerhouse

The iPad has come such a long way since Steve Jobs introduced it in 2010. For years, the iPad was a great device for consuming, whether you were listening to music, reading books, browsing the web, shopping, watching videos, TV, and movies, or playing games. Now the iPad is also a great productivity device, and with the great multitasking features in iPadOS, you might be surprised at how much you can do.

In this chapter, we show you some of the great multitouch features built into iPadOS, including split view, the importance of external accessories, and some of the great productivity apps available.

Working with Multitouch and Gestures

We explain in Chapter 2 the main gestures and multitouch commands you can use on your iPad. If you need to, take a moment and refresh yourself about those gestures now. It's okay; we'll wait until you return.

In this chapter, we talk about the *importance* of those gestures and multitouch commands. Swiping, tapping, tapping and dragging, tapping and holding, multifinger swipes, pinching, and zooming — these features are key to getting the most from your iPad. And after you make gestures and multitouch commands habitual, navigating and controlling your iPad will be faster, more efficient, and easier than ever.

In our experience it doesn't take too much practice for those gestures and multitouch controls to become second nature. We've been amazed at how intuitive even young children find gestures, and those of us with a few more years under our belts quickly get to the point where we don't even think about the gestures we're using.

TIP

As gestures become second nature, don't be surprised if you find yourself swiping and tapping places where you can't use them. Bryan, for instance, has tapped a word in a physical book to look up its definition. You may also start expecting every screen to be a touchscreen. If you find yourself doing that sort of thing, just laugh it off and remind yourself that it's a sign of how life-changing your iPad really is.

TECHNICAL STUFF

THE POWER INSIDE YOUR iPad

iPads are unbelievably powerful. In some ways they're even faster than a lot of MacBook and PC models, with amazing raw processing and graphics capabilities.

All that power starts with Apple's homegrown chip designs and how the company can use those chips in ways no other company can because Apple controls the hardware and the software. You don't have to know the ins and out of these processors to take advantage of your iPad's power, but for those curious about why we say the iPad is powerful, let's take a closer look.

Apple designed its own line of processors for the iPad and iPhone that are based on the ARM (Advanced RISC Machines) architecture. ARM processors are especially good for mobile devices because they use less power than the x86 processors that power most Macs and PCs today. Apple has its own team of chip designers who have quietly revolutionized the mobile processing space.

At the time we were putting this book together, the Apple A12X Bionic CPU powered the iPad Pro (11-inch) and iPad Pro 12.9-inch (3rd generation). iPad Air (2019) and iPad mini (5th generation) use the A12 Bionic processor, while iPad (2019) uses the A10 Fusion processor. All three processors are 64-bit, and Apple was the first company to bring 64-bit processing to mobile devices. You, gentle reader, don't need to know what 64-bit processing is to enjoy your iPad, but the really simple explanation is that 64-bit processors can use more RAM.

Another technology that makes today's iPads powerful is that they contain the M-series motion embedded coprocessors. Again, you don't really have to know what an embedded coprocessor does to enjoy the fruits of its labor, but the short version is that they take data from all the sensors inside your iPad and make it easier for your apps to use that data.

The Neural Engine is another amazing feature of the Apple A12X processor in iPad Pro (11-inch) and iPad Pro 12.9-inch (3rd generation). The Neural Engine handles a lot of the machine learning your iPad does, including Siri tasks, image analyzing, and more.

We can't forget the graphics capabilities of the processors inside the current lineup of iPads. Multiple cores and Apple's Metal technology — special calculations developers can use for advanced graphics — mean that Apple's iPads offer the best graphics and image processing of any tablet on the market.

Whew! Look at all that technical stuff! But here's what it all means: Apple's iPads are powerful devices capable of doing some heavy lifting. You can edit photos and movies, create spreadsheets and presentations, write, produce music, and when you need a break, play some great games. Hey, mental relaxation is an important part of staying productive, and you can tell your boss we said so. Just don't get mad if your boss disagrees.

Checking Out Split View and Slide Over

One of the most important multitasking features Apple brought to the iPad is split view and slide over. We showed you how to do both in Chapter 2. Here, we go into how these features can increase your productivity.

Many activities on your iPad work best as full-screen apps. But other activities are much easier, more efficient, or more productive when you can have apps running side by side, as shown in Figure 13-1. For instance, taking notes on a book, from a web page, or maybe about an image can be much easier when you have the source material open on one part of your screen and your note-taking app open in the other part of your screen.

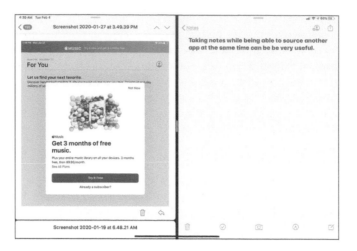

FIGURE 13-1:
Split view
greatly
increases
productivity on
your iPad.

Or imagine wanting to paint an image based on a photograph. Having the photo open on one part of your screen is probably way better for you than switching back and forth between apps. Web developers might have their coding environment open in one part of their screen and the live web page open in the other.

Even keeping Messages or another messaging app open for a chat while you're working in another app can be convenient — and the same is true with Slack, Trello, and other collaborative apps.

The possibilities are endless when using split view and slide over, and iPadOS makes it easy. If you need to refresh yourself on how they work, head back to Chapter 2 and check it out.

Increasing Your Productivity with a Keyboard

If you want to do a lot of typing on your iPad, consider using an external keyboard. We talk about Apple's Smart Keyboard and Magic Keyboard in Chapter 17, and many third-party iPad keyboards are available, too.

The built-in virtual keyboard that is part of iPadOS is fine for many circumstances, especially for short tasks such as entering search terms, sending iMessages, and even making notes and entering information in Calendar. And, in a pinch, even writing much longer passages is doable on the virtual keyboard.

But if you want to write papers, essays, reports, or other longer documents, an external keyboard can be a real game changer. The larger keyboard, the tactile feedback of physical keys, and more screen real estate dedicated to your work (rather than to the virtual keyboard) can dramatically increase your productivity.

TIP

If you're going to use a physical keyboard with your iPad, make sure you have a stand or case with a built-in kickstand (see Figure 13-2) so you can prop your iPad up while you use the keyboard. We show you some stands and cases in Chapter 17.

And we'll take a moment to emphasize the possibilities inherent in something you might already have lying around: any old Bluetooth keyboard. If you can connect it to your iPad, you can use it to input text. For instance, our friend Kelly Guimont from *The Mac Observer* throws her Apple Magic Keyboard — the short, aluminum wireless keyboard without a number keypad — into her bag when she goes out to work on her iPad, and it works perfectly for her. Plus, she already owned it, meaning she didn't have to pay for something new.

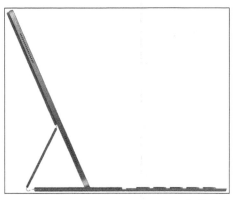

Credit: Apple

FIGURE 13-2:
Apple's Smart Keyboard Folio has a built-in kickstand for a good viewing angle.

Looking at Productivity Apps

We close our look at the iPad as a productivity and multitasking powerhouse by talking about some important productivity apps:

>> **Pages, Numbers, and Keynote:** Apple's productivity suite — Pages, Numbers, and Keynote — is terrific. In fact, we believe most people will find these apps to be everything they need for all but the most specific business tasks. Lists, budgets, letters, newsletters, flyers, spreadsheets, and what are demonstrably the best looking presentations can all be built with Apple's apps. And they're free. Just download them from the App Store if you don't already have them.

>> **Microsoft Office Apps:** Microsoft Office remains the king of business productivity suites, and while we stand by our assertion that most people will find Apple's apps to be everything they need, some people need, or just want,

to use Microsoft's tools. Word, Excel, PowerPoint, OneNote, and OneDrive are all available for iPad, allowing you to work on corporate documents right on your iPad. Complete feature access for these apps requires an Office 365 subscription.

>> **Adobe Photoshop and Adobe Lightroom:** Adobe launched Photoshop on iPad in 2019, and while it's been met with mixed reviews (3.8 rating on the App Store as of this writing), it does bring support for Photoshop Documents (PSD files) to iPad. For many people, that alone is worth the monthly subscription necessary for full feature access. Lightroom — Adobe's asset manager app — is also available in the App Store, and it's a must-have for many creative professionals who are heavily invested in Adobe's creative professional apps.

>> **GarageBand:** The iPad is a great music creation and mixing device, and Apple's GarageBand for iPad is a big part of that. With GarageBand, you can do multitrack recording, capture input from MIDI instruments and microphones (with external accessories), use effects and other filters, and a lot more. If you're interested in making music on your iPad, check out Bob's *GarageBand For Dummies,* 2nd Edition (Wiley). Oh, and GarageBand is free in the App Store.

>> **PDF Expert:** Reading and editing PDF documents is important for many users; one of our favorite apps is PDF Expert by Readdle. PDF Expert allows you to read, annotate, edit, and share PDF documents. It has an intuitive interface and is a free download, with in-app purchases starting at $6.99 for unlocking different features.

>> **Scrivener:** Literature & Latte's Scrivener is Bryan's favorite writing app on the Mac and on the iPad, too. Its organizing features are legendary, and it lets you view your manuscript in chapters or scenes or as index cards. Scrivener also offers a ton of formatting and labeling options. And you can save states and do comparisons between those states — really, Scrivener is just amazing, and if you're serious about any type of long-form writing, check it out. Scrivener for iPad is $19.99.

>> **Procreate:** If art is your thing, you have some great apps to choose from. Procreate is one of the best for sketching and painting; we've heard artists rave about it for years. It's amazing with Apple Pencil, too. Procreate features tons of brushes and pallets, high-definition canvases, shapes, layers, vector text, onion skinning for animations, and a whole lot more. And it's just $9.99.

There are many more great productivity apps, creative apps, organizing apps, to-do apps, and other apps that will let you do more and more of your digital work on your iPad. Explore the App Store for the different areas that appeal to you, and you'll find something that will make you more productive on your iPad.

Chapter **14**

Taking iPad Controls Siri-ously

PadOS offers two main ways of controlling your iPad. The first is Control Center, a handy set of device settings you're most likely to use frequently. Features such as volume, airplane mode, quick music playback controls, brightness, screen locks, and mute are just a swipe down from the upper-right corner of your screen.

And then there's our first digital love, Siri, the intelligent, voice-activated virtual personal assistant living like a genie inside your iPad. She not only hears what you have to say but also attempts to figure out the intent of your words. Siri then does her darnedest to respond to your wishes. She — yes, it's a female voice unless you change it — can help you dictate and send a message, get directions, call a friend, discover who won the ballgame, tell you when a movie is playing, ID the song playing in the background, arrange a wake-up call, search the web, find a decent place to eat, help you pay money to a friend, remind you to do something based on your location, and lots more. Siri talks back, too, sometimes with humor and other times with attitude. And Apple is constantly making her smarter and more capable.

We'll resist saying much more about Siri until later in this chapter because first we're going to dive into Control Center.

Controlling Control Center

As its name suggests, Control Center is a repository for controls, tools, and settings you'll need frequently. To access Control Center, swipe down from the upper-right corner of your screen — any screen, even the lock screen.

Unless — and we bet you were waiting for some kind of *but* — an app disallows access to Control Center. If that's the case, you'll have to close that app by pressing the Home button or swiping up from the bottom of your screen to go back to your Home screen, and then swiping down from the upper-right corner.

NEW

The biggest change with Control Center in iPadOS is that it's no longer tied to App Switcher. When you open it by swiping down from the upper-right corner of your screen, it's just you, a blurry background version of whatever you had on your screen when you opened Control Center, and Control Center itself.

When you open Control Center, two group of icons appear, along with several more individual buttons. The first group is for the iPad's radios: airplane mode, cellular data (if your iPad is a Wi-Fi + Cellular model), Wi-Fi, and Bluetooth. If you have a Wi-Fi–only iPad, the cellular data icon is replaced with an AirDrop icon, as shown in Figure 14-1. If you press and hold down on that group, you'll get expanded controls that add AirDrop and Personal Hotspot, as shown in Figure 14-2, which was taken on an iPad with Wi-Fi + Cellular.

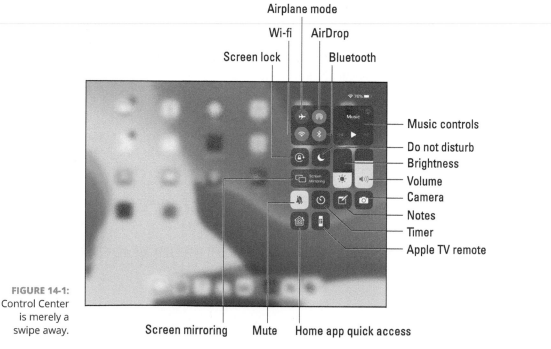

FIGURE 14-1:
Control Center
is merely a
swipe away.

The ability to tap and hold buttons or button groupings is a hallmark feature in Control Center. It allows iPadOS to give you expanded access when you need it, while keeping Control Center neat and tidy the rest of the time. Take a second to tap and hold all the buttons to see what's there!

TIP

Tapping the Wi-Fi or Bluetooth button in iPadOS's Control Center does not turn off those radios on your iPad. Instead, it disconnects your iPad from any connected Wi-Fi network or Bluetooth devices, respectively, while leaving the radios themselves on. To truly turn off those radios — say, to save battery life — you need to go to Settings.

FIGURE 14-2:
Expand Control Center groups and buttons by tapping and holding down.

Next to the radio controls are the music controls: previous, play, and next. Tap and hold down the music control block, and you get a volume slider, a slider for controlling where you are in the song, a list of AirPlay speakers or Apple TVs on your network, and an additional AirPlay icon for a different way of choosing AirPlay output.

Immediately below the music controls are brightness and volume sliders that look more like a thermometer metaphor than a slider metaphor. Tap and slide up or down on either control to change screen brightness and volume, respectively. If you tap and hold down on the volume slider, you'll just get a bigger volume slider and additional controls for AirPods Pro, if they're connected to your iPad. Tapping and holding down on the brightness slider will add buttons for Night Shift and True Tone, which we discuss in more depth in Chapter 15.

Stay with us, because there's more! To the left of the brightness and volume sliders are the screen lock icon and the do not disturb icon. You can tap the do not disturb icon to immediately activate or deactivate that mode, or tap and hold the icon for additional do not disturb options. Below these icons is an icon for activating screen mirroring, where you can choose an Apple TV or other compatible device to mirror your iPad's screen.

Below these icons a collection of other icons, a sort of a catch-all for everything else: mute, timer, notes, camera, Home app, and Apple TV remote, as shown in Figure 14-1. Not shown in Figure 14-1 is the flashlight icon, which is available on iPads with a rear camera flash. All of these icons expand when you tap and hold them. The expanded camera control is particularly useful because it has options for Take Selfie, Record Video, Record Slo-Mo, and Take Photo.

And this is where things get customizable. Choose Settings ⇨ Control Center ⇨ Customize Controls. You'll get a list of controls specific to your iPad that you can remove or add, including Accessibility Shortcuts, Alarm, Dark Mode, Guided Access, Magnifier, Hearing, Screen Recording, Stopwatch, and Text Size. Tap the red circle with a minus sign to remove a control. Tap the green circle with a plus sign to add a control. You can add all of them if you want, but your Control Center will be a mess. Also, you can rearrange the order of these icons by tapping the three little lines next to any control and dragging it where you want.

TIP

You can permit or deny access to Control Center on the lock screen in Settings. Go to Settings ⇨ Touch ID & Passcode ⇨ Allow Access When Locked, and toggle Control Center on or off.

Summoning Siri

TIP

REMEMBER

WARNING

You can't turn Siri off, but you can control how you access her in Settings ⇨ Siri & Search. You'll see toggles for Listen for "Hey Siri," Press Home for Siri, and Allow Siri When Locked. We look at each of these methods in this section.

Siri requires Internet access.

A lot of factors go into Siri's accuracy in understanding you, including surrounding noises and unfamiliar accents. You also need to be comfortable with the fact that Apple is recording what you say, though the company anonymizes Siri data through something called differential privacy, which allows Apple to collect anonymized data and mix it with noise in such a way that it can't be tracked back to individual users.

You can call Siri into action in a few ways. The traditional way is to press and hold down the Home button (or the sleep/wake button if you own an iPad Pro with Face ID) until you hear a tone. Pretty simple, eh? Siri will then listen for your query, as shown in Figure 14-3. Start talking, and your question appears on-screen.

FIGURE 14-3:
Siri is eager to respond.

You can also summon Siri by merely saying, "Hey Siri." You can even keep going with your question or command by saying something like, "Hey Siri, FaceTime Mom."

Siri also responds when you press and hold down the call button on most Bluetooth headsets. If you have Apple AirPods, two sharp taps on the outside of either AirPod will activate Siri. If you have AirPods Pro, you can use "Hey Siri."

What happens next is up to you. You can ask a wide range of questions or issue voice commands. If you didn't get your words out fast enough or you were misunderstood, tap the microphone icon at the bottom of the screen and try again.

Siri relies on voice recognition and artificial intelligence (hers, not yours). The voice genie responds in a conversational manner, and Siri sounds amazing in iPadOS. But using Siri isn't always a hands-free experience. Spoken words are sometimes supplemented by information on the iPad screen (as you see in the next section).

Siri seeks answers using sources such as Google, Wikipedia, Yelp, Yahoo!, Open Table, Twitter, and WolframAlpha, making Siri your personal search agent for your iPad's content or outside information. For instance, ask Siri to find all the videos you shot at your kid's graduation party and she'll oblige (at least if you tagged them correctly).

Siri on the iPad can also launch apps — Apple's own as well as third-party apps. From your contacts, Siri might be able to determine who your spouse, coworkers, and friends are, as well as knowing where you live. You might say, "Show me how to get home," and Siri will fire up Maps to help you on your way. Or you can say, "Find a good Italian restaurant near Barbara's house," and Siri will serve up a list, sorted by Yelp rating. Using Open Table, Siri can even make a restaurant reservation.

Apple has also opened up Siri to third-party app producers. For example, you can have Siri arrange a ride through Uber or Lyft, or pay a debt on your behalf through apps such as Venmo or Square Cash, or through Apple Pay.

If you ask about a favorite sports team, Siri will retrieve the score of the team's last game or the game in progress. And if you're rummaging through a longish email that you can't quite get through at the moment, you can have Siri set a reminder for you to follow up later in the evening.

TIP

If you don't want Siri to have access to a particular app, just turn it off. For a list of apps, tap Settings ⇨ Siri & Search. Then tap any of your apps and you can turn off Siri support within that app.

Figuring Out What to Ask

The beauty of Siri is that there's no designated protocol you must follow when talking to her. Asking, "Will I need an umbrella tomorrow?" produces the same result as, "What is the weather forecast around here?" Although competing digital assistant platforms such as Amazon Alexa rely on training the user to say exactly the right thing to get a result, Siri has been trained to understand you. She makes her share of mistakes, of course, but Apple's long-view approach is making Siri better at understanding the meaning of your words.

Another cool feature is that Siri can identify the name and artist of the musical track that's playing. Just ask Siri what song is playing and she'll name that tune. When the song is properly identified, you even get a chance to buy it or play it.

If you're not sure what to ask, tap the ?-in-a-circle to list sample questions or commands, some shown in Figure 14-4. You can tap any of these examples to see even more samples.

FIGURE 14-4:
Siri can help out in many ways.

Here are some ways Siri can lend a hand . . . um, we mean a voice:

>> **FaceTime:** "FaceTime *phone number* my wife."

>> **Music:** "Play Frank Sinatra" or "Play Apple Music." "What song is this?" "Rate this song three stars."

>> **Messages:** "Send a message to Nancy to reschedule lunch."

>> **Apple Pay:** "Apple Pay $10 to Johnny Appleseed."

>> **Translation:** "Translate 'I miss you so' in French."

>> **Sports:** "Did the Warriors win?"

>> **Calendar:** "Set up a meeting for 9 a.m. to discuss funding."

>> **Reminders:** "Remind me to take my medicine at 8 a.m. tomorrow."

- **Maps:** "Find an ATM near here."
- **Mail:** "Mail the tenant about the recent rent check."
- **Photos:** "Show me the photos I took at Samuel's birthday party."
- **Stocks:** "What's Apple's stock price?"
- **Web search:** "Who was the 19th president of the United States?"
- **WolframAlpha:** "How many calories are in a blueberry muffin?"
- **Clock:** "Wake me up at 8:30 in the morning."
- **Trivia:** "Who won the Academy Award for Best Actor in 2003?"
- **Twitter:** "Send tweet, 'Going on vacation,' smiley-face emoticon" or "What is trending on Twitter?"

Correcting Mistakes

As we point out earlier, as good as Siri is, she sometimes needs to be corrected. Fortunately, you can correct her mistakes fairly easily. The simplest way is to tap the microphone icon and try your query again.

You can also tap your question on your iPad's screen to edit or fix what Siri thinks you said. If a word or phrase is underlined, you can use the keyboard to make a correction. Apple will also offer suggestions when you tap the underlined material: "Maybe you meant . . . ." After you have make the edit, tap Done on the virtual keyboard, and Siri will give you a new response based on that edit.

Siri also seeks your permission before sending a dictated message. That's a safeguard you might come to appreciate. If you need to modify the message, you can do so by saying such things as, "Change Tuesday to Wednesday" or "Add: I'm excited to see you, exclamation mark" — obligingly, *I'm excited to see you!* will be added.

Using Dictation

All iPads that run iPadOS offer a dictation function, so you can speak to your iPad and have the words you say translated into text. It's easy and works pretty well. Even if you're comfortable with the virtual keyboard or use an accessory keyboard, dictation is often the fastest way to get your words into your iPad.

When you want to use your voice to enter text, tap the microphone key on the virtual keyboard that appears in the app you're using. Begin speaking right away. A sound wave appears in place of the virtual keyboard as you talk.

The first time you tap the microphone key, a dialog appears asking if you want to enable dictation. Your humble authors are never shy about using our voices, so we happily agree. But why might you choose otherwise? Your voice input, contacts, and location are shared with Apple, which makes some people uncomfortable.

You can always enable or disable dictation later. Go to Settings ⇨ General ⇨ Keyboard and tap to turn the Enable Dictation switch on or off. You won't see the mic key on the keyboard.

REMEMBER

Dictation works only if you're connected to the Internet. If you're not connected, the microphone key will appear dimmed.

Some apps don't display the microphone key on the keyboard. If you don't see a microphone key, the app doesn't accept dictated input.

When you've finished dictating your text, tap Done to end the dictation and return to your regular keyboard.

TIP

Here are a couple of ways you can improve your dictation experience:

» You can speak punctuation by saying it. So, remember to say, "period," "question mark," or whatever at the end of your sentences. You can also insert commas, semicolons, dashes, and other punctuation by saying their names.

» The better your iPad hears you, the better your results will be:

• A wired headset with a microphone is great when you have a lot of ambient noise nearby.

• A Bluetooth headset or Apple's AirPods or AirPods Pro may be better than the built-in microphone.

• If you use the iPad's built-in mic, make sure the iPad case or your fingers aren't covering it.

WARNING

When dictation is enabled, information is shared with Apple's servers. This hasn't stopped your authors from taking advantage of dictation, but if you have particular privacy concerns, it's helpful to keep this in mind.

Making Siri Smarter

From Settings ⇨ Siri & Search ⇨ Language, you can tell Siri which language you want to converse in. Siri is available in English (with many country variations), as well as versions of Chinese, Danish, Dutch, Finnish, French, German, Hebrew, Italian, Japanese, Korean, Malay, Norwegian, Portuguese, Russian, Spanish, Swedish, Thai, and Turkish.

You can also request voice feedback from Siri all the time, or just when you're using a hands-free headset. If you want, you can silence the feedback when the mute switch is on. You'll still get voice feedback if using the Hey Siri command.

In the My Info field in Settings, you can tell Siri who you are. When you tap My Info, your contacts list appears. Tap your own name in Contacts.

You can also choose whether Siri has a male or female voice. If you're using English, you can even choose Siri's accent: American, Australian, British, Indian, Irish, or South African.

WARNING

You can call upon Siri from the lock screen too. (That's the default setting, anyway.) Consider this feature a mixed blessing. Not having to type a passcode to get Siri to do her thing is convenient. On the other hand, if your iPad ends up with the wrong person, he or she would be able to use Siri to send an email or message in your name, post to Facebook, or tweet, bypassing whatever passcode security you thought was in place. If you find this potential scenario scary, tap Settings ⇨ Siri & Search and turn off the option for Allow Siri When Locked so that it's white instead of green. For more on Settings, read Chapter 15.

5
The Undiscovered iPad

Explore every single iPad setting that's not discussed in depth elsewhere in the book. By the time you finish reading Chapter 15, you'll know how to customize every part of your iPad that can be customized.

Peruse our comprehensive guide to troubleshooting the iPad, which details what to do when almost anything goes wrong, complete with step-by-step instructions for specific situations.

Gaze longingly at some of the iPad accessories we use and recommend, including physical keyboards, earphones and headphones, and speakers. No, this stuff's not included with your iPad, but we consider most of it essential just the same.

IN THIS CHAPTER

» **Apple ID settings**

» **Taking off in airplane mode**

» **Figuring out your location**

» **Keeping the clan together through Family Sharing**

» **Finding a lost iPad**

Chapter **15**

Setting You Straight on Settings

D
o you consider yourself a control freak? The type of person who has to have it your way? Boy, have you landed in the right chapter.

Settings is kind of the makeover factory for the iPad. You open Settings by tapping its Home screen icon; from there, you can do things such as change the tablet's background or wallpaper and specify your search engine of choice. You can also alter security settings in Safari, tailor email to your liking (among other modifications), and get a handle on how to fetch or push new data.

TIP

The Settings area on the iPad is roughly analogous to System Preferences on a Mac or the Control Panel in Windows, with a hearty serving of app preferences thrown in for good measure.

But you won't have to visit Settings in every case because Control Center (see Chapter 14) grants you immediate access to several commonly used settings and controls. That includes airplane mode, sound, and display brightness, which we address in this chapter. But even with Control Center, expect to make some tweaks in Settings from time to time. Because we cover some settings elsewhere in this book, we don't dwell on every setting here. Nor do we describe every setting in the order in which Apple lists them. But you still have plenty to digest to help you make the iPad your own.

Checking Out the Settings Screen

When you first open Settings, you see a display that looks something like Figure 15-1, with a scrollable list on the left side of the screen and a pane on the right that corresponds to whichever setting is highlighted in blue. We say "something like" because Settings on your iPad may differ slightly from what is shown here.

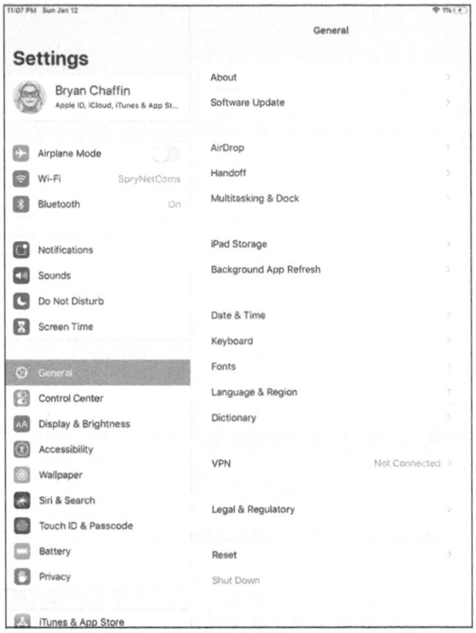

You must scroll down to see the entire list. Also, if you see a greater-than symbol (>) to the right of a listing, the listing has a bunch of options. Throughout this chapter, you tap the > symbol to check out those options.

As you scroll to the bottom of the list on the left, you come to all the settings pertaining to some of the specific third-party apps you've added to the iPad. (See Chapter 10.) These settings aren't visible in Figure 15-1.

FIGURE 15-1:
Your list of settings.

Everybody has a different collection of apps on his or her iPad, so settings related to those programs will also be different.

Apple ID Settings

The first thing you'll notice in the Settings app is the section at the top with your Apple ID info. You'll see your name, the avatar you selected when you set up your device, and a partial description of the settings available in your Apple ID settings.

Tap your Apple ID settings, and you'll find a variety of settings for both your Apple ID and Apple services, as shown in Figure 15-2:

>> **Personal details:** Edit your name, phone numbers, and email addresses associated with your Apple ID.

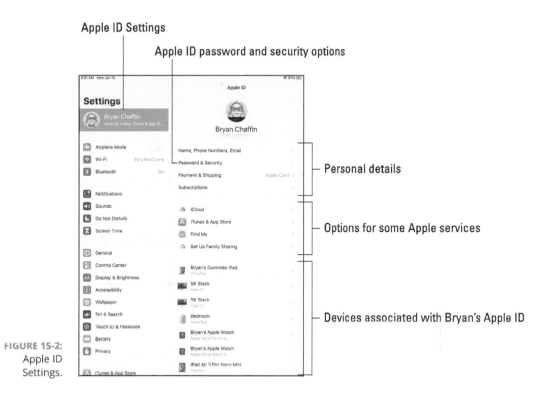

Apple ID Settings

Apple ID password and security options

Personal details

Options for some Apple services

Devices associated with Bryan's Apple ID

FIGURE 15-2:
Apple ID
Settings.

>> **Password & Security:** Reset your password, manage a trusted phone number for your Apple ID account, and turn on or off two-factor authentication. (We recommend that you turn it on.)

>> **Payment & Shipping:** Manage which credit cards you have attached to your iCloud account, including a place for you to enter your shipping address for Apple Store purchases.

>> **iCloud:** The amount of total and available storage. Tap Manage Storage to, well, manage your iCloud storage, taking note of all your iOS and iPadOS backups. If need be, you can buy more storage. Tap Change Storage Plan to get started.

>> **iTunes & App Store:** A shortcut to the iTunes & App Store section, described later in this chapter.

>> **Find My:** Manage the Find My feature specific to the device you're using at the moment. You can also set which of your Apple devices is used to determine where you are when it comes to sharing your location. You can also see everyone you might have shared your location with.

>> **Set Up Family Sharing:** Manage or set up your iCloud Family Sharing plan.

>> **Device list:** View a handy list of every device associated with your Apple ID. Tap through to any of them and you'll see the device's Find My settings, model name, operating system version, and serial number. You can also remove any device from your account except the iPad you're using.

>> **Sign Out:** Sign out of your Apple ID and erase data on the iPad associated with that Apple ID. You may have to scroll down to see this option.

Flying with Sky-High Settings

Your iPad offers settings to keep you on the good side of air-traffic communications systems. No matter which iPad you have — Wi-Fi only or a model with cellular — you have airplane mode.

Using a cellular radio or Wi-Fi on an airplane is restricted to when the pilot says it's okay. But nothing is wrong with using an iPad on a plane to read, listen to music, watch videos, peek at pictures, or play games. To do so, however, you first need to enable airplane mode by tapping the toggle next to Airplane Mode in Settings. You'll know it's on rather than off when you see green instead of gray on the switch.

Enabling airplane mode disables each of the iPad's wireless radios: Wi-Fi, cellular, and Bluetooth (depending on the model). While your iPad is in airplane mode, you can't surf the web, get a map location, send or receive emails, sync through iCloud, use the iTunes or App Store, or do anything else that requires an Internet connection. If a silver lining exists here, it's that the iPad's long-lasting battery will last even longer — good news if the flight you're on is taking you halfway around the planet.

 The appearance of a tiny airplane icon on the status bar at the upper-right corner of the screen reminds you that airplane mode is turned on. Just remember to turn it off when you're back on the ground.

TIP
If in-flight Wi-Fi is available on your flight, which is increasingly the case, you can turn on Wi-Fi independently, leaving the rest of your iPad's wireless radio safely disabled. And it's a breeze to do by toggling the setting in Control Center. Bluetooth, which we get to shortly, can also be enabled independently.

Controlling Wi-Fi Connections

Wi-Fi is typically the fastest wireless network you can use to surf the web, send email, and perform other Internet tricks on the iPad. You use the Wi-Fi setting to determine which Wi-Fi networks are available to you and which one to join.

Tap Wi-Fi so that the setting is on, and all Wi-Fi networks in range are displayed, as shown in Figure 15-3.

TIP

Tap the Wi-Fi switch off (gray) whenever you don't have access to a network and don't want to drain the battery. You can easily toggle Wi-Fi on and off in Control Center. When you're in a hotel, at an airport, or at another location, you might still have to enter a password after joining even if the lock link is not present.

A signal-strength indicator can help you choose the network to connect to if more than one is listed; tap the appropriate Wi-Fi network when you reach a decision. If a network is password-protected, you see a lock icon and need the passcode to access it.

FIGURE 15-3:
Check out your Wi-Fi options.

WARNING

Be careful when joining open networks (such as those in coffee shops or other public places) as well as networks you don't know. Malicious actors might try to snoop on any unencrypted data on a network you don't control.

You can also turn on and off the Ask to Join Networks setting. However, networks your iPad is already familiar with are joined automatically, whether the Ask to Join Networks feature is toggled on or off. If the Ask feature is off and no known networks are available, you have to select a new network manually. If the Ask feature is on, your iPad will ask if you want to join new networks as they become available. Either way, you see a list with the same Wi-Fi networks in range.

The iPad also remembers passwords for frequently used networks.

If you used a particular network automatically in the past but no longer want your iPad to join it, tap the *i*-in-a-circle next to the network in question (in Wi-Fi settings) and then tap Forget This Network. The iPad develops a quick case of selective amnesia.

TECHNICAL STUFF

In some instances, you have to supply other technical information about a network you hope to glom onto. You encounter a bunch of nasty-sounding terms: DHCP, BootP, Static, IP Address, Subnet Mask, Router, DNS, Search Domains, Client ID, and HTTP Proxy. Chances are none of this info is on the tip of your tongue — but that's okay. For one thing, it's a good bet that you'll never need to know this stuff. What's more, even if you *do* have to fill in or adjust these settings, a network administrator or techie friend can probably help you.

Sometimes you may want to connect to a network that's closed and not shown on the Wi-Fi list. If that's the case, tap Other and use the keyboard to enter the network name. Then tap to choose the type of security setting the network is using (if any). Your choices are WEP, WPA, WPA2, WPA Enterprise, and WPA2 Enterprise. Again, the terminology isn't the friendliest, but we figure that someone nearby can lend a hand.

WARNING

Connecting to unfamiliar open networks carries risks. Malicious hackers may be able to get to your personal or business data. Be careful when joining unknown networks, especially open ones.

If no Wi-Fi network is available, you have to rely on a cellular connection if you have capable models. If you don't — or you're out of reach of a cellular network — you can't rocket into cyberspace until you regain access to a network.

Getting Fired Up over Bluetooth

Of all the peculiar terms you may encounter in techdom, *Bluetooth* is one of our favorites. The name is derived from Harald Blåtand, a tenth-century Danish monarch, who, the story goes, helped unite warring factions. And, we're told, *Blåtand* translates to *Bluetooth* in English. (Bluetooth is all about collaboration between different types of devices — get it?)

Blåtand was ahead of his time. Although we can't imagine he ever used a tablet computer, he now has an entire short-range wireless technology named in his honor. On the iPad, you can use Bluetooth to communicate wirelessly with a compatible Bluetooth headset, such as Apple's AirPods and AirPods Pro, or to use an optional wireless keyboard, such as Apple's Smart Keyboard. Such accessories are made by Apple and others.

To ensure that your iPad works with a Bluetooth device, it typically has to be wirelessly *paired*, or coupled, with the chosen device. If you're using a third-party accessory, follow the instructions that came with that device so it becomes *discoverable*, or ready to be paired with your iPad. Then turn on Bluetooth (on the Settings screen) so that the iPad can find such nearby devices and the device can find the iPad.

In Figure 15-4, an Apple wireless keyboard and the iPad are successfully paired when you enter a designated passkey on the keyboard. You won't need a passkey to pair every kind of device, though. You can't, for example, enter a passkey when pairing the iPad with a wireless speaker. Most Bluetooth devices work up to a range of about 30 feet and don't require line of sight.

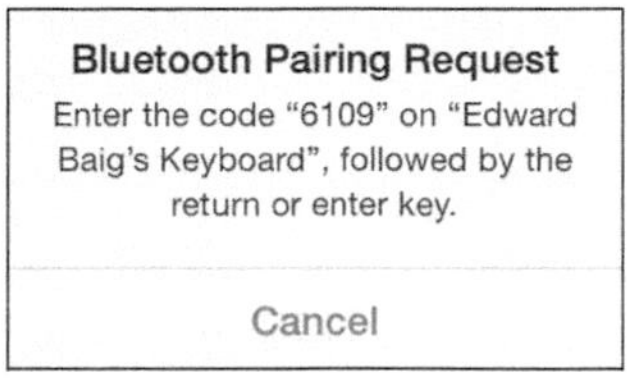

Bluetooth Pairing Request

Enter the code "6109" on "Edward Baig's Keyboard", followed by the return or enter key.

Cancel

FIGURE 15-4:
Pairing an Apple wireless keyboard with the iPad.

Unless you turn it off, Bluetooth is on by default. To see if it's on, pull down from the top-right corner of the screen to access Control Center. The Bluetooth icon (shown in the margin) shows blue in Control Center when Bluetooth is on. Tap the Bluetooth icon in Control Center so that it turns white to disconnect any Bluetooth devices currently connected to your iPad. Note, however, that this does not turn off Bluetooth on your iPad — it only disconnects from connected devices. To turn off Bluetooth, which saves battery life, go to Settings ⇨ Bluetooth and toggle Bluetooth from green to gray.

While you're in Settings ⇨ Bluetooth, check out the list of Bluetooth devices you've previously paired to your iPad. To unpair a device, select it from the device list by tapping the *i*-in-a-circle icon, and then tap Forget This Device. We guess breaking up *isn't* hard to do.

The iPad can tap into Bluetooth in other ways. One is through *peer-to-peer* connectivity, so you can engage in multiplayer games with other nearby iPad, iPhone, or iPod touch users. You can also exchange business cards, share pictures, and send short notes. In addition, you don't even have to pair the devices as you do with a headset or wireless keyboard.

TECHNICAL STUFF

You can't use Bluetooth to exchange files or sync between an iPad and a computer. Nor can you use it to print stuff from the iPad on a Bluetooth printer (although the AirPrint feature handles that chore in some instances). That's because the iPad doesn't support any of the Bluetooth *profiles* (or specifications) required to allow such wireless stunts to take place — at least not as of this writing. We think that's a shame.

You may also see devices that communicate with the iPad through a flavor of Bluetooth called Bluetooth Low Energy (BLE), Bluetooth Smart, or Bluetooth Smart Ready. Apple's iBeacon technology is based on BLE and is a way to tap into your location, another topic for later in this chapter.

You can wirelessly share files also through AirDrop, as noted in Chapter 12 and elsewhere in this book.

Roaming among Cellular Data Options

You see another group of settings only if you have a cellular model iPad. The options appear on the right pane of the Settings screen when you highlight Cellular Data on the left:

>> **Cellular Data:** If you know you don't need the cellular network when you're out and about or are in an area where you don't have access to the network, turn it off. Your battery will thank you later. But even if you have access to a speedy cellular network, be prudent; in a 4G environment where you can easily consume gobs of data, your data allowance may run out all too quickly. And if you haven't set up your cellular data plan yet, you can get started by tapping the carrier of your choice directly in Settings ⇨ Cellular Data. Data rates apply.

>> **Data Roaming:** You may unwittingly rack up lofty roaming fees when exchanging email, surfing with Safari, or engaging in other data-heavy activities while traveling abroad. Turn off Data Roaming to avoid such potential charges.

TIP

>> **Manage Account:** Tap Manage *your carrier* Account to see or edit your account information or to add more data.

>> **Add a SIM PIN:** The tiny *SIM,* or *Subscriber Identity Module,* card inside your iPad with cellular holds important data about your cellular account. To add a PIN or a passcode to lock your SIM card, tap SIM PIN. That way, if someone gets hold of your SIM, he or she can't use it in another iPad without the passcode.

REMEMBER

If you assign a PIN to your SIM, you have to enter it to turn the iPad on or off, which some might consider a minor hassle. And be aware that the SIM PIN is different from and may be in addition to any passcode you set for the iPad, as described later in this chapter.

>> **Cellular Data:** You can use your cellular connection for iCloud documents, iTunes, a Safari reading list, and most third-party apps. You can see just how much data you're using on your apps and, if need be, shut down an app that's

sucking up way too much. You can also decide whether or not to use cellular connections for FaceTime. Use the setting at the bottom of the Cellular Data panel to turn on Wi-Fi Assist, which lets your iPad automatically employ cellular data when your Wi-Fi connection is poor.

>> **Personal Hotspot:** Share your iPad's data connection with any other devices you carry. Just know that extra charges may apply — and even if they don't, you'll rack up that much extra data. You or the owner of the device piggybacking on your Internet connection must enter the designated password generated by the iPad for the Hotspot connection to make nice. You can use the hotspot feature via Wi-Fi or Bluetooth, or by connecting a Lightning-to-USB cable. See Chapter 12 to find out how to use Personal Hotspot.

Managing Notifications

Developers can send you alerts related to the apps you've installed on your iPad. Such alerts are typically in text form but may include sounds as well. The idea is that you'll receive notifications even when the app they apply to isn't running. Notifications may also appear as numbered badges on their corresponding Home screen icon. The downside to keeping push notifications turned on is that they can be distracting.

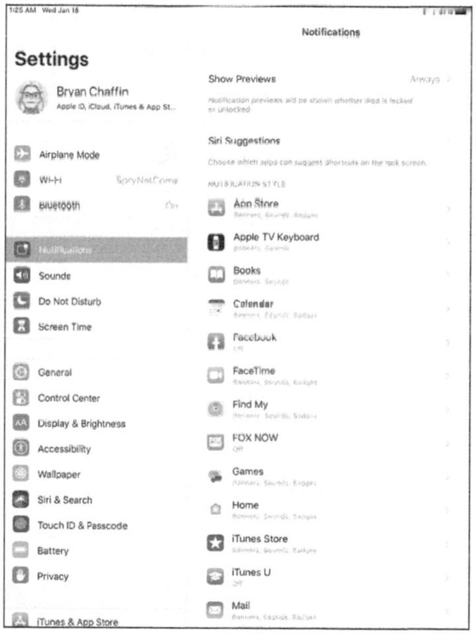

You manage notifications on an app-by-app basis. To do so, tap Notifications on the left side of the Settings screen, and then tap the app you want to manage. All installed apps that can take advantage of notifications (see Chapter 12) appear on the right, as shown in Figure 15-5. Tap an app and choose whether to Allow Notifications by enabling that option. If you choose

FIGURE 15-5:
Notify the iPad of your notification intentions.

not to permit notifications for select apps, you'll see the word *Off* in the list next to those app names.

Tap any app to adjust its settings. In Figure 15-6, you see notification settings for the Instagram app, as indicated by the word *Instagram* at the top of the screen. Some apps offer other options, including sound alerts, and other apps may offer fewer options.

To help you get started, here's a rundown of the options shown in Figure 15-6, starting at the top:

FIGURE 15-6:
Notification settings for Instagram.

>> **Allow Notifications:** Enable or disable notifications for the selected app. Straightforward enough.

>> **Alerts:** When notifications are allowed, all alert options — Lock Screen, Notification Center, and Banners — are enabled by default. Tap each one to activate or deactivate that style of alerts. Tap Banner Style at the bottom of the Alerts section to choose between temporary banners, which stay at the top of your screen for a few seconds before automatically disappearing, and persistent banners, which stay at the top of your screen until you perform an action, such as flicking them away or tapping them to go to the app.

>> **Sounds:** Choose from a variety of sounds for many Apple notifications. Apps such as Instagram, however, give you control over only whether or not you hear the sound they chose.

>> **Badges:** Display the number of pending alerts on the app's icon on your Home screen.

>> **Show Previews:** See a preview of whatever you're being notified about. In the case of Instagram, the preview would be a thumbnail image of the post you're being alerted about.

>> **Notification Grouping:** Choose between allowing your iPad to group notifications as it sees fit, to group them by app, or to simply turn Notification Grouping off for the selected app.

Apps that don't take advantage of the settings in Settings ➪ Notifications can still offer notifications, but you'll have to scroll down to the Apps section on the left side of Settings and tap the app you want to alter.

TIP

If you find you went overboard with notifications at first to the point where they become annoying or distracting, don't fret. You can always go back and redo any notifications you've set up.

Many notifications are interactive, so you can respond to them on the spot. For example, you can reply to an incoming email or iMessage without having to drop by the underlying app.

In the today view, you can make modifications without paying a separate visit to Settings. Open the today view by swiping from left to right on the lock screen, tap Edit at the bottom of the screen, and choose the widgets that should appear in this view. Tap the green circled + to add an available widget or the red circled dash to remove a widget. You can also determine the order in which widgets appear and whether to display them in the right or left column of the today view.

Sounds

Consider the Sounds settings area the iPad's soundstage. There, you can turn audio alerts on or off for a variety of functions: ringtones, text tones, new email, sent mail, calendar and reminder alerts, Facebook posts, tweets, and AirDrop. You can also decide whether you want to hear lock sounds and keyboard clicks.

You can alter the ringtone you hear for FaceTime calls and the text tone you hear for iMessages. If you want more, visit the iTunes Store to buy more, typically for $0.99 and $1.29 a pop. You can also create your own ringtones in GarageBand on an iPad.

TIP

To set a custom tone for individuals in the Contacts app, tap Contacts ➪ *your contact* ➪ Edit, and then tap either the Ringtone or the Text Tone option. Tap Done when you're finished.

To raise the decibel level of alerts, drag the ringer and alerts volume slider to the right. Drag in the opposite direction to bring down the noise. An alternative way to adjust sound levels is to use the physical volume buttons on the side of the iPad, as long as you're not already using the iPad's Music or Videos player to listen to music or watch video, respectively.

You can enable and disable the use of physical buttons to alter the volume by using the Change with Buttons switch, below the volume slider.

Do not disturb

Apple understands that sometimes you don't want to be bothered by notifications or other distractions, no matter how unobtrusive they might be. The result is a feature aptly named do not disturb, which you can find by tapping Settings ⇨ Do Not Disturb. Tap the toggle on Do Not Disturb to turn it on (green), and a moon icon appears in the status bar (shown in the margin). With do not disturb on, you can rest assured that your alerts are silenced until you turn the setting off. You can also activate and deactivate do not disturb by swiping down from the top-right corner of your screen to open Control Center and then tapping the moon icon to turn it on (white icon) or off (gray icon).

Other options in Settings ⇨ Do Not Disturb allow you to schedule when do not disturb kicks in and when it turns off. You can also tap Allow Calls From to permit incoming FaceTime calls or messages from everyone (or no one). If you enable the Repeated Calls switch, a second incoming FaceTime call from the same person within three minutes will not be silenced; the rationale is if the person is trying to reach you that badly, the call must be really important.

You get to make one more choice here: silence FaceTime calls and notifications always or only when the iPad is locked.

Location, Location, Location Services

By using the onboard Maps, Camera, or Find Friends app (or any number of third-party apps), the iPad makes good use of knowing where you are. With Location Services turned on, your iPad has the capability to deliver traffic information and suggest popular destinations in your vicinity. And at your discretion, you can share your location with others.

iPads with cellular capabilities use built-in GPS to help determine your location. The Wi-Fi–only iPad can find your general whereabouts by triangulating signals from Wi-Fi base stations.

If such statements creep you out a little, don't fret. To protect your right to privacy, individual apps pop up quick messages (similar to the warning presented by Maps, shown in Figure 15-7) asking whether you want them to use your current location. You can also turn off Location Services in Settings ⇨ Privacy ⇨ Locations Services.

FIGURE 15-7:
Maps wants to know where you are.

TIP

Be aware as well that some apps will ask for access when you're in the midst of using them. Consider the request carefully before allowing such access.

While visiting the Privacy setting, you may want to consult the privacy listings for individual apps and functions on your iPad: If any third-party apps request access to these services, they show up here.

Meantime, tap Settings ⇨ Privacy ⇨ Location Services to enable or disable various other location preferences, ranging from compass calibration to location-based Apple ads.

You can also choose to share your location with family members and friends in the Messages and Find My Friends apps, and as part of Family Sharing.

From time to time on the iPad, you can land in the same destination multiple ways. For example, you can access the same privacy settings via the restrictions settings that we address later in this chapter.

Settings for Your Senses

A number of settings control what the iPad looks and sounds like.

Display & Brightness

The brightness slider shown in Figure 15-8 appears when the Display & Brightness setting is highlighted. Who doesn't want a bright, vibrant screen? Alas, the brightest screens exact a trade-off: Before you drag the control to the max, remember that brighter screens sap the life from your battery more quickly.

TIP

That's why we recommend activating Auto-Brightness in Settings ⇨ Display & Brightness. This setting automatically adjusts the screen according to the lighting environment in which you're using the iPad, saving considerable battery power.

FIGURE 15-8:
Sliding this control adjusts screen brightness.

Another setting you'll find in Display & Brightness (for iPad Pro models) is True Tone. Turn it on and the iPad display can automatically adapt to ambient lighting conditions using special sensors in your iPad Pro.

The Night Shift setting is also found here (as well as in Control Center). As a reminder, it shifts the colors of the display after dark to help you get a good night's sleep, or so the theory goes.

If the app you're spending time in supports dynamic type, you can adjust the type size by dragging a slider. Under Display & Brightness, you'll also find a switch for making text bold.

Tap Auto-Lock under Display & Brightness, and you can set how much time elapses before the iPad automatically locks or turns off the display. Your choices are 15 minutes, 10 minutes, 5 minutes, or 2 minutes. Or you can set it so the iPad never locks automatically.

TIP

If you work for a company that insists on a passcode (see the next section), the Never Auto-Lock option isn't in the list that your iPad displays.

Home Screen & Dock

The Home Screen & Dock section has four different settings that can significantly change your overall iPad experience:

>> **App Icons:** Apple made it simple with this setting. Tap More to have smaller but more icons on each of your Home screens. Tap Bigger to have larger but fewer icons on each Home screen.

>> **Keep Today View on Home Screen:** Keep the today view slide-over panel on your Home screen at all times. In our experience, this works best with larger iPads, or in landscape mode, or both. Your mileage may vary, so experiment with it to see if you like it.

>> **Multitasking:** Reveal three key multitasking features, Allow Multiple Apps (learn more in Chapter 13), Picture in Picture (see Chapter 2), and Gestures (see Chapter 2). We recommend you enable all three of these features if they aren't on by default.

>> **Show Suggested and Recent Apps in Dock:** Display on the right side of the dock apps that Siri thinks you might want, as well as recently opened apps. Learn more about this feature in Chapter 1.

Accessibility

The Accessibility tools on your iPad are targeted at helping people with certain needs. There's a lot to dig into, so we encourage you to explore the various choices on your own, especially if you or a loved one have a particular area of need.

VoiceOver

The VoiceOver screen reader describes aloud what's on the screen. It can read email messages, web pages, and more. With VoiceOver active, you tap an item on the screen to select it. VoiceOver places a black rectangle around the item and either speaks the name or describes an item. For example, if you tap Display & Brightness, the VoiceOver voice speaks the words "Display and brightness button." VoiceOver even lets you know when you position the iPad in landscape or portrait mode and when your screen is locked or unlocked.

Within the VoiceOver setting, you have several options. For instance, you can drag a Speaking Rate slider to speed up or slow down the speech. You can also determine the kind of typing feedback you get: characters, words, characters and words, or no feedback. Additional switches let you turn on sound effects, change the pitch, and choose the default speech dialect. For example, you can choose an English dialect common to Australia, the United Kingdom, Ireland, or South Africa, along with, of course, the United States. You have additional speech choices from within these countries.

You have to know a new set of finger gestures when VoiceOver is on, which may seem difficult, especially when you first start using VoiceOver. This requirement makes a lot of sense because you want to be able to hear descriptions on the screen before you activate buttons. Different VoiceOver gestures use different numbers of fingers, and Apple recommends that you experiment with different techniques to see what works best for you. A VoiceOver Practice button is provided for this purpose.

We list just a few of the many available gestures here:

>> **Tap:** Select the item.

>> **Rotate two fingers:** This gesture has multiple outcomes that depend on how you set the rotor control gesture. To select your options, head to Settings ⇨ Accessibility ⇨ VoiceOver ⇨ Rotor. The rotor control gesture is similar to turning a dial: You rotate two fingertips on the screen. The purpose is to switch to a different set of commands or features. Suppose you're reading text in an email. By alternately spinning the rotor, you can switch between hearing the body of a message read aloud word by word or character by character. After you set the parameters, flick up or down to hear stuff read back. When you

type an email, the flicking up and down gestures serve a different purpose: The gestures move the cursor left or right within the text.

» **Two-finger tap:** Stop speaking.

» **Two-finger swipe up:** Read everything from the top of the screen.

» **Two-finger swipe down:** Read everything from your current position on the screen.

» **Three-finger swipe up or down:** Scroll a page.

» **Double-tap:** Activate a selected icon or button to launch an app, turn a switch from on to off, and more.

Zoom

The Zoom feature offers a screen magnifier for those who are visually challenged. To zoom, double-tap the screen with *three* fingers. Drag three fingers to move around the screen. To increase magnification, use three fingers to tap and drag up. Tap with three fingers and drag down to decrease magnification. You can tap a Zoom Controller switch for quick access to zoom controls. You can also choose to zoom full screen or zoom only a window. And you can drag a slider to choose your maximum zoom level, up to 15x.

Magnifier

With this feature, you can use your iPad's camera as a magnifier to take a closer look at real-world objects, like a label with print too small to read it. Tap the Magnifier tab and then toggle the Magnifier switch to green to enable this feature. To then activate the magnifier feature, triple-tap your sleep/wake button, and your screen will be taken over by a blown up view from your iPad's rear camera. You can also toggle the Auto-Adjust Exposure switch to green to automatically adjust brightness and contrast based on ambient light. Note that this setting affects only the magnifier feature.

Display & Text Size

This section offers a variety of controls for changing your text size, making it bolder, adding shapes to text-based buttons, reducing transparency, and a lot more.

Motion

We think the parallax effect of icons and alerts is cool, but your neighbor may not agree. Tap the Motion section to reveal controls for Reduce Motion, Auto-Play Message Effects, Auto-Play Video Previews, and Limit Frame Rate.

Spoken Content

Tap the Spoken Content section to reveal controls for Speak Selection Speak Screen, Typing Feedback, Voices, Speaking Rate, and Pronunciations. When the Speak Selection setting is on, the iPad speaks any text you select. With Speak Screen enabled, you can swipe down with two fingers from the top of the screen to have all the contents of the current screen read out loud. Typing Feedback allows you to hear what you type as you type it, and there are several controls for fine-tuning this feature. A slider control allows you to adjust the speaking rate for all of the spoken content. And the Pronunciations section allows you to fine-tune how specific phrases and words are pronounced.

Audio Descriptions

Toggling the Audio Descriptions switch enables the iPad to automatically play audio descriptions when available.

Touch

Tap the Touch section to find controls for enabling the following features:

>> **Assistive Touch:** Use an adaptive accessory, such as a joystick, because of difficulties touching the screen. A movable dot appears; tap the dot to access certain features, such as notifications or Home. You can also create custom gestures through AssistiveTouch.

>> **Touch Accommodations:** Customize the touch sensitivity of your iPad. For example, you can change the amount of time you must touch the screen before your touch is recognized. You can also change how long your iPad treats multiple touches as a single touch. And you can enable a Tap Assistance option to allow any single finger gesture to perform a tap before a timeout period, which you can customize, expires.

>> **Tap to Wake (iPad Pro only):** Tap your screen to wake it up, a must on iPad Pro models with Face ID and no Home button.

>> **Shake to Undo:** Undo your typing with a shake of your iPad. In our experience, this experience sounds neat but few people use it.

>> **Call Audio Routing:** This feature is set to Automatic by default, and we recommend you leave it there. Tap it, however, to manually set where audio phone calls you answer on your iPad get routed, regardless of the speakers or headset you are using when the call comes in. When set to Automatic, your iPad will intelligently send audio phone calls to whatever speakers you are using.

Face ID & Attention (iPad Pro models with Face ID only)

Tap the Face ID & Attention section to reveal controls that allow you to turn off Require Attention for Face ID. We recommend you leave this on, as it is by default. When activated, your iPad will verify that you are actually looking at your iPad before unlocking it with Face ID. Another setting here is Attention Aware Features. When activated (green), this feature will check to see if you're looking at your iPad before dimming the screen.

Switch Control

Several controls are represented under the Switch Control setting. The general idea is that you can use a single switch or multiple switches to select text, tap, drag, type, and perform other functions. However, turning on Switch Control changes the gestures and techniques you use to control your tablet and are presumably already familiar with. For example, the iPad can scan by or highlight items on the screen until you select one. Or you can take advantage of scanning crosshairs to select a location on the screen. You can also manually move from item to item by using multiple switches, with each switch set to handle a specific action. We recommend poking around this setting to examine these and other options.

Voice Control

When activated, Voice Control allows you to control your iPad with your voice. This way of interacting with and controlling your iPad is different than the usual method, and you'll see multiple controls for customizing this feature.

Top Button (iPad Pro models with Face ID) or Home Button

Tap this section for controls that change the how your sleep/wake button works:

>> **Click Speed:** Choose between Default, Slow, and Slowest to change how fast your iPad should interpret when you press the sleep/wake button. This setting is relevant when you press the sleep/wake button more than one time to activate a feature.

>> **Press and Hold to Speak:** On by default, press and holding down your sleep/wake button will enable Siri. Tap this setting to Off to disable Siri when pressing and holding down the sleep/wake button.

>> **Use Passcode for Payments:** Toggle this switch to green if you want to force your iPad to always require your iTunes password for purchases instead of allowing you to use Face ID or Touch ID to authorize purchases.

Apple TV Remote

Tap the Apple TV Remote option to use directional buttons instead of swipe gestures when using the Apple TV Remote app on your iPad. Toggle it to green to use directional buttons or leave it white to use swiping gestures by default.

Keyboards

Tap the Keyboards section for access to controls that change the way hardware keyboards perform. There is also a control for having virtual keyboards display lowercase letters when the Shift key isn't pressed.

AirPods

The AirPods section of Accessibility settings allows you to control press speed, press and hold down duration, and noise cancellation with one AirPod if you have AirPod Pros.

Hearing Devices

The Hearing Devices section allows you to connect to Apple-certified hearing aids through Bluetooth. The Hearing Aid Compatibility setting improves audio quality with some connected hearing aids.

RTT

Tap the RTT section to enable the ability to make and receive RTT calls through FaceTime on your iPad.

Audio & Visual

The Audio & Visual section of Accessibility has three controls:

- **Mono Audio:** Combine the right and left audio channels so that both channels can be heard in either earbud of any headset you plug in. This setting is helpful if you suffer hearing loss in one ear.

- **Balance:** A slider control adjusts how much audio is combined and to which ear it is directed.

- **Visual:** Toggle the LED Flash for Alerts to have the LED on the back of your iPad flash for any alerts. (iPads with rear LED flashes only.)

Subtitles and Captioning

The Subtitles and Captioning setting lets you turn on a closed captions + SDH switch to summon closed-captioning or subtitles. You can also choose and preview the subtitle style and create your own subtitle style.

Guided Access

Parents of autistic kids know how challenging it can be to keep their child focused on a given task. The Guided Access setting can limit iPad usage to a single app and also restrict touch input on certain areas of the screen. You can set a passcode to use when Guided Access is enabled and use Touch ID (on compatible models) to end it.

Siri

The Siri section of Accessibility has the following two controls:

>> **Type to Siri:** Siri allows you to type your requests when you press and hold down the sleep/wake button. When enabled, the ability to type your Siri requests is in addition to Siri listening as normal.

>> **Voice Feedback:** Choose between Always On and Hands-Free Only for Siri responding to you with voice feedback when your iPad is muted.

Accessibility Shortcut

Double-clicking the Home button launches multitasking. But you can set up the iPad so that triple-tapping the button turns on certain accessibility features. By doing so, you can turn on or off Guided Access, VoiceOver, Invert Colors, Color Filters, Reduce White Point, Zoom, Switch Control, and AssistiveTouch.

Wallpaper

Choosing wallpaper is a neat way to dress up the iPad according to your aesthetic preferences. You'll find colorful dynamic animated wallpapers with floating bubbles that add a subtle dizzying effect. But stunning as they are, these images may not hold a candle to the masterpieces in your own photo albums (more about those in Chapter 9). And animations consume more power.

You can sample the pretty patterns and dynamic designs that the iPad has already chosen for you, as follows:

1. **Tap Settings ⇨ Wallpaper and then tap Choose a New Wallpaper.**

   A list of your photo albums appears, along with Apple's own wallpaper.

2. **Tap Dynamic or Stills, or tap one of your own photo albums in the list.**

   We chose Stills to bring up the thumbnails shown in Figure 15-9.

3. **Tap a thumbnail image.**

   That image fills the screen.

4. **When an image is full-screen, choose among the following options, which appear at the bottom of the screen:**

   - *Cancel:* Return to the thumbnail page without changing your Home or lock screen.

   - *Perspective Zoom:* Turn this motion effect on or off. Note that this is not an option if you're setting a dynamic wallpaper image.

   - *Set:* Choose between Set Lock Screen, Set Home Screen, or Set Both.

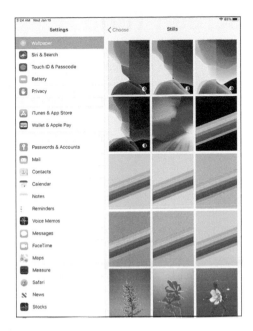

FIGURE 15-9:
Choosing a majestic background.

Siri & Search

We love Siri, the chatty personal digital assistant who can remind you whether to take an umbrella or clue you in on how the Giants are faring in the NFL, and we devote a good chunk of Chapter 14 to learning more about her. Here in Settings, you can change her voice from female to male, choose a default language, let Siri know your name, and decide whether to summon her through the "Hey Siri" command.

You can also tell the iPad which apps you want to search for by flipping the switch for each one. There are switches here to turn on Siri Suggestions for Search, Lookup, and your lock screen.

We address Search in Chapter 2 and Siri in Chapter 14. As a reminder, you can initiate a search on the iPad by dragging down from near the top of the screen.

Screen Time

NEW

Screen Time consists of two sets of tools. One shows you how much time you're spending on your iPad, and the other allows you to set restrictions on how much time you, your children, your employees, or your students spend on their iPad:

» **Screen Time:** See a report of your daily average use of your iPad for the current week. Tap See All Activity to get a more detailed report, including how much time you've spent in individual apps. You can also see the average number of times you've picked up your iPad, as well as the average number of notifications you received. All of these tools are designed to help you take control of your own screen time, or the screen time of your children, employees, or students.

» **Restrictions:** Screen Time allows you to set restrictions on how and when your iPad is used:

- *Downtime:* Set limits on when your iPad can be used. You can block your iPad from use at different times and days of the week — or every day of the week.

- *App Limits:* Choose apps you want to limit on your iPad. You can limit individual apps, a category of apps, or all apps. When you've selected the apps you want to limit, tap Next to set the number of minutes or hours (or both) that those apps can be used during a given day.

- *Always Allow:* Choose apps that can always be accessed on your iPad, regardless of other restrictions you've set.

- *Content & Privacy Restrictions:* Dive deep into a number of settings designed to protect your privacy or the privacy of your children, employees, or students. A vast number of settings are here, and we encourage you to explore them fully.

You can also set a passcode for accessing Screen Time. If you're setting a passcode for your children, employees, or students, it should be different than the passcode that unlocks your iPad to prevent them from undoing the restrictions you so carefully set.

Further down in the Screen Time settings is Share Across Devices. Toggle the switch green if you want to copy your Screen Time settings across every device signed into your iCloud account. Choose the Family option if you want to set up Screen Time only for iCloud accounts set up for Family Sharing.

If you want to turn off Screen Time, tap Settings ⇨ Screen Time ⇨ Turn Off Screen Time at the bottom of the Screen Time settings.

Exploring Settings in General

Certain miscellaneous settings are difficult to pigeonhole. Apple wisely lumped these under the General settings moniker. Here's a closer look at your options.

About About

You aren't seeing double. This section, as shown in Figure 15-10, is all about the About setting. And About is full of trivial (and not-so-trivial) information *about* the device. What you find here is straightforward:

>> **Name:** The name of your device, which you can edit. This name will appear on your network and in the share interface when using AirDrop to transfer files.

>> **Software version:** As this book goes to press, we're up to version 13.1.3. In parentheses next to the version number, a string of numbers and letters, such as 14B55c, tells you more precisely what software version you have, though this won't have a practical effect for most iPad users.

>> **Model Name:** Apple's official name for your iPad model.

>> **Model Number:** The official model number for your iPad.

>> **Serial Number:** The serial number of your iPad.

FIGURE 15-10:
You find info about your iPad under About.

>> **Network:** The cellular network you are subscribed to, if any. This entry is only for iPads with cellular capabilities.

>> **Songs:** The number of songs stored on your iPad.

>> **Videos:** The number of videos stored on your iPad.

>> **Photos:** The number of photos stored on your iPad.

>> **Applications:** The number of apps installed on your iPad.

>> **Capacity:** Because of the way the device is formatted, you always have a little less storage than the advertised amount of flash memory.

- **Available:** The amount of storage you haven't yet used on your iPad.

- **Carrier (Wi-Fi + Cellular versions only):** This may seem redundant with the Network entry described earlier in this list, but it's the difference between which company you are paying and which network your iPad is connected to.

- **Cellular Data Number:** For billing purposes only.

- **Wi-Fi address:** The address assigned to your internal Wi-Fi radio. You aren't likely to ever need to know this.

- **Bluetooth address:** The address assigned to your internal Bluetooth radio. You aren't likely to ever need to know this.

- **IMEI, ICCID, MEID, and CSN:** International Mobile Equipment Identifier, International Circuit Card Identifier, Mobile Equipment Identifier, and Chip Serial Number, respectively. All live up to their geeky acronyms by helping to identify your specific device.

- **Modern Firmware:** The version of your iPad's firmware, which is a combination of hardware and software that helps your iPad function as an iPad.

- **SEID:** An identifier for the Secure Element used in the Apple Pay mobile payments system.

- **EID:** An identifier tied to your SIM card. For Wi-Fi + Cellular versions only.

- **Certificate Trust Settings:** Esoteric information relating to security and encrypted data.

Software Update

The Software Update section is self-explanatory. When Apple unleashes an update, you can find it here.

AirDrop

In the AirDrop setting, tap Receiving Off to turn off AirDrop on your iPad. Tap Contacts Only so that only people you know can send you an AirDrop file. Tap Everyone to allow any Tom, Dick, or Harry to send you files — we don't recommend this option.

AirPlay & Handoff

The Handoff feature lets you start a task (such as typing an email) on your iPad, on another device running iOS 8 or later (including iPadOS), or on a Mac computer running macOS Yosemite or later, and resume the task on another compatible iOS device, iPadOS device, or Mac. All the devices have to be running the same iCloud account. On the tablet, you'll be able to resume with the app from your lock screen or app switcher. On a Mac, you'll see the appropriate app on the dock.

iPad Storage

The About setting (covered earlier) gives you a lot of information about your device. But after you back out of About and return to the main General settings, you can find out how your iPad is using its storage. You can see what type of files take up how much space, and even see which apps are hogging the most storage and delete those you're no longer using.

Background App Refresh

Some apps continue to run in the background even when you're not actively engaged with them. If you flip the Background App Refresh switch so that green is showing, you can allow such apps to update content when an active Wi-Fi or cellular connection is available. The potential downside to leaving this switch turned on is a hit on battery life.

As it turns out, your iPad is pretty smart about when to refresh apps. iPadOS detects patterns based on how you use your iPad. It learns when your tablet is typically inactive — at night perhaps when you're in slumberland. And in some cases, apps are refreshed when you enter a particular location.

You can also turn on or off Background App Refresh for any individual app listed under this setting. Flip the switch to make the determination for each given app.

Date & Time

Tap Date & Time to reveal several settings for your iPad's clock:

>> **24-Hour Time:** Display a 24-hour clock. Toggle to white if you prefer a 12-hour clock.

>> **Show AM/PM in Status Bar:** Include the AM/PM designation. This setting is visible only if you are using a 12-hour clock.

>> **Show Date in Status Bar:** Display today's date in the status bar.

>> **Set Automatically:** Set the clock to the time on Apple's servers. We strongly recommend you use this feature.

>> **Time Zone:** Manually set your time zone. If you are using the Set Automatically feature, this option will show your current time zone, and you can't change it.

Keyboard

Tap Settings ⇨ General ⇨ Keyboard settings to see the following options covering typing on your virtual keyboard:

» **Keyboards:** Use an international keyboard (see Chapter 2). You can also choose the layout of your English keyboards in this settings, substitute the default keyboard on your iPad to, for example, Swype, SwiftKey, or Fleksy. For more on adding a third-party keyboard, consult Chapter 2.

» **Text Replacement:** Create shortcuts that will expand into longer text. The default entry is "omw." If you leave this entry as it is, whenever you type "omw," it will automatically expand to "On my way!" Tap the + icon at the top right of the screen to add your own text replacements. Tap the Edit button at the bottom of the screen to delete text replacement entries.

» **Auto-Capitalization:** Automatically capitalize the first letter of the first word you type after ending the preceding sentence with a period, a question mark, or an exclamation point. Auto-capitalization is on by default.

» **Auto-Correction:** The iPad takes a stab at what it thinks you meant to type.

» **Enable Caps Lock:** All letters are uppercased LIKE THIS if you double-tap the shift key. (The shift key is the one with the arrow pointing up.) Tap shift again to exit caps lock.

» **Shortcuts:** The iPad's virtual keyboard will display a shortcut bar with controls to copy and paste the text you've selected text, or to make that text bold, italic, or underline. Don't confuse this Shortcuts setting with the "." Shortcut setting described later.

» **Smart Punctuation:** Your iPad will automatically format smart quotes and smart apostrophes as you type.

» **Enable Key Flicks:** Use a flick to type alternate characters on your keyboard.

» **"." Shortcut:** A period is inserted followed by a space when you double-tap the space bar. This setting is turned on by default; if you've never tried it, give it a shot.

» **Check Spelling:** The keyboard checks spelling while you type.

» **Predictive:** The iPad keyboard suggests certain words that you might want to type next. Tap a suggested word to accept it. You can also flip the Predictive switch on or off from the keyboard itself.

» **Slide on Floating Keyboard to Type:** Slide your finger across your iPad's floating keyboard to type.

>> **Delete Slide-to-Type by Word:** Delete entire words from Slide-to-Type when you use the delete key, as opposed to deleting one letter at a time.

>> **Enable Dictation:** Use your iPad's microphone — or the microphone in a connected headset — to dictate your textual input.

>> **Memoji Stickers:** Enable memoji stickers in your keyboard. See Chapter 6 for more on memoji stickers.

TIP

You'll see another type of shortcut option, called Text Replacement, in which the keyboard presents a full phrase when you type a few letters. For example, typing the letters *omw* yields *On my way!* Tap the + under the Text Replacement setting to add a new phrase and the optional shortcut for that phrase. Saving a few letters is economical, don't you think?

Font

Your iPad comes with multiple fonts installed, but you can also find fonts in the App Store (both free and not). Tap the Font setting to see any third-party fonts you've installed and to see a link to the App Store where you can search for more fonts.

Language & Region

In the Language & Region section, you can set the language in which the iPad displays text, plus the date and time format for the region in question. You can choose a Gregorian, Japanese, or Buddhist calendar, too.

Dictionary

Tap the Dictionary setting to see both the dictionaries enabled on your iPad by default and the long list of optional dictionaries you can enable. Choosing an international keyboard will often enable additional dictionaries.

VPN

Tap Settings ⇨ General ⇨ VPN to set up or manage a VPN.

TECHNICAL STUFF

A *VPN,* or *virtual private network,* is a way for you to securely access your company's network behind the firewall — using an encrypted Internet connection that acts as a secure tunnel for data. Some people use VPNs to encrypt their traffic or evade regional restrictions on content.

You can configure a VPN on the iPad by following these steps:

1. **Tap Settings ⇨ General ⇨ VPN ⇨ Add VPN Configuration.**

2. **Tap one of the protocol options.**

   The iPad software supports the protocols *IKEv2* (Internet Key Exchange), *L2TP* (Layer 2 Tunneling Protocol), and *IPSec,* which apparently provides the kind of security that satisfies network administrators.

3. **Using configuration settings provided by your company or VPN provider, fill in the appropriate server information, account, password, and other information.**

4. **Choose whether to turn on RSA SecurID authentication, if the option presents itself.**

   Better yet, lend your iPad to the techies where you work and let them fill in the blanks on your behalf.

After you configure your iPad for VPN usage, you can turn that capability on or off by tapping (yep) the VPN switch in Settings.

Legal & Regulatory

If you find yourself unable to sleep, be sure and tap the Legal & Regulatory section to read all the fine print that legions of lawyers have managed to cram into your iPad. Yeah, it's that exciting.

Reset

As little kids playing sports, we ended an argument by agreeing to a do-over. Well, the Reset settings, found by tapping Settings ⇨ General ⇨ Reset on the iPad, are one big do-over. Now that you're (presumably) grown up, think long and hard about the consequences before implementing do-over settings. Regardless, you may encounter good reasons for starting over; some of these are addressed in Chapter 16.

Here are your reset options:

>> **Reset All Settings:** Reset all settings, but no data or media is deleted.

>> **Erase All Content and Settings:** Reset all settings *and* wipe out all your data.

- **>> Reset Network Settings:** Delete the current network settings and restores them to their factory defaults.

- **>> Subscriber Services:** Reprovision (or refresh) your account and reset your authentication code. It will not show up on all models.

- **>> Reset Keyboard Dictionary:** Remove added words from the dictionary. Remember that the iPad keyboard is intelligent. One reason why it's so smart is that it learns from you. So when you reject words that the iPad keyboard suggests, it figures that the words you specifically banged out ought to be added to the keyboard dictionary.

- **>> Reset Home Screen Layout:** Revert all icons to the way they were at the factory.

- **>> Reset Location & Privacy:** Restore factory defaults.

Shut Down

In addition to being able to use your wake/sleep and Home buttons, or wake/sleep and volume up buttons, to shut down your iPad, you can also use the Shut Down setting in your General settings to shut down your device. To shut down your iPad, tap Shut Down, then slide the slide to power off slider from left to right. Your iPad will promptly shut down. Tap the cancel button at the bottom of your screen to back out of the shutdown process.

Controlling Control Center

In Chapter 14, we sing the praises of Control Center, the convenient utility that is no farther away than a down swipe from the upper-right corner of the screen. In Settings ⇨ Control Center, you get to decide whether to make Control Center accessible from the lock screen and whether you can access it within apps. The switches for making these determinations are pretty straightforward.

Touch ID (or Face ID) & Passcode

If you want to prevent others from using your iPad, you can set a passcode by tapping Settings ⇨ Touch ID & Passcode (or just Passcode on models without Touch ID) and then tapping Turn Passcode On. iPad Pro models with Face ID will instead have a Face ID & Passcode setting. By default, you use the virtual keypad to enter and confirm your passcode. After you do so, you'll see options for when and how you use Touch ID or Face ID, as well as options for changing your passcode and resetting Touch ID or Face ID.

If you've already set up Touch ID or Face ID, you'll see options for using that feature for iPad Unlock, iTunes & App Store, Apple Pay, and Password Autofill. By default, these options are toggled on (green). You can toggle each option off if you want, but we recommend that you leave them on.

Below those toggles are settings that control your fingerprint scan. By default, you have just the one fingerprint you initially set up for Touch ID, probably called Finger 1. Tap Settings ➪ Touch ID & Passcode ➪ Finger 1 to rename that finger-print scan or delete it.

You can add up to five fingerprints (yours and people you trust with whom you share the iPad). Tap Add a Fingerprint and go through the training session that you likely encountered back when you set up your iPad (consult Chapter 2 for details). If the iPad doesn't recognize your finger, you see Try Again at the top of the screen. You get three wrong tries before you're forced to use a traditional passcode instead, at least for this session.

If you have Face ID, you can reset Face ID or set up an alternate appearance. This might be useful if Face ID has a hard time recognizing you in sunglasses, for instance.

You can also determine whether a passcode is required immediately, after 1 minute, after 5 minutes, 15 minutes, 1 hour, or 4 hours. Shorter times are more secure, of course. On the topic of security, the iPad can be set to automatically erase your data if someone makes ten failed passcode attempts.

You can also change the passcode or turn it off later (unless your employer dic-tates otherwise), but you need to know the present passcode to apply any changes. If you forget the passcode, you have to restore the iPad software, as we describe in Chapter 16.

From the Touch ID & Passcode setting, you can determine whether to allow access to the today view, the notifications view, or Siri, or Home control when the iPad is locked.

As an added security measure, a regular passcode is required the first time you try to get past a lock screen after restarting the tablet.

Promoting Harmony through Family Sharing

Earlier under Screen Time, we show you how to impose an iron fist when it comes to permitting iPad usage at home. Now we're going to try to make everybody in the clan happy again. Visit iCloud settings and consider setting up Family Sharing with up to six members of your family. Adults and kids can partake, but one grown-up must take charge as the family organizer. We figure it might as well be you, the person reading this book. You'll be the person presenting your iCloud Apple ID username and password, and the one on the hook for paying for iTunes, Books, and App Store purchases. As the family organizer, you can turn on Ask to Buy so that you can approve (or deny) purchases or download requests from other members of your clan.

When Family Sharing has been implemented, you can all share a calendar, photos, reminders, and your respective locations. Family Sharing may also help find a missing device through the important Find My iPad feature, which we describe at the end of this chapter.

WARNING

Should you leave Family Sharing, your account is removed from the group and you can no longer share content with everybody else. You won't be able to use DRM-protected music, movies, TV shows, books, or apps that another member purchased. And you won't be able to access the family calendar, reminders, or photos.

Family Sharing works on devices with iOS 8 and later, including iPadOS, and macOS Yosemite and later on a Mac.

Sorting and displaying contacts

Do you think of us as Ed, Bob, and Bryan or Baig, LeVitus, and Chaffin? The answer to that question will probably determine whether you choose to sort your contacts list alphabetically by last name or first name.

In Settings, tap Contacts; scroll down to the Contacts section; and peek at Sort Order. Then tap Last, First or First, Last. You can determine whether you want to display a first name or last name first by tapping Display Order and then choosing First, Last or Last, First. You can also go with a short name to fit more names on the screen. You can choose a first name and last initial, first initial and last name, first name only, or last name only. If you prefer nicknames, you can choose those instead, when available.

You'll also see a Contacts Found in Apps switch that when disabled will remove unconfirmed contact suggestions. You won't see such autocomplete suggestions in Mail, the incoming call screens, or the Contacts app.

Transactional Settings

You use your iPad to shop and pay for stuff, areas where the following settings apply.

iTunes & App Store

In the iTunes & App Store section, you decide whether your iPad should automatically download music, apps, books, audiobooks, and updates. And if you give the okay, you can choose whether to tap into your cellular network (if applicable) when downloading these items.

Wallet & Apple Pay

If you have an iPad with Touch ID or Face ID and want to take advantage of Apple Pay (Apple's mobile payments system), add a new credit or debit card in the Wallet & Apple Pay section. Apple Pay lets you make secure online purchases right from your tablet.

You can also manage your Apple Cash settings, including tying in a bank for sending and receiving money through Messages using Apple Pay. For an in-depth discussion of Apple Pay and Apple Pay Cash, see Chapter 6.

Find My iPad

We hope you never have to use the Find My iPad feature — though we have to say that it's darn cool. If you inadvertently leave your iPad in a taxi or restaurant, Find My iPad may just help you retrieve it. You need a free iCloud account and your iPad must be connected to a network of some kind.

Well, that's *almost* all you need. Tap Settings ➪ Apple ID ➪ Find My and make sure Find My iPad is switched on.

Now, suppose you lost your tablet — and we can only assume that you're beside yourself. Follow these steps to see whether Find My iPad can help you:

1. **Log on to your iCloud account at** www.icloud.com **from any browser on your computer.**

2. **Click the Find iPhone icon.**

   Yes, even though the feature is Find My iPad on the iPad, it shows up as Find iPhone on the iCloud site. Don't worry; it will still locate your iPad — and, for that matter, a lost iPhone, a Mac, and sometimes even lost AirPods or AirPods Pro.

   Assuming your tablet is turned on and in the coverage area, its general whereabouts turn up on a map in standard or satellite view, or a hybrid of the two. In our tests, Find My iPad found our iPads quickly.

   Even seeing your iPad on a map may not help you much, especially if the device is lost somewhere in midtown Manhattan. Take heart.

3. **At the iCloud site, click the Lost Mode button.**

4. **Type a phone number at which you can be reached, as well as a plea to the Good Samaritan who (you hope) picked up your iPad.**

   Apple has already prepared a simple message indicating that the iPad is lost, but you can change or remove the message and substitute your own plea for the return of your tablet.

   The message appears on the lost iPad's screen.

TIP

To get someone's attention, you can also sound an alarm that plays for two minutes, even if the volume is off. Tap Play Sound to make it happen. Hey, that alarm may come in handy if the iPad turns up under a couch in your house. Stranger things have happened.

We also recommend turning on the Send Last Location setting in Find My iPad because it automatically sends the tablet's location to Apple when the device's battery is critically low. That way, you still have a puncher's chance of getting back a lost iPad even when the battery is knocked out.

TIP

Find My iPhone (which finds any iOS or iPadOS device, as well as any friends or family who have shared their location with you) is also available as a free app.

After all this labor, if the iPad is seemingly gone for good, click Erase iPad at the iCloud site to delete your personal data from afar and return the iPad to its factory settings. (A somewhat less drastic measure is to remotely lock your iPad by using a passcode.)

Meanwhile, the person who found (or possibly stole) your iPad cannot reactivate the device to use as his or her own, or to peddle, unless he or she successfully types in *your* Apple ID.

Even if you choose to erase the device remotely, it can still display a custom message with the information needed for someone to return it to you. If, indeed, you ever get your iPad back, you can always restore the information from an iTunes backup on your Mac or PC or iCloud.

We authors love a happy ending.

Chapter **16**

When Good iPads Go Bad

n our experience, Apple devices are reliable. But every so often, a good iPad might just go bad. So, in this chapter, we look at the types of bad things that can happen, along with suggestions for fixing them.

What kind of bad things are we talking about? Well, we're referring to problems involving

» Frozen or dead iPads

» Wireless networks

» Synchronization with computers (both Mac and PC) or iTunes

After all the troubleshooting, we tell you how to get even more help if nothing we suggest does the trick. Finally, if your iPad is so badly hosed it needs to go back to the mother ship for repairs, we offer ways to survive the experience with a minimum of stress or fuss, including how to restore your stuff from an iTunes, Finder, or iCloud backup.

Resuscitating an iPad with Issues

Our first category of troubleshooting techniques applies to an iPad that's frozen or otherwise acting up. The recommended procedure for a frozen iPad is to perform the seven *R*s in sequence.

1. Recharge
2. Restart
3. Reset your iPad
4. Remove your content
5. Reset settings and content
6. Restore
7. Recovery mode

But before you even start those procedures, Apple recommends you take these steps:

1. **Verify that you have the current version of iTunes installed on your Mac or PC.**

   You can download the latest and greatest version here: www.apple.com/itunes/download.

2. **Verify that you're connecting your iPad to your computer using a USB port.**

TIP

   If you encounter difficulties here, we implore you to read the paragraph in the next section that begins with this:

   - *"Don't* plug the iPad's dock connector or Lightning–to–USB cable into a USB port on your keyboard, monitor, or unpowered USB hub."

3. **Make sure your iPad software is up to date.**

   To check using iTunes on your Mac or PC:

   a. *Connect the iPad to the computer and launch iTunes, if it doesn't launch automatically.* If you connect more than one iDevice to this computer simultaneously, the button will say the number of devices (for example, *5 Devices*) rather than *iPad.* Click the button to display a drop-down list and select the device you want.

   b. *Click the Summary tab and then click the Check for Update button.*

To check with your iPad:

a. *On the Home screen, tap Settings.*

b. *In the Settings list on the left side of the screen, tap General.*

c. *On the right side of the screen, tap Software Update.*

If your iPad requires an update, you receive instructions for doing so. Otherwise, please continue.

If your iPad is still acting up — if it freezes, doesn't wake up from sleep, doesn't do something it used to do, or in any other way acts improperly — don't panic. The following sections describe the things you should try, in the order we (and Apple) recommend.

If the first technique doesn't do the trick, go on to the second. If the second one doesn't work, try the third. And so on.

Recharge

If your iPad acts up in any way, shape, or form, the first thing you should try is to give its battery a full recharge before you proceed.

REMEMBER

Don't plug the iPad's dock connector or Lightning–to–USB cable into a USB port on your keyboard, monitor, or an unpowered USB hub. You *must* plug the cable into a USB charging brick like the one that came with your iPad, or one of the USB ports on your computer itself because the USB ports on your computer supply more power than the other ports.

If your computer is more than a few years old, even your built-in USB ports may not supply enough juice to recharge your iPad. It'll sync just fine; it just won't recharge. If you see *Not Charging* next to the battery icon at the top of the screen, use the included USB power adapter to recharge your iPad from an AC outlet rather than from a computer.

TIP

Most *powered* USB hubs, the kind you plug into an AC outlet, will charge your iPad just fine. But *passive* or *unpowered* hubs — ones that don't plug into the wall for power — won't cut it when it comes to charging your iPad.

TIP

If you're in a hurry, charge your iPad for a minimum of 20 minutes. We think a full charge is a better idea, but a charge of 20 minutes is better than no charge at all. And for faster charging in any circumstances, turn off your iPad completely while it charges or at least put it in airplane mode. It's fine to use your iPad while it charges, but it will charge faster if you turn it off or put it in airplane mode.

Restart

If you recharge your iPad and it still misbehaves, the next thing to try is restarting. Start by restarting a recalcitrant app. If your iPad has a Home button, double-click that Home button and swipe up on the misbehaving app in App Switcher. If your iPad doesn't have a Home Button, swipe up from the bottom of your screen to go to your Home screen, swipe up and hold to pull up App Switcher, and then swipe up on the misbehaving app.

You know how restarting a computer often fixes problems? Well, restarting your iPad sometimes works wonders, too, so that's what to try next.

Here's how to restart your iPad if it has a Home button:

1. Hold down the sleep/wake button.
2. When the slider appears, slide it to turn off the iPad and then wait a few seconds.
3. Press the sleep/wake button again until the Apple logo appears on the screen.
4. If your iPad is still frozen, misbehaves, or doesn't start, hold down the Home button for six to ten seconds to force any frozen applications to quit.
5. Repeat Steps 1–4 again.

Here's how to restart your iPad if it does *not* have a Home button:

1. Hold down the sleep/wake button and the volume up button.
2. When the slider appears, slide it to turn off the iPad and then wait a few seconds.
3. Press the sleep/wake button again until the Apple logo appears on the screen.
4. If your iPad is still frozen, misbehaves, or doesn't start, hold down the Home button for six to ten seconds to force any frozen applications to quit.
5. Repeat Steps 1–4 again.

TIP

If your Home or sleep/wake button is acting up and you can't power down the usual way, try enabling Assistive Touch in Settings ⇨ Accessibility ⇨ Touch ⇨ AssistiveTouch. Toggle the AssistiveTouch button so it changes from white (off) to green (on). A gray circle will appear on your screen; tap the gray circle and several options including on-screen versions of the Home and sleep/wake buttons appear. You can try to use these virtual buttons to power down your iPad, though it may or may not help depending on why your physical buttons weren't working properly in the first place.

If these steps don't get your iPad back up and running, move on to the third R: resetting your iPad.

Reset your iPad

You can also do what many people call a hard, or hardware, reset. A hard reset requires you to push specific buttons in the right sequence to force your iPad to shut down and restart.

To perform a hard reset on an iPad with a Home button, merely hold down the sleep/wake button and then the Home button, continuing to keep both buttons down for at least ten seconds. When you see the Apple logo, release both buttons.

To perform a hard reset on an iPad that doesn't have a Home button, press and quickly release the volume up button, then press and quickly release the volume down button, and then press and hold down the sleep/wake button. When the Apple logo appears, release the sleep/wake button.

Resetting your iPad is like forcing your computer to restart after a crash. Your data shouldn't be affected by a reset — and in many cases, the reset cures whatever was ailing your iPad. So don't be shy about giving this technique a try. In many cases, your iPad goes back to normal after you reset it this way.

TIP

Sometimes you have to hold down the sleep/wake button *before* you hold down the Home button. If you press both at exactly the same time, you create a *screen shot* — a picture of whatever is on your screen at the time — rather than reset your iPad.

Unfortunately, sometimes resetting *doesn't* do the trick. When that's the case, you have to take stronger measures.

TIP

At this point, it's a good idea to back up your iPad's contents. On your iPad, go to Settings ➪ iCloud ➪ iCloud Backup and tap the Back Up Now button. Or connect your iPad to your computer and look in the Backup section of the Summary pane in iTunes (macOS Mojave and earlier) or in Finder for macOS Catalina. The Backup pane in either iTunes or Finder will also tell you when the last backup occurred.

Remove content

Nothing you've tried so far should have taken more than a few minutes (or 20 if you tried the 20-minute recharge). We hate to tell you, but that's about to change because the next thing you should try is removing some or all of your data to see whether it's causing your troubles.

To do so, you need to sync your iPad and then reconfigure it so some or all of your files are *not* synchronized (which removes them from the iPad). The problem could be contacts, calendar data, songs, photos, videos, or podcasts. You can apply one of two strategies to this troubleshooting task:

>> **If you suspect a particular data type** — for example, you suspect your photos because your iPad freezes whenever you tap the Photos icon on the Home screen — try removing that data first.

>> **If you have no suspicions,** deselect every item and then sync. When you're finished, your iPad should have no data on it. If that method fixes your iPad, try restoring your data, one type at a time. If the problem returns, you have to keep experimenting to determine which particular data type or file is causing the problem.

If you're still having problems, the next step is to reset your iPad's settings and content.

Reset settings and content

Resetting involves two steps: The first one, resetting your iPad settings, resets every iPad *setting* to its default — the way the iPad was when you took it out of the box. Resetting the iPad's settings doesn't erase any of your data or media, so you can try this step without trepidation. The only downside is you may have to change some settings back to where you want them afterwards. To reset your settings, tap the Settings icon on the Home screen and then tap Settings ⇨ General ⇨ Reset ⇨ Reset All Settings.

WARNING

Be careful *not* to tap Erase All Content and Settings, at least not yet. Erasing all content takes more time to recover from (because your next sync takes a long time), so try Reset All Settings first.

If you're having network or connectivity issues, try Settings ⇨ General ⇨ Reset ⇨ Reset Network Settings. Next, if resetting all settings or network settings didn't cure your iPad, you have to try Erase All Content and Settings. Read the next warning paragraph first. Then tap Settings ⇨ General ⇨ Reset ⇨ Erase All Content and Settings.

The Erase All Content strategy deletes everything from your iPad — all your data, media, and settings. Because all these items are stored on your computer or the cloud — at least in theory — you should be able to put things back the way they were by restoring your latest backup and then syncing after the reset. But you may lose any photos or screen shots you've taken, as well as any contacts, calendar events, reminders, playlists, and anything else you've created or modified on the iPad since it last synced.

After using Erase All Content and Settings, check to see whether your iPad works properly. If that didn't cure what ailed your iPad, the next-to-the-last R, restoring your iPad using iTunes, may help.

Restore

Before you give up on your poor, sick iPad, you can try to restore it. To restore, connect your iPad to your computer as though you were about to sync. But when the iPad icon appears in iTunes (macOS Mojave and earlier) or Finder (macOS Catalina), click the Summary tab and then click the Restore button. This action erases all your data and media and resets all your settings.

If your computer isn't available, you can also trigger a restore from your iPad by tapping Settings ➪ General ➪ Reset ➪ Erase All Content and Settings.

If Find My iPad (Settings ➪ iCloud ➪ Find My) is enabled, you'll see a message to disable it before you restore your iPad.

If you've backed up your iPad, all your data and media still exists on your computer (except for photos or screen shots you've taken, as well as email, contacts, calendar events, playlists, and anything else you've created or modified on the iPad since your last sync). That means you shouldn't lose anything by restoring. Your next sync will take longer than usual, and you may have to reset settings you've changed since you got your iPad. But other than those inconveniences, restoring shouldn't cause you any additional trouble.

Performing a restore deletes everything on your iPad — all your data, media, and settings. You *should* be able to put things back the way they were with your next sync; if that doesn't happen, for whatever reason, you can't say we didn't warn you. That said, you may still be able to restore from an iTunes, Finder, or iCloud backup as described in this chapter's thrilling conclusion, a scintillating section we call, "Dude, Where's My Stuff?"

Recovery mode

So, if you've tried all the other steps or you couldn't try some or all of them because your iPad is so messed up, you can try one last thing: Recovery mode. Here's how it works:

1. Connect your iPad to your Mac or PC with a Lightning or USB-C cable.

2. Force restart your iPad:

- *If your iPad if has a Home button:* Press and hold down both the Home and the wake/sleep buttons at the same time. Continue holding down until you see the Connect to iTunes screen.

- *If your iPad doesn't have a Home button:* Press and quickly release the volume up button, then press and quickly release the volume down button, and then press and hold down the wake/sleep button until you see the Connect to iTunes screen.

If you see a battery icon like the one shown in the margin, you need to let your iPad charge for at least 10 to 15 minutes. When the battery picture goes away or turns green instead of red, go back to Step 2 and try again.

If you don't see the Connect to iTunes screen on your iPad, try Steps 1 and 2 again.

3. Do one of the following:

- *On Windows PCs or Macs running macOS Mojave and earlier:* If iTunes didn't open automatically, launch it now.

- *On Macs running macOS Catalina:* Go to Finder and select your iPad. You should see a recovery mode alert on your computer screen saying your iPad is in recovery mode and you must restore it before it can be used with iTunes.

4. Use iTunes or Finder to restore the device, as we describe in the preceding section.

Okay. So that's the gamut of things you can do when your iPad acts up. If you tried all our tips and techniques and none of them worked, skim through the rest of this chapter to see whether anything else we recommend looks like it might help. If not, your iPad probably needs to go into the shop for repairs.

Never fear, gentle reader. Be sure to read the "If Nothing We Suggest Helps" section, later in this chapter. Your iPad may be quite sick, but we help ease the pain by sharing some tips on how to minimize the discomfort.

Problems with Networks

If you're having problems with Wi-Fi or your wireless carrier's data network (Wi-Fi + Cellular models only), this section may help. The techniques here are short and sweet — except for the last one, restore. Restore, which we describe in a previous section, is inconvenient and time-consuming, and entails erasing all your data and media and then restoring it.

First, here are some simple steps that may help:

» **Make sure you have sufficient Wi-Fi or cellular signal strength.**

» **Try moving around.** Changing your location by as little as a few feet can sometimes mean the difference between great wireless reception and no wireless reception. If you're inside, try moving around even a step or two in one direction. If you're outside, try moving 10 or 20 paces in any direction. Keep an eye on the cell signal or Wi-Fi icon as you move around, and stop when you see more bars than you saw before.

» **Restart your iPad.** If you've forgotten how, refer to the "Restart" section, earlier in this chapter. As we mention, restarting your iPad is often all it takes to fix whatever is wrong.

If you have a Wi-Fi + Cellular iPad, try the following:

» **Make sure you haven't left your iPad in airplane mode, as we describe in Chapter 15.** In airplane mode, all network-dependent features are disabled, so you can't send or receive messages or use any of the apps that require a Wi-Fi or data-network connection (that is, Mail, Safari, Maps, and the iTunes and App Store apps).

» **Toggle airplane mode on and off.** Turn on airplane mode by swiping down from the upper-right corner of the screen to bring up Control Center and then tapping the airplane icon. Wait 15 or 20 seconds and then tap the airplane icon again to turn airplane mode off.

Toggling airplane mode on and off resets both the Wi-Fi and wireless data-network connections. If your network connection was the problem, toggling airplane mode on and off may correct it.

Apple offers two good articles that may help you with Wi-Fi issues. The first, at http://support.apple.com/kb/TS3237, offers some general troubleshooting tips and hints. The second, at http://support.apple.com/kb/IIT1365, discusses potential sources of interference for wireless devices and networks.

If none of these suggestions fix your network issues, try resetting your network settings by tapping Settings ⇨ General ⇨ Reset ⇨ Reset Network Settings.

Finally, if nothing else has fixed your issue, you can try restoring your iPad, as we describe previously in the "Restore" section.

WARNING

Performing a restore deletes everything on your iPad — all your data, media, and settings. You should be able to put things back the way they were with your next sync. If that doesn't happen, well, consider yourself forewarned.

Sync, Computer, or iTunes Issues

The last category of troubleshooting techniques in this chapter applies to issues that involve synchronization and computer–iPad relations. If you're having problems syncing or your computer doesn't recognize your iPad when you connect it, here are some things to try.

We suggest you try these procedures in the order they're presented here:

1. **Recharge your iPad.**

   If you didn't try it previously, try it now. Go to the "Resuscitating an iPad with Issues" section, earlier in this chapter, and read what we say about recharging your iPad. Every word there applies here.

2. **Try a different USB port or a different cable if you have one available.**

   It doesn't happen often, but occasionally USB ports and cables go bad. When they do, they invariably cause sync and connection problems. Always make sure that a bad USB port or cable isn't to blame.

   If you don't remember what we said about using USB ports on your computer rather than the ones on your keyboard, monitor, or hub, we suggest you reread the "Recharge" section, earlier in this chapter.

3. **Restart your iPad and try to sync again.**

   We describe restarting in full and loving detail in the "Restart" section, earlier in this chapter. You might also want to restart your computer, just in case.

4. **Reinstall iTunes (Windows PC or Mac running macOS Mojave or earlier) or use Finder (Macs running macOS Catalina) to manage iPad syncing.**

TIP

Even if you have an iTunes installer handy, you probably should visit the Apple website and download the latest-and-greatest version, just in case. You can find the latest version of iTunes at www.apple.com/itunes/download.

More Help on the Apple Website

If you try everything we suggest earlier in this chapter and still have problems, don't give up just yet. This section describes a few more places you may find help. We recommend you check them out before you throw in the towel and smash your iPad into tiny little pieces (or ship it back to Apple for repairs, as we describe in the next section).

First, Apple offers an excellent set of support resources on its website at www. apple.com/support/ipad/setup. You can browse support issues by category, search for a problem by keyword, read or download technical manuals, and scan the discussion forums.

Speaking of the discussion forums, you can go directly to them at http:// discussions.apple.com. They're chock-full of useful questions and answers from other iPad users. If you can't find an answer to a support question elsewhere, you can often find it in these forums. You can browse by category or search by keyword. Either way, you find thousands of discussions about almost every aspect of using your iPad.

Now for the best part: If you can't find a solution by browsing or searching, you can post your question in the appropriate Apple discussion forum. Check back in a few days (or even in a few hours), and some helpful iPad user may well have replied with the solution. If you've never tried this fabulous tool, you're missing out on one of the greatest support resources available anywhere.

Last, but certainly not least, you might want to try a carefully worded Google search. You might just find the solution.

If Nothing We Suggest Helps

If you tried every trick in the book (this book) and still have a malfunctioning iPad, consider shipping it off to the iPad hospital (better known as Apple, Inc.). The repair is free if your iPad is still under its one-year limited warranty.

TIP

You can extend your warranty for as long as two years from the original purchase date, if you want. To do so, you need to buy AppleCare+ for your iPad. You don't have to do it when you buy your iPad, but you must buy it before your one-year limited warranty expires. AppleCare+ for iPad, iPad Air, and iPad mini is $3.49 per month for 24 months, or $69 if you pay up front. AppleCare+ for iPad Pro is $6 per month for 24 months or $129 if you pay up front.

Here are some things you need to know before you take your iPad in to be repaired:

>> *Your iPad may be erased during its repair,* so you should sync your iPad with iTunes, Finder, or iCloud and make a backup before you take it in, if you can. If you can't and you entered data on the iPad since your last sync, such as a contact or an appointment, the data may not be there when you restore your iPad upon its return.

>> Remove any accessories, such as a case or screen protector.

TIP

Although you may be able to get your iPad serviced by Best Buy or another authorized Apple reseller, we recommend you take or ship it to your nearest Apple Store, for two reasons:

>> **No one knows your iPad like Apple.** One of the Geniuses at the Apple Store may be able to fix whatever is wrong without sending your iPad away for repairs.

>> **The Apple Store will, in some cases, swap out your wonky iPad for a brand-new one on the spot.** You can't win if you don't play, which is why we always visit our local Apple Store when something goes wrong (with our iPads, iPhones, iPods, and even our laptops and iMacs).

If you've done everything we've suggested, we're relatively certain you're now holding an iPad that works flawlessly. Again.

That said, some or all of your stuff may not be on it. If that's the case, the following section offers a two-trick solution that usually works.

Dude, Where's My Stuff?

If you performed a restore or had your iPad replaced or repaired, you have one more task to accomplish. Your iPad may work flawlessly at this point, but some or all of your stuff — your music, movies, contacts, iMessages, or whatever — is missing. You're not sunk, at least not yet. You still have a couple of tricks up your sleeve.

>> **Trick 1: Sync your iPad with iTunes or Finder and then sync it again.** That's right — sync and sync again. Why? Because sometimes stuff doesn't get synced properly on the first try. Just do it.

>> **Trick 2: Restore from backup.** Click the Summary tab in iTunes and then click Restore Backup. If Find My iPad (Settings ⇨ iCloud ⇨ Find My iPad) is enabled, you'll first see a message to disable it before you restore your iPad. Then the Restore from Backup dialog appears and offers you a choice of backups, as shown in Figure 16-1. Select the one you want, click the Restore button, and let the iPad work some magic.

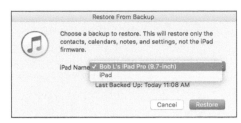

Restore From Backup

Choose a backup to restore. This will restore only the contacts, calendars, notes, and settings, not the iPad firmware.

iPad Name ✓ Bob L's iPad Pro (9.7-inch)
iPad

Last Backed Up: Today 11:08 AM

Cancel   Restore

FIGURE 16-1:
Select the appropriate backup and click the Restore button.

TIP

If you have more than one backup for a device, as Bob has for his iPads in Figure 16-1, try the most recent (undated) one first. If it doesn't work or you're still missing files, try restoring from any other backups before you throw in the towel.

These backups include photos in the camera roll, text messages, notes, contact favorites, sound settings, and more, but not media you've synced, such as music, videos, or photos. If media is missing, try performing Trick 1 again.

If you aren't holding an iPad that works flawlessly and has most (if not all) of your stuff, it's time to make an appointment with a Genius at your local Apple Store, call the support hotline (800-275-2273), or visit the support web page at www. apple.com/support/ipad.

Chapter **17**

Accessorize Your iPad

A nyone who has purchased a new car in recent years is aware that it's not always a picnic trying to escape the showroom without the salesperson trying to get you to part with a few extra bucks. You can only imagine what the markup is on roof racks and navigation systems.

We don't suppose you'll get a hard sell when you snap up a new iPad at an Apple Store (or elsewhere). But Apple and several other companies are all too happy to outfit whichever iPad model you choose with extra doodads, from wireless keyboards and stands to battery chargers and carrying cases. So just as your car might benefit from dealer (or third-party) options, so too might your iPad benefit from a variety of spare parts.

Accessories from Apple

Our roster of worthwhile accessories begin with the options that carry the Apple logo:

>> **Apple Smart Cover:** No iPad has ever shipped with a case in the box, which has helped build a thriving industry of third-party cases in addition to Apple's optional cases and covers. Let's start with Apple's *Smart Cover*, an ultra-thin

cover for just the screen that attaches to your iPad magnetically. Flip the cover open (even just a little), and your iPad wakes instantly; flip it shut, and your iPad goes right to sleep. The Smart Cover is available in numerous bright colors in polyurethane ($39–$49) or leather ($69).

>> **Apple Magic Keyboard:** The various virtual keyboards that pop up just as you need them on the iPad are fine for shorter typing tasks, whether it's composing emails or tapping a few notes. For longer assignments, however, we writers are more comfortable pounding away on a real-deal physical keyboard.

The $99 Apple Magic Keyboard — a Mac keyboard that also works with iPad — is a way to use a decent-enough aluminum physical keyboard without physically tethering it to the iPad. It operates from up to 30 feet away from the iPad via Bluetooth, the wireless technology we discuss in Chapter 15. The keyboard has a built-in lithium-ion battery, which you can charge by plugging it into the supplied Lightning–to–USB port on a computer or (via an adapter) to your iPad. Apple claims battery life of a month or more.

That said, many compatible Bluetooth keyboards and keyboard covers and cases can be used with any iPad, plus smarter cases for Pro models and iPad 10.2-inch, such as . . .

>> **Apple Smart Keyboard:** Apple's special keyboard-and-cover combinations for iPad are the aptly named Smart Keyboard folio for iPad Pro and Smart Keyboard for iPad Air (2019) and iPad (10.2-inch). Pricing for Apple's current iPad models are $159 (iPad Air and iPad), $179 (iPad Pro 11-inch), and $199 (iPad Pro 12.9-inch).

The keyboard connects to the iPad via the smart connector on the edge of the Smart Keyboard and on the side of the iPad models just listed. And beyond typing, you get the added benefit of using the Smart Keyboard as your Smart Cover.

>> **Camera connector:** iPads don't include a USB port or an SD memory card slot, which happen to be the most popular methods for getting pictures (and videos) from a digital camera onto a computer. Apple offers the Lightning–to–USB camera adapter ($29), the Lightning–to–USB-3 camera adapter ($39), the Lightning–to–SD-card camera reader ($29), and the USB-C–to–SD-card reader ($39).

>> **Travel adapter:** If you're traveling abroad, consider the Apple World Travel Adapter Kit. The $29 kit includes the proper prongs and adapters for numerous countries around the globe, and it lets you juice up not only your iPad but also iPhones, iPod touches, and Macs.

Listening and Talking

You've surely noticed that your iPad didn't include earphones or a headset. Fortunately, you can find a seemingly unlimited number of third-party options, as well as Apple's popular AirPods and AirPods Pro. We talk about some of our favorite options in the next section.

Wired headphones, earphones, and headsets

Search Amazon for *headphones, earphones,* or *headsets,* and you'll find thousands of each available at prices ranging from $10 to more than $1,000. Or if you prefer to shop in a bricks-and-mortar store, Target, Best Buy, and the Apple Store all have decent selections, with prices starting at less than $20.

TIP

Much as we love the shopping experience at Apple Stores, you won't find any bargains there because Apple-branded products are rarely discounted, including the company's own Beats brand of headphones.

Lots of wired earphones and headphones are on the markets. Past editions of this book have focused on wired earphones and headphones. For instance, Bryan loves his Mix-Fi headphones from Blue Microphones ($299). Find out more at www. bluedesigns.com. You can find a myriad of options for a lot less money, too.

But, and we know you felt a *but* coming, wireless earphones and headphones are all the rage these days, and we tell you more about them in the next section.

Bluetooth stereo headphones, earphones, and headsets

Bluetooth headphones have steadily improved over the years. You get higher audio quality if you're using expensive wired headphones, but unless you're an audiophile, you'll probably find that Bluetooth headsets sound good. Apple's Beats by Dre have wireless earphones starting at $99.95, and Apple's own AirPods are $159. Bob and Bryan both love their AirPods Pro, priced at $249. AirPods Pro add an in-ear seal, active noise cancellation, and higher sound quality than the original AirPods.

Hundreds of models from other companies are available for a lot less, too. Do a search on Amazon, and you'll find many options under $100, with some starting at just $11.88. You can also find Bluetooth over-the-ear or on-ear headphones, with many models as low as $40.

Listening with Speakers

You can connect just about any speakers to your iPad, but if you want decent sound, we suggest you look only at *powered* speakers, not *passive* (unpowered) ones. Powered speakers contain their own amplification circuitry and can deliver much better (and louder) sound than unpowered speakers. Prices range from well under $100 to hundreds (or even thousands) of dollars. Most speaker systems designed for use with your computer, iPod, or iPhone work well as long as they have an auxiliary input or a dock connector that can accommodate your iPad.

Desktop speakers

Logitech (www.logitech.com) makes a range of desktop speaker systems priced from less than $25 to more than $300. But that $300 system is overkill for listening to music or video on your iPad, which doesn't support surround sound anyway. If you're looking for something inexpensive, you can't go wrong with a Logitech-powered speaker system.

Bob and Bryan are both big fans of Audioengine (www.audioengineusa.com) desktop speakers. They deliver superior audio at prices that are reasonable for speakers that sound this good. Audioengine A5+ is the premium product priced at $399 per pair; Audioengine A2+ is its smaller but still excellent sibling priced at $219 per pair. They're available only direct from the manufacturer, but the company is so confident you'll love them that it offers a free audition for the speaker systems.

Bluetooth speakers

Like Bluetooth headsets, Bluetooth speakers are immensely popular and let you listen to music up to 33 feet away from your iPad. They're great for listening by the pool or hot tub or anywhere else you might not want to take your iPad.

Bryan likes JBL's Pulse 3 ($230 from JBL or $120 from Amazon) and Pulse 4 ($200) portable Bluetooth speakers. Bob has the Ultimate Ears Mega Boom wireless speaker/speakerphone, which he says is the best-sounding $200 Bluetooth speaker he has ever tested. The newest version, Ultimate Ears Mega Boom 3, lists for $200 but we found it on Amazon for as little as $170.

AirPlay speakers

The newest type of speakers you might choose for your iPad support Apple's proprietary AirPlay protocol, which takes advantage of your existing Wi-Fi network to stream audio and video from your iPad (or other compatible iDevice) to a single AirPlay-enabled speaker or audio/video receiver. The biggest differences between AirPlay and Bluetooth speakers are

>> Bluetooth can stream music only in a compressed form; AirPlay can stream music (and video) uncompressed. So, a speaker with AirPlay should sound better than a similar speaker with Bluetooth.

>> Bluetooth's range is roughly 30 feet; AirPlay's range is up to 300 feet. You can't extend Bluetooth's range, but Wi-Fi networks can be extended with additional Wi-Fi routers.

>> iTunes (on your computer) can use AirPlay to stream audio or video to multiple speakers or audio/video receivers, with individual volume controls for each device; Bluetooth streams to only one device at a time.

Wrapping Your iPad in Third-Party Cases

Much as we like the Apple iPad case, other vendors offer some excellent, different options:

>> Speck Presidio Pro, www.speckproducts.com

>> Targus, www.targus.com.

>> Griffin Technology, www.griffintechnology.com

>> iLuv, www.i-luv.com

>> Zero Chroma Vario, at www.zerochroma.com

>> Twelve South BookBook, www.twelvesouth.com

>> LifeProof nüüd, www.lifeproof.com

>> Gumdrop Hideaway for iPad, www.gumdropcases.com

>> Burkley Case's Turner Smart Leather Folio Cover, www.burkleycase.com

>> Vaja Cases, www.vajacases.com

Standing Up Your iPad

The Griffin Tablet Stand ($29.99) is so unusual that we just had to include it (see Figure 17-1). It's a dual-purpose desktop stand made of heavy-duty aluminum. You can open it to hold your iPad in either portrait or landscape mode for video watching, displaying pictures (a great way to exploit picture frame mode, as we describe in Chapter 9), or even reading. In upright mode, it's also the perfect companion for the Apple wireless keyboard (or any other Bluetooth keyboard). Or close the legs and lay it down, and it puts your iPad at the perfect angle for typing on the on-screen keyboard.

The iKlip Studio Stand (www.ikmultimedia.com; $29.99), shown in Figure 17-2, may not look as cool as Griffin's, but it's lightweight and folds flat. And it has rubber feet that don't slide around when you tap the screen. Bob says: "I love my iKlip Studio Stand. Wherever my iPad goes, my iKlip Studio Stand goes with it."

Courtesy of Griffin Technology

Courtesy of IK Multimedia

FIGURE 17-1:
The Griffin Tablet Stand is a unique, dual-purpose tabletop stand for your iPad.

FIGURE 17-2:
iKlip Studio Stand is adjustable, portable, and easy to set up and use.

6

The Part of Tens

Explore our ten favorite free apps in the App Store. You'll find clever apps that serve as a superb way to enjoy digital comics, settle disputes over any movie, ever, and even help you identify the name of an unfamiliar song.

Peruse our ten favorite not-for-free apps for the iPad, including one very addictive game and apps that let you create and mail picture postcards, make your own movies with Hollywood-style special effects, and control your Mac or PC remotely from your iPad.

Check out ten of our favorite tips and tricks for making the most of your iPad.

IN THIS CHAPTER

» TripCase, Shazam, and Flipboard

» Movie and TV apps

» Comixology and Epicurious

» Evernote and Pandora Radio

Chapter **18**

Ten Appetizing and Free Apps

K*iller app* is familiar jargon to anyone who has spent any time around computers. The term refers to an application so sweet or so useful that just about everybody wants or must have it.

You could make the argument that the most compelling killer app on the iPad is the very App Store itself. This online emporium has an abundance of splendid programs — dare we say killer apps in their own right? — many of which are free. These cover everything from food (hey, you gotta eat) to showbiz. Okay, so some rotten apples (aren't we clever) are in the bunch, too. But we're here to accentuate the positive.

With that in mind, in this chapter, we offer ten of our favorite free iPad apps. In Chapter 19, we tell you about our favorite iPad apps that aren't free but are worth every penny.

We show you ours, and we encourage you to show us yours. If you discover your own killer iPad apps, by all means, let us know — our email addresses are at the end of the Introduction to this book — so that we can check them out.

TripCase

We travel more than most people, and what we wished and hoped for was a single intelligent repository for travel-related information, one that was smart enough to alert us of gate changes, weather delays, flight cancellations, and the like, and one that was easy to configure, convenient to use, and free.

What we found is TripCase, which is all that and more. It's a free app (and website) that organizes details of each trip in one place, with reminders and flight alerts delivered directly to your iPad.

TripCase has a lot to like, but one thing we like best is that it's drop-dead simple to add your travel events — without copying and pasting or even typing. We merely forward our confirmation emails — for flights, hotels, rental cars, and other travel-related services — to trips@tripcase.com. TripCase parses the details, creates an itinerary, and sends us an email to confirm that our trip is ready to view in TripCase. We've forwarded confirmations from at least a half dozen travel providers, and TripCase has never failed to interpret them correctly. (And you can always enter details the old-fashioned way — by copying and pasting or typing.)

After TripCase has your info, you can view it in the TripCase app or in any web browser. The app is well-organized, with a timeline view of the itinerary (as shown in Figure 18-1), and details are but a tap away (as shown in Figure 18-2). TripCase also includes an action view with flight alerts, reminders, and other messages. Any way you look at it, TripCase does most of the work for you.

TripCase can even help you locate an alternate flight based on your original reservation should your flight be cancelled or delayed. And it reminds you to check in and print boarding passes 24 hours before each flight. Sweet!

TripCase's motto is "stress-free travel." Although it may not make travel stress free — or increase the legroom in and around a cramped airline seat — it definitely makes travel less stressful.

And one more note about TripCase. If you purchase its Receipts feature ($5.99), you can take pictures of your receipts, and TripCase will collect them for you until you're ready to download them as a PDF. Handy!

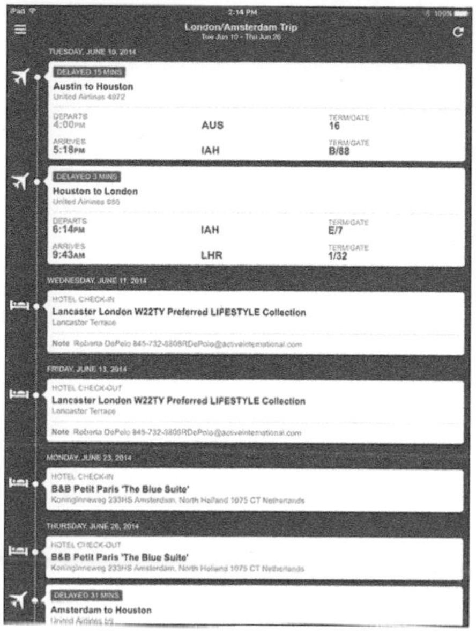

FIGURE 18-1:
The timeline view shows you everything you need in the order you're likely to need it.

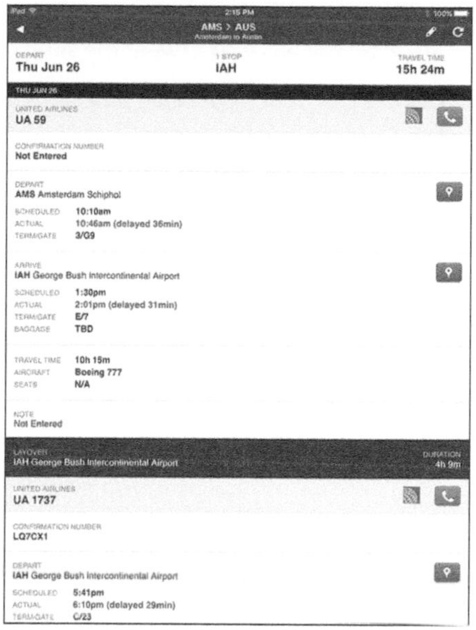

FIGURE 18-2:
Tap any item in the timeline to see its details.

Shazam

Ever heard a song on the radio or television, in a store, or at a club and wondered what it was called or who was singing it? With the Shazam app, you may never wonder again. Just launch Shazam and point your iPad's microphone at the source of the music. In a few seconds, the song title and artist's name magically appear on your iPad screen, as shown in Figure 18-3.

In Shazam parlance, that song has been *tagged*. Now, if tagging were all Shazam could do, that would surely be enough. But wait, there's more. After Shazam tags a song, you can

>> Buy the song at the iTunes Store

>> Watch related videos on YouTube

FIGURE 18-3:
Shazam can even identify indie songs like this one by Bryan's old band, The Atomic Love Bombs.

>> Tweet the song on Twitter if you set up Twitter in Settings

>> Read a biography, a discography, or lyrics

>> Take a photo and attach it to the tagged item in Shazam

>> Email a tag to a friend

Shazam isn't great at identifying classical music, jazz, show tunes, or opera. But if you use it primarily to identify popular music, it rocks (pun intended). It has worked for us in noisy airport terminals, crowded shopping malls, and even once at a wedding ceremony.

Oh, and one more thing: You can have Siri (with Shazam's assistance) identify a song for you even if you don't have the Shazam app installed.

Flipboard

Flipboard is a socially oriented personal magazine app we're confident news and information junkies will like a lot.

To get started with Flipboard, tap the topics you're interested in: business, technology, sports, arts & culture, wine tasting, music, cute animals, and a lot more — over 30,000 topics, in fact.

Flipboard then delivers articles based on your selections, all presented in a handsome, intuitive interface. Swipe left and right to move from page to page. Tap on the articles you want to read. Fine-tune the articles that Flipboard delivers by tapping a thumbs-up (more like this) or a thumbs-down (less like this) icon.

By choosing "weird" as one of his topics, Ed was able to read articles he was unlikely to stumble upon otherwise, including a story out of the Daily Mail in the UK that revealed "The weirdest things dentists have found in patients' mouths."

Trust us, you'll find articles in Flipboard that are a lot more appetizing than that one. As a bonus, you can link Flipboard to various social media accounts.

Movies by Flixster

We like movies, so we use the Flixster app a lot. Feed it your zip code and then browse local theaters by movie, showtimes, rating, or distance from your current location. Or browse to find a movie you like and then tap to find theaters, showtimes, and other info, as shown in Figure 18-4. Another nice feature is the capability to buy tickets to most movies from your iPad with just a few additional taps.

We appreciate that we can read reviews, play movie trailers, and email movie listings to others with a single tap. We also enjoy the movie trailers for soon-to-be-released films and DVDs. Other free movie showtime apps are out there, but we like Flixster the most.

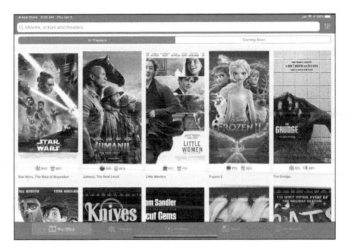

FIGURE 18-4: Find out showtimes, watch trailers, get more info on the director or cast, and more.

IMDb Movies & TV

While we're on the subject of the silver screen, we couldn't resist opening IMDb, shorthand for Internet Movie Database (owned by Amazon). And what a database it is, especially for the avid filmgoer. This vast and delightful repository of all things cinema is the place to go for complete cast/crew listings, actor/filmmaker bios, plot summaries, movie trailers, critics' reviews, user ratings, parental guidance, famous quotations, and all kinds of trivia.

You can always search for movies, TV shows, actors, directors, and so on by typing a name in the search field at the top of the screen. You can also browse various menu choices to find current movies by showtimes, what's coming soon, or what's popular. You can browse TV recaps, too, or find people born on the day you happen to be looking and poking around the app. It's also fun to check out Trending Celebrities on IMDb. The recent roster included Jaimie Alexander, Tom

Hardy, Alexandra Daddario, Priyanka Chopra, Emilia Clarke, Johnny Depp, Leonardo DiCaprio, Marion Cotillard, Natalie Dormer, Michael Fassbender, Rooney Mara, among many others.

One piece of advice to movie buffs: Avoid IMDb if you have a lot of work to do. You'll have a hard time closing the curtain on this marvelous app.

Netflix

Flixster, IMDb, and now Netflix. You've no doubt detected a real trend by now, and that trend is indeed our affection for movies and TV shows. If you love TV and movies, too, you're sure to be a fan of the Netflix app. From the iPad, you have more or less instant access to thousands of movies and TV shows on demand as well as Netflix's original content. You can search by *genre* (classics, comedy, drama, and so on) and *subgenre* (courtroom dramas, political dramas, romantic dramas, and so on).

Netflix Originals include popular shows such as *Orange Is The New Black,* the huge hit *Stranger Things, Jessica Jones, The Irishman,* the *Lost in Space* reboot, *The Witcher, Mindhunter,* and *The Crown.*

Although the app is free, you have to pay Netflix streaming subscription fees that start at $8.99 a month. You also need an Internet connection, preferably through Wi-Fi, though it will stream over cellular networks, too.

WARNING

Remember what we tell you about streaming movies over 3G or 4G and be mindful of your data plan.

Comixology

The Comixology app is a fantastic way to read comic books on a touchscreen. Its online store features thousands of comics and comic series from dozens of publishers, including Arcana, Archie, Marvel, Devil's Due, Digital Webbing, Red 5, DC Comics, and Zenescope, as well as hundreds of free comics.

Furthermore, many titles are classics, like issue #1 of *The Amazing Spider-Man.* Released in 1963 for $0.12, a copy in excellent condition goes for at least $25,000 today! We're enjoying this out-of-print classic in pristine condition on our iPads, as shown in Figure 18-5, for a mere $16.99 (or free with a $5.99 unlimited monthly subscription).

Other comics are priced from $0.99 per issue, though many issues of many series are available for free as a teaser.

Finally, this app provides a great way to organize the comics you own on your iPad so that you can find the one you want quickly and easily.

New releases are available every Wednesday, so visit the web store often to check out the latest and greatest offerings. Both the store and your personal comic collection are well organized and easy to use. And reading comics in Comixology is a pleasure you won't want to miss if you're a fan of comics or graphic novels.

FIGURE 18-5:
Comixology is the best way to read comics on your iPad.

Epicurious Recipes & Shopping List

We love to eat. But we're writers, not gourmet chefs, so we'll take all the help we can get when it comes to preparing a great meal. And we get a lot of that culinary assistance from Epicurious, which easily lives up to its billing as the "Cook's Companion." This tasty recipe app comes courtesy of Condé Nast Digital.

With more than 33,000 recipes to choose from, we're confident you'll find a yummy one in no time. From the Home screen, you can browse categories, often timed to the season. Around the time we were writing this book, recipe collection categories included Halloween Treats, Vegetarian Thanksgiving, Lunches Kids Love, and Chocolate Desserts. To which we say, "Yum." Some recipes carry reviews.

If you tap Search instead, you can fine-tune your search for a recipe by food or drink, by main ingredient (for example, banana, chicken, pasta), by cuisine type, and by dietary consideration (low-carb, vegan, kosher, and so on), among other parameters.

When you discover a recipe you like, you can add it to a collection of favorites, email it to a friend, pass along the ingredients to your shopping list, summon nutritional information, or share it on Facebook and Twitter.

If you want to sync favorite recipes on your iPhone and iPad through a personal recipe box on Epicurious.com, you can now do so for free.

Bon appétit.

Evernote

Before we even talk about the Evernote iPad app, let's take a quick look at the problem Evernote resolves for us: storing our little bits of digital information — text, pictures, screen shots, scanned images, receipts, bills, email messages, web pages, and other info we might want to recall someday — and synchronizing all the data among all our devices and the cloud.

Evernote (`www.evernote.com`) is all that and more, with excellent free apps for iOS, macOS, Android, and Windows, plus a killer web interface that works in most browsers.

You can create notes of any length on your iPad by typing, dictating, or photographing. You can add unlimited tags to a note, and create unlimited notebooks to organize your rapidly growing collection of notes.

Getting words and images into Evernote couldn't be much easier, but the info will be useless if you can't find it when you need it. Evernote won't let you down, with myriad options for finding and working with your stored data. In addition to the aforementioned tags and notebooks, Evernote offers searching and filtering (Tags and Notebooks) to help you find the note you need, as shown in Figure 18-6.

Two other nice touches are worth noting:

FIGURE 18-6:
Evernote's main screen only hints at how easy it is to create and find notes.

>> Notes are automatically tagged with your current location (as long as you create them on your iPad or other location-enabled device), so you can filter by Places.

>> You can attach reminders to notes and receive notifications on the date and time you chose. Best of all, you'll be notified on your iPad as well as on your other iDevices, Macs, PCs, and on the Evernote website!

Our two favorite features are that Evernote syncs notes with all your devices and the cloud automatically and that everything we've mentioned so far — creating, organizing, and syncing notes — is free.

Bob likes Evernote so much that he recently upgraded to the premium plan ($7.99/month), primarily to increase his monthly upload limit to 10GB and to get the capability to search for text in PDFs.

Pandora Radio

We've long been fans of Pandora on other computers and mobile devices, so we're practically delirious that this custom Internet radio service is available *gratis* on the iPad. And you can play Pandora music in the background while doing other stuff.

Pandora works on the iPad in much the same way that it does on a Mac or PC. In the box at the upper left, tap + Create Station and type the name of a favorite artist, song title, or composer via the iPad keyboard, and Pandora creates an instant personalized radio station with selections that exemplify the style you chose. Pandora will also suggest some stations you might like based on the stations you've already established, and you can browse genre stations.

Suppose you type *Beatles*. Pandora's instant Beatles station includes performances from John, Paul, George, and Ringo, as well as tunes from other acts.

And say you type a song title, such as *Have I Told You Lately*. Pandora constructs a station with similar music after you tell it whether to base tunes on the Van Morrison, Rod Stewart, or another rendition.

You can help fine-tune the music Pandora plays by tapping the thumbs-up or thumbs-down icon at the bottom of the screen associated with the music you've been listening to during the current session.

Pandora also takes advantage of the generous screen real estate of the iPad to deliver artist profiles, lyrics, and more. (Refer to Figure 18-7.) You may see ads, too, unless you opt for Pandora Plus ($4.99 a month) or Pandora Premium ($9.99 a month), premium upgrades that eliminate them. Both plans add other benefits as well, such as permitting you to more often skip music you don't like, on-demand listening, and more.

TIP

If you tap the share icon below an album cover of the currently playing song, you can write a message about the song, and then share it on Facebook or Twitter or email it. Other options in Pandora let you bookmark the song or artist that's playing or head to iTunes to purchase the song or other material from the artist directly on the iPad (if available). You can instantly create stations from artists or tracks or also indicate when you're tired of a track.

FIGURE 18-7:
Have we told you lately how much we like Pandora?

Chapter **19**

Ten Apps Worth Paying For

I f you read Chapter 18, you know that lots of great free apps are available for your iPad. But as the cliché goes, some things are worth paying for. Still, none of the ten for-pay apps we've chosen as some of our favorites are likely to break the bank. As you're about to discover, some apps in this list are practical, and some are downright silly. The common theme? We think you'll like carrying these apps around on your iPad.

PhotoCard by Bill Atkinson

Who is Bill Atkinson? He had a hand (or both hands) in the first Macintosh computer, as well as the MacPaint and HyperCard Mac applications. Today he's a world-renowned nature photographer, which brings us to his app. PhotoCard by Bill Atkinson is a free app that lets you create gorgeous high-resolution postcards and send them via either email or the US Postal Service.

But the reason we love it is that you can have printed postcards sent via USPS for $1.50 to $2.00 per postcard, depending on how many print-and-mail credits you purchase. The 8.25-x-5.5-inch postcards are, in a word, stunning. Printed on heavy glossy stock on a state-of-the-art HP Indigo Digital Press and then laminated for protection, they're as beautiful as any postcard you've ever seen.

You can use one of the 200 included Bill Atkinson nature photos, as shown in Figure 19-1, or you can use any picture in your Photos library. You can add stickers and stamps, as shown in Figure 19-1, and you can even add voice notes to emailed cards.

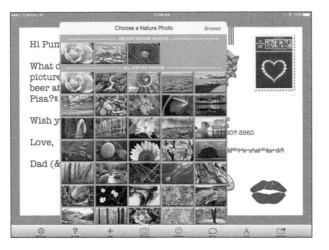

FIGURE 19-1:
Your postcard can feature one of Bill Atkinson's gorgeous nature photos.

TIP

If you're still uncertain, download the app (it's free) and try it. Send an email postcard or two to yourself. After you've seen how gorgeous these cards can be and how easy the app is to use, we think you'll spring for some print-and-mail credits and take your iPad on your next vacation as Bob always does.

Words with Friends — Word Game

This brings us to perhaps the only time in this entire book that two of your authors had a disagreement. Bob and Ed love word games and puzzles, but Bob loves Words with Friends — Word Game, whereas Ed prefers the real thing: namely, SCRABBLE.

Words with Friends — Word Game is the most social game Bob has found — and a ton of fun, too. Because it's turn-based, you can make a move and then quit the app and do other stuff. When your friend makes his next move, you can choose to be notified that it's your turn by sound, on-screen alert, a number on the Words with Friends icon on your Home screen, or any combination.

TIP

Although this app sold for $2.99 previously, when we checked the price for this edition we noticed that it was now free, but some features require in-app purchases. There's no guarantee it'll remain free, so if you like word games, it's worthwhile to see if you can still grab a copy for $0.

Bob says: "Even if you can't, it's easily worth three bucks. After you have a copy, feel free to challenge me if you like; my username is `boblevitus` (although I often have the maximum 20 games going, so keep trying if I don't accept your challenge right away)."

ArtStudio for iPad — Paint & Draw

Do you fancy yourself an artist? We know our artistic talent is limited, but if we were talented, ArtStudio for iPad — Paint & Draw is the program we'd use to paint our masterpieces. Even if you have limited artistic talent, you can see that this app has everything you need to create awesome artwork.

We were embarrassed to show you our creations, so instead we whipped up Figure 19-2, which shows just the options for just one of ArtStudio's tools (there are dozens and dozens more).

Here are just some of ArtStudio's features:

FIGURE 19-2:
ArtStudio for iPad's Wet Paint Brush Settings and brush options.

>> Offers 25 brushes, including pencils, a smudge tool, bucket fill, and an airbrush. Brushes are resizable and simulate brush pressure.

>> Allows up to five layers with options, such as delete, reorder, duplicate, merge, and transparency.

>> Provides filters, such as blur, sharpen, detect edges, and sepia.

At $4.99, it's a heck of a deal for a thoughtfully designed and full-featured drawing and painting app. If you're not ready to invest $4.99, check out ArtStudio LITE, a free version that offers a taste of the real deal but with smaller canvases, limited layer and export support, and fewer custom brushes. And ArtStudio Pro ($11.99) offers additional features, a new engine that powers all the graphical features of the app, full iCloud integration, and more.

Pinball Crystal Caliburn II

Good pinball games require supremely realistic physics, and Pinball Crystal Caliburn II ($3.99) nails it. The way the ball moves around the table and interacts with bumpers and flippers is so realistic that you'll think you're at an arcade. The app is so realistic, in fact, that you can shake the table to influence the ball's movement.

Another hallmark of a great pinball game is great sound effects, and this game doesn't disappoint. The sounds the ball makes when it bounces off a bumper, is hit with a flipper, or passes through a rollover are spot-on and authentic.

If you like pinball, we think you'll love Pinball Crystal Caliburn II on your iPad. LittleWing (the developer) recently released an iOS version of its original pinball hit, Tristan, which also sports realistic physics and sounds and is also a lot of fun.

Art Authority for iPad

We've already admitted to being artistically challenged, but that applies only to making art. We appreciate good art as much as the next person. That's why we're so enthusiastic about Art Authority, even at $4.99.

Art Authority is like an art museum you hold in your hand; it contains more than 100,000 paintings and sculptures by more than 1,500 of the world's greatest artists. The works are organized into period-specific rooms, such as Early (up to the 1400s), Baroque, Romanticism, Modern, and American. In each room, the artworks are subdivided by movement. For example, as Figure 19-3 shows, the Modern room has works of Surrealism, Cubism, Fauvism, Dadaism, sculpture, and several more.

You'll find period overviews, movement overviews, timelines, and slideshows, plus a searchable index of all 1,500+ artists and separate indices for each room.

Developer Open Door Networks includes an Art Near Me feature, which lets you search for art in your vicinity. And the Art Real Size feature adds the perspective of understanding how big or small a work really is. Video has also been added for hundreds of major works. If you love art, check it out.

The kid-friendly version called Art Authority K-12 for iPad still has close to 100,000 paintings and sculptures. It costs $7.99; "inappropriate" nudity for the youngsters has been eliminated.

Solar Walk

We like to gaze at the heavens, but we often have no clue what we're looking at. Solar Walk, a handsome animated $4.99 guide to the night sky from Vito Technology, will delight astronomy students and anyone fascinated by outer space, even if purists scoff that Pluto, no longer considered a planet, is included in the model of the solar system. Note that at the time of this writing, the official name of the app is Solar Walk — Planets Explorer. But the App Store has several other Solar Walk apps, each focusing on a different astronomy niche. If you like Solar Walk — Planets Explorer, check out the others, too.

From the start, you're taken on a virtual tour through the galaxy. You can search planets — Figure 19-4 shows Saturn — satellites, stars, and more. You can even travel through time and space with a time machine feature. Animated movies cover topics such as Earth's cycles, solar eclipse, and the moon's phases.

What's more, the app can exploit 3D, provided you supply your own *anaglyph*-style cyan-red 3D glasses. And if you hook the iPad up to a 3D TV using an HDMI adapter, you can get a true sense of the depth and sheer size of the solar system in 3D, while controlling what you see on the screen through the iPad.

Without 3D, you can use AirPlay to mirror what's on the iPad screen on the bigger TV screen, provided you have an Apple TV.

FIGURE 19-4:
Learning about beautiful Saturn in Solar Walk.

One thing we find frustrating: Solar Walk is heavy on in-app purchases. For example, you'll have to pay 99¢ to watch a 3D animation showing a repair of the Hubble telescope, though you can get a high-resolution bundle with numerous extras for $2.99.

Action Movie FX

With Action Movie FX, it's a breeze to add big-budget Hollywood-style special effects to video you shoot with your iPad. Action Movie FX comes from producer J. J. Abrams's Bad Robot Productions, best known for TV shows such as *Alias* and *Fringe* and feature films including *Star Trek* and *Star Wars: The Rise of Skywalker*. We expected the app to be pretty good, and it is — it may well be the most fun app we've ever used to make videos with an iPad.

The free version features eight big-budget movie effects, such as missile attack, avalanche, and meteor from outer space, as well as phaser fight and photon torpedoes from Abrams's epic theatrical release *Star Trek into Darkness*. More recently, you can add FX packs with *Star Wars* effects. In other words, Action Movie FX lets you add Hollywood-style special effects to your videos so you can "destroy" people, places, pets, and other stuff in a variety of fun and interesting ways.

Making a video with Action Movie FX couldn't be easier. Just launch the app, select the scene you want to use, tap Start, and shoot a minimum of five seconds of video. It's better if the footage is of someone or something that will remain still, unlike Bob's dog Zeke, the slightly blurry miniature vizsla in Figure 19-5.

When you've finished filming, you can adjust the timing as well as resize and reposition the special effects. When you're satisfied with your creation, your masterpiece appears after a bit of processing; you can then share it, save it to your Camera Roll album, adjust its timing again, or shoot another video.

The free effects are great, but we found ourselves wanting more and have purchased most of the ten currently available FX packs, for $0.99 each. They're mostly great, but our absolute favorites are the Jet (shown in Figure 19-6) and Alien Burst (refer to Figure 19-5).

The videos are HD, and look great in a text message or an email displayed on any device. The videos look fabulous on your iPad, but also look surprisingly good on a bigger display such as the one on a Mac, a PC, or an HDTV.

Finally, you just can't beat the price — your first eight effects are free. But we're betting that you'll like it enough to pop for one or more $0.99 FX packs. Either way, we're pretty sure you'll have as much fun as we have adding special FX to your videos.

Masterclass

Masterclass is aptly named. With this app, you can listen to one-on-one lectures from some of the top people in several fields. Interested in writing? Neil Gaiman's masterclass, shown in Figure 19-7, has 19 lessons covering almost 5 hours of material. Writing rules, editing, writer's block, descriptions, humor this stuff is invaluable. Ron Howard will teach you filmmaking. Neil DeGrasse Tyson will teach you science. Gordon Ramsey will teach how to make pasta (and other cooking tips). Annie Leibovitz will teach you photography. Poker-playing legend Daniel Negraneau has a masterclass on poker. Chess. Wine appreciation. Making music. Singing. Acting. Architecture. The list goes on, and these are truly treasure troves of great information.

FIGURE 19-7: Neil Gaiman has great lessons on writing in Masterclass.

Everything is broken down into individual lessons, and most have subchapters. The controls are easy to use, and the production value of the lessons is outstanding. At $15 per month, billed annually, Masterclass is the most expensive app in our list of apps worth paying for, but boy is it worth it. Think about all the things you could learn more about during that year!

Dark Sky Weather

You can find many fine weather apps in the App Store. We rely on Dark Sky a lot because of the app's uncanny capability to inform us not only whether it will rain or snow at our current location but also when it will rain or snow pretty much down to the minute and within one hour of the time that you begged the question. Figure 19-8 shows what the main Dark Sky screen looks like.

If you've ever been caught in a downpour without a raincoat or an umbrella — and who hasn't?— you'll wish you had sprung for this $3.99 app.

You get some basic weather info, too, including a detailed daily forecast, a seven-day forecast, and details on wind, precipitation, humidity, and pressure. Dark Sky will also let you know when the sun will rise and when it will set. Through some cool simulations, you can map the path of

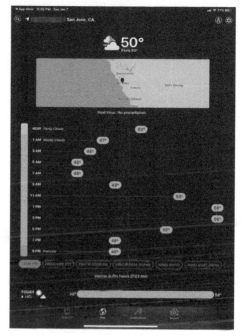

FIGURE 19-8:
Dark Sky Weather makes it easy to see hour by-hour forecasts.

upcoming precipitation or even go back a few days. You can also report your real-time local conditions; other people's submissions help make Dark Sky so accurate. But for us, the real draw is the down-to-the-minute prediction feature, which in our experience has been right more often than wrong.

It's not necessary to keep the app open to get word of an impending storm; Dark Sky can dispatch a notification shortly before rain or snow is supposed to start. Dark Sky is powered by a homegrown and aptly named weather service called Forecast.

Parallels Access

Parallels Access is practically magic. It lets you access your Mac or PC desktop — and even use the apps on those computers — right from your iPad. For some people, Parallels Access may eliminate the need to carry a laptop.

What sets Parallels Access apart from other apps that provide remote access to computers is that you can use *all* the programs that reside on your PC or Mac, including the proprietary software that your company may employ. Moreover, you can interact with those applications on the tablet as if each were designed for the iPad.

Parallels, as the company puts it, "applifies" PC/Mac programs so that the software is modified on the tablet to display iPad-style buttons for actions such as copy, paste, and select. And touch gestures on the iPad substitute for mouse moves on your computer. For example, tapping is like clicking with a mouse; two-finger tapping is equivalent to a right-click. Hold your finger against the display in an Excel spreadsheet, say, and an iPad magnifying glass appears.

You can use your voice to dictate text remotely onto the home or office computer. And you can listen to music on the iPad that resides on your faraway computer, too — no, the folks back home or in the office will not hear what you're hearing; the app is set up so as not to disturb them.

Parallels Access can't completely make up for the lack of a physical keyboard on the iPad. But the on-screen Mac or Windows keyboards that appear in the app display any dedicated special keys unique to Mac or Windows keyboards.

The Parallels Access app is free to download, as is the agent program you must install on each Mac or PC that you choose to access. A single-user Parallels Access subscription is $19.99 per year for an unlimited number of devices (iPads and iPhones running iOS 11 or higher, Android tablets and phones running Android 5 or higher, Kindle Fire devices running Fire OS 3.0 or later, and any device with an HTML5 web browser), and up to five computers (PCs running Windows 7, 8.1, or 10, and Macs running macOS Sierra or later).

Chapter **20**

Ten Hints, Tips, and Shortcuts

There are so many great things about our iPads, and some of them are easy to overlook or forget. We've put together ten of our favorite hints, tips, and shortcuts, and we think you'll want to study and learn them all.

Use Do Not Disturb for Others

You probably think of the do not disturb (DND) feature as a way of keeping your iPad from bugging you while you are sleeping, in a meeting, or just don't want to be bothered. But DND can also help you be considerate to your family, roommates, or fellow office workers. If you're going to leave your iPad behind when you go somewhere, activate do not disturb to keep your notifications from bothering everyone else! You can activate DND by swiping down from the upper-right corner of the screen to open Control Center and then tapping the quarter moon icon, as we explain in Chapter 15.

Create a Website Home Screen Shortcut

You can add any web page as an icon to your Home screen, and then open the icon with a tap, like any app icon. In Safari, pull up the page you want to save to your Home screen, then tap the Share icon on the right side of the screen next to the address bar. Scroll down if necessary to the add to home screen icon, which is a + inside a square. You'll see a preview of the icon. Tap Add to complete the process. Your Home screen appears, sporting your new shortcut. Tap it any time to open that web page.

Edit Today View

We love today view in iPadOS. It's the slide-over view where you can get quick access to recently used apps, see headlines from the News app, see reminders, check out your AirPod battery levels, and more. From the main Home screen, swipe your finger from the left to the right to open today view. Scroll to the bottom of today view, and then tap the Edit button to display a list of all today view widgets you're using and not using. First, get rid of the widgets you don't use. They don't need to be in your way. Next, add any widgets you think you might like — just don't forget to go back and remove them later if you find you don't want them.

Customize Your Dock with Your Most Used Apps

The dock is one of the most used elements of iPadOS. It comes with five apps by default, as we describe in Chapter 2, but you can also add up to 15 apps to the dock.

To add an app to the dock, tap and hold down on the icon on your Home screen, and then drag the icon to the dock. It's that easy! Don't be shy — add your most commonly used apps to the dock for quick access to them from anywhere.

Type on a Floating Keyboard

Have you ever wanted the virtual keyboard in iPadOS to be smaller? You can do that, and it's easy. In any app that uses the virtual keyboard, just pinch the keyboard using two fingers (or a finger and a thumb), and it will shrink to less than half its normal size. The keyboard will also be set to float, so you can move it anywhere on the screen.

To move your floating keyboard, tap and drag the gray bar at the bottom of the keyboard. To expand the keyboard back to its full size and re-dock it to the bottom of your screen, either unpinch it or drag it to the bottom of your screen. It will automatically expand to its normal dimensions and position.

Look Up Words

We love words. Okay, we're writers, but we know many of you love words, too. One of the things we love most about our iPads is the ability to look up a word any time we want.

To look up a word, tap and hold down on the word to select it. Your word will be highlighted with handles on either end that allow you to adjust the selected word. Tap and drag either handle to reposition it. Above your selection will be a contextual menu that lets you copy, look up, or share the selection. Tap Look Up to bring up the definition of the word, as well as relevant searches, Siri suggested websites, and more. After you get used to this feature, you'll miss it any time you're reading legacy media, such as printed books, newspapers, or magazines.

Find Almost Anything Using Spotlight

Spotlight is another feature that can easily be overlooked. If you need to find something on your iPad or do a quick web search without opening Safari first, swipe down from the middle of your Home screen to open Spotlight. Type your search term, and you'll get relevant results from your iPad, apps on your iPad, and Siri suggestions for websites.

Tap and Hold Down on Home Screen Icons

You can tap and hold down on any Home screen icon for quick access to actions specific to that app. Some apps will have more — or fewer — actions available. For instance, tapping and holding down on the News app icon will give you quick access to some of the news sites you follow. Tapping and holding down on the Maps app gives you quick access to marking your location, sharing your location, and searching nearby. Apple's Measure app, on the other hand, has no special actions available, but every app will give you the option to Edit Home Screen or Delete App.

Lock Your Screen's Rotation

You can unlock and lock your iPad's screen rotation when needed. This feature is handy; we use it frequently. For instance, when lying down and reading, we lock our screen because we don't want our iPad rotating the screen every time we move. But when we are doing many other activities, we might want to be free to rotate the screen at any time. To lock or unlock your screen rotation, swipe down from the upper-right corner and tap the screen rotation lock icon, as described in greater detail in Chapter 2.

Use the Volume Button as a Camera Shutter

When taking photographs with your iPad, you can use either the volume up or volume down button as a camera shutter button. Many times, we just can't reach the on-screen shutter button, and this handy trick has really helped us out.

Index

About the Authors

Edward C. Baig writes the Personal Technology column in *USA TODAY* and makes regular video appearances on the web and TV. Ed is also the author of *Macs For Dummies,* 10th Edition, and cowriter (with Bob LeVitus) of *iPhone For Dummies.* Before joining *USA TODAY* as a columnist and reporter in 1999, Ed was on the editorial staff at *Business Week, U.S. News & World Report,* and *Fortune* magazine.

Bob LeVitus, better known as "Dr. Mac," has written or cowritten nearly 90 popular computer books, selling millions of copies worldwide. His most recent titles include his *Working Smarter for Mac Users* for Working Smarter 4 Productions and *macOS Catalina For Dummies* for Wiley. In addition to books, Bob has penned columns in the *Houston Chronicle* and *Mac Observer* for more than 20 years after writing for pretty much every magazine that has ever used the word *Mac* in its title.

Bryan Chaffin is the cofounder and editor-in-chief of *The Mac Observer,* as well as the cohost of The Apple Context Machine podcast and Pop.0 video podcast. In addition to writing for several print magazines, he has contributed to or coauthored five *Dummies* titles, including *Incredible iPad Apps For Dummies.* Bryan is shopping his first novel, *Accidental Intelligence.*

Dedications

I dedicate this book to my beautiful and amazingly supportive wife, Janie, and to my incredible kids: daughter Sydney, son Samuel, and canine Sadie. The book is also written in the memory of my "doggie son," Eddie, Jr., and my mom and dad, Lucille and Sam. I love you all.

— Ed Baig

As always, this book is dedicated to my wife, Lisa LeVitus, who taught me everything I know about pretty much everything I know (except, perhaps, technology). She's put up with me for more than 30 years and she's still the best. Also, as always, I dedicate this book to my now-adult kids, Allison and Jacob, who love their Apple devices almost as much as I love them (my kids, not my devices).

— Bob LeVitus

I dedicate this book to Laura, an amazing woman who challenges, supports, encourages, excites, and confounds me every day. Not sure I could have made it through the 11th edition of this book without her in my life.

— Bryan Chaffin

Authors' Acknowledgments

Special thanks to everyone at Apple who helped us turn this book around so quickly: Steve Dowling, Greg (Joz) Joswiak, John Richey, Keri Walker, Trudy Muller, Tom Neumayr, Janette Barrios, Christine Monaghan, Andy Bowman, and everyone else. We couldn't have done it without you. We apologize if we missed anybody.

Big-time thanks to the gang at Wiley: Steve "Still Pretty Mellow All Things Considered" Hayes, Susan "just one more little thing. . ." Pink, and technical editor Michelle Krazniak, who has no humorous nickname yet but did a rocking job. We also want to thank our invaluable proofreader, Debbye "Hawkeye" Butler, who again did a tremendous job. Finally, thanks to everyone at Wiley we don't know by name or humorous nickname. If you helped with this project in any way, you have our everlasting thanks.

Bob adds: Extra special thanks to my super-agent of 30 years, Carole "Swifty" Jelen. And also to Bryan Chaffin, for his exceptional editorial contributions under pressure. Nicely done, Bryan!

Ed adds: Thanks to my agent, Matt Wagner, for again turning me into a *For Dummies* author. I'd also like to thank my *USA TODAY* friends and colleagues for your enormous support. Most of all, thanks to my loving family for understanding my nightly (and weekend) disappearances as we raced to get this project completed on time. They all keep me sane.

And finally, thanks to you, gentle reader, for buying our book.

Publisher's Acknowledgments

Executive Editor: Steve Hayes

Project Editor: Susan Pink

Copy Editor: Susan Pink

Technical Editor: Michelle Krazniak

Proofreader: Debbye Butler

Sr. Editorial Assistant: Cherie Case

Production Editor: Magesh Elangovan

Cover Image: © Kaspars Grinvalds/Shutterstock

Take dummies with you everywhere you go!

Whether you are excited about e-books, want more from the web, must have your mobile apps, or are swept up in social media, dummies makes everything easier.

Find us online!

dummies.com

Leverage the power

Dummies is the global leader in the reference category and one of the most trusted and highly regarded brands in the world. No longer just focused on books, customers now have access to the dummies content they need in the format they want. Together we'll craft a solution that engages your customers, stands out from the competition, and helps you meet your goals.

Advertising & Sponsorships

Connect with an engaged audience on a powerful multimedia site, and position your message alongside expert how-to content. Dummies.com is a one-stop shop for free, online information and know-how curated by a team of experts.

- Targeted ads
- Video
- Email Marketing
- Microsites
- Sweepstakes sponsorship

20 MILLION PAGE VIEWS EVERY SINGLE MONTH

15 MILLION UNIQUE VISITORS PER MONTH

43% OF ALL VISITORS ACCESS THE SITE VIA THEIR MOBILE DEVICES

700,000 NEWSLETTER SUBSCRIPTIONS TO THE INBOXES OF *300,000* UNIQUE INDIVIDUALS EVERY WEEK

# of dummies

Custom Publishing

Reach a global audience in any language by creating a solution that will differentiate you from competitors, amplify your message, and encourage customers to make a buying decision.

- Apps
- Books
- eBooks
- Video
- Audio
- Webinars

Brand Licensing & Content

Leverage the strength of the world's most popular reference brand to reach new audiences and channels of distribution.

For more information, visit dummies.com/biz

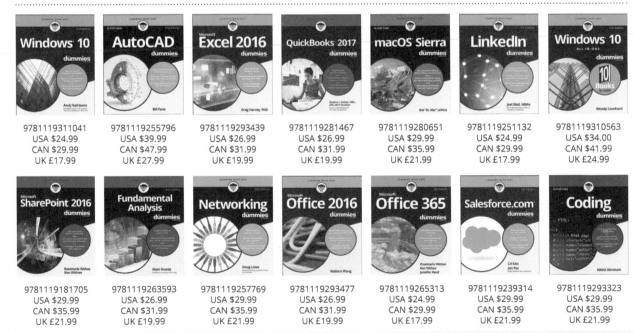

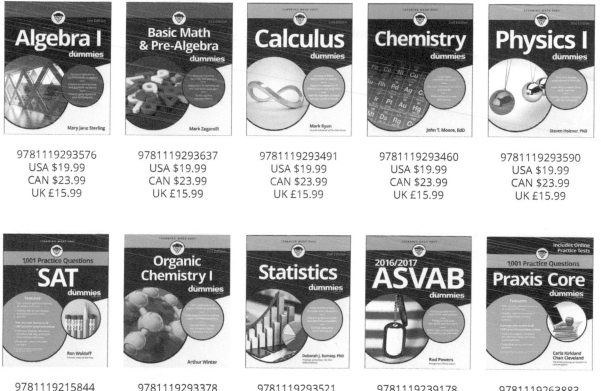

Small books for big imaginations